Juan Ponce de León

and the

Spanish Discovery of Puerto Rico and Florida

Juan Ponce de León

and the Spanish Discovery of
Puerto Rico and Florida

by

Robert H. Fuson

The McDonald & Woodward Publishing Company

Blacksburg, Virginia

2000

The McDonald & Woodward Publishing Company
P. O. Box 10308, Blacksburg, Virginia 24062

*Juan Ponce de León
and the Spanish Discovery of Puerto Rico and Florida*

All rights reserved. First printing April 2000
Printed in the United States of America by
McNaughton & Gunn, Inc., Saline, MI

09 08 07 06 05 04 03 02 01 00   10 9 8 7 6 5 4 3 2 1

Library of Congress Cataloging-in-Publication Data

Fuson, Robert Henderson
   Juan Ponce de León and the Spanish discovery of Puerto Rico and
   Florida / by Robert H. Fuson.
      p. cm.
   Includes bibliographical references and index.
      ISBN 0-939923-84-X; ISBN 0-939923-82-3 (pbk.) (alk. paper)
      1. Ponce de Leân, Juan, 1460?-1521. 2. Explorers--America--Biog-
   raphy. 3. Explorers--Spain--Biography. 4. Florida--Discovery and
   exploration--Spanish. 5. Puerto Rico--Discovery and exploration--
   Spanish. I. Title.
   E125.P7 F87 2000
   975.9'092--dc21
   [B]
                                                         99-056164

Contents

For
my very special granddaughters,
with love

Lindsey Ann Fuson
Ashley Beth Buchsbaum
Victoria Lea Fuson

Acknowledgments

As with any book of this complexity, one does not know who to thank for fear someone will be overlooked. But allow me to first cite the librarians at the University of South Florida. I am also grateful for the support of David and June Cussen of Pineapple Press in Sarasota, Florida. Pineapple Press not only gave permission to reprint material from my recent book *Legendary Islands of the Ocean Sea,* which it published, but actively encouraged this effort. Carla Rahn Phillips allowed me to quote at length from her 1986 lecture *Life at Sea in the Sixteenth Century.* Dr. Phillips, a historian at the University of Minnesota, is one of the preeminent authorities on Spanish colonial ships and shipping. I am truly indebted to Dr. Phillips for permission to use this delightful piece. George and Fran Barford literally went the extra mile for me — they went all of the way to Caparra, in Puerto Rico, to photograph the ruins of Juan Ponce de León's house near San Juan. Several of their photographs appear in the following pages, and I cannot sufficiently express my gratitude for their help. Dr. Fernando Ferrán B., Fundación Dominicana de Desarrollo, Santo Domingo, DR, and Sr. Salvador González, Instituto de Turismo de España - TURESPAÑA, Madrid, Spain provided me with much useful information. As with all of my past literary efforts, I do not know how I would have succeeded without the assistance of the linguistic ability of my wife, Amelia. Her ability to speak fluent Spanish has pulled me over many hurdles.

I also wish to acknowledge the assistance provided by McDonald and Woodward Publishing Company in bringing this project to completion. I greatly appreciate the editorial and production contributions of Carol Boone, Ellen Compton-Gooding, Judy Moore, and Jerry McDonald. Furthermore, I want to express my gratitude to Milagros Flores, San Juan National Historic Site, and Craig Morris, Fort Caroline National Memorial, for providing the publisher with several photographs and other illustrative materials that have been used herein.

And last, but certainly not least, I want to thank my granddaughter Lindsey for her computer skills. I can honestly say that without her assistance much of this book would still be in the computer. What would Juan Ponce de León say about that?

Preface

In the spring of 1992, I sailed from the Madeira Islands in the eastern Atlantic Ocean to Cádiz, Spain, aboard the tall ship *Sea Cloud*, retracing the Atlantic routes of Christopher Columbus in a backwards and somewhat scrambled fashion. Little did I realize that the notion to write this book would seize me as *Sea Cloud* entered the historic Bay of Cádiz on that sunny morning in May.

One of the reasons I went to Cádiz in the first place was to visit this oldest city in the Western World. Another reason was

Figure 1. Tall ship S/Y *Sea Cloud* on which the author retraced portions of Christopher Columbus's and Juan Ponce de León's routes in the Canary Islands and the Bay of Cádiz. (Courtesy Sea Cloud Cruises, Ltd., Valletta, Malta)

that two of Christopher Columbus's four voyages to America — the New World — had departed from Cádiz, and he had returned to that port twice — once in chains. Also, almost every Spaniard that had anything to do with the Ocean Sea and the New World during the fifteenth and sixteenth centuries had some connection to Cádiz or to one of its sister cities on the adjacent bay. One of the Spaniards who passed that way was a young man on his way to Florida and his place in history by way of what are today the Dominican Republic and Puerto Rico. That young man was named Juan Ponce de León.

Juan Ponce — who traveled to the West Indies on the Second Voyage of Columbus — was to be the central character in a chapter of a book I was writing that was still in the manuscript stage in 1992. That book, *Legendary Islands of the Ocean Sea*, was published in 1995, and the chapter about Juan Ponce, "The Island of Flowers," clearly revealed one thing to me as I researched it — very little had ever been written about the man.

After I returned home from Spain I began to read everything I could that pertained to Ponce de León. There were only three or four books written about him by Puerto Ricans and even fewer by Florida authors. I was surprised to find that most writers — other than those who had written specifically about Juan Ponce — considered the founding of Saint Augustine in 1565 to be the *real* beginning of Florida's history.

Beginning in 1993 I set out on a quest of sorts to locate every place that Juan Ponce might have visited in the New World. In very short order I discovered that there was a paucity of historical markers and monuments in two of the three places most closely associated with him. Puerto Rico commemorates its founder and first governor in many ways, but one hears and sees very little of Juan Ponce in the Dominican Republic unless he or she ventures to the easternmost province of La Altagracia, where he had his home. In Florida the absence of accurate information, and the presence of misinformation, about Juan Ponce is even more pronounced. Myth has replaced fact, and only in Saint Augustine — a place Juan Ponce never saw — is there any attempt to honor the first governor of Florida. Juan Ponce is not commemorated at any of the places he actually visited.

The primary objective of this book is to document, as much as possible, the life of Juan Ponce de León and to accurately identify his true contributions to the history of the Dominican Republic, Puerto Rico, and Florida. In addition, I hope to dispose of the myths about Juan Ponce and the early Spanish history of Florida, and to fill in that gap in Florida's history between the Spaniards' first inkling that a landmass existed somewhere west of the Bahamas and their eventual settlement of Saint Augustine. The period that begins with Saint Augustine is thoroughly documented, and even the prehistory (before the coming of the Spanish) of Florida is rather well understood and becoming clearer every day. A few of the Spanish campaigns that took place before the founding of Saint Augustine, such as the ill-fated excursions of Pánfilo de Narváez and Hernando de Soto, have been carefully examined and there are eye-witness accounts of these adventures to guide the interested reader and researcher. Nevertheless, the first documented Spanish forays to Florida have remained obscure, and no one seems to have provided an uninterrupted history of European activity in the region between the First Voyage of Columbus in 1492 and the establishment of Saint Augustine in 1565. Hopefully, this book will rectify that problem.

In the pages that follow I will try to answer the oft-asked question, "Who was Ponce de León, anyway?" He was not a madman seeking a mystical fountain, but he was the young adventurer present when Columbus first sighted and landed on Puerto Rico; the successful farmer on Española who envisioned, then implemented, the Castilian colonization of Puerto Rico; the explorer who discovered the Gulf Stream, Biscayne Bay, the Florida Keys, the Dry Tortugas, Charlotte Harbor, and Tampa Bay; the man who gave Florida its present name; and the first governor of Florida. He was not a greedy slave-trader who lusted for gold, but he was primarily a farmer who was fair in his treatment of both Indian and European. He never used his family connections in Castilla to advance his cause in the New World. He was a good husband and father of four children. He was loyal to his God and sovereigns and he was a moral person in an age of immorality.

Perhaps Juan Ponce de León was as much a victim of his time as he was a product of it. He lived in a period of stark brutality, not only as Europeans related to Indians, but as Indians related to Indians and Europeans related to Europeans. One of Juan Ponce's closest friends, Vasco Núñez de Balboa, was cut down in the prime of life by his own people. A truly larger-than-life hero of the early sixteenth century, Ferdinand Magellan, was butchered by Filipino natives while his companions idly stood by. Hernán Cortés defied his governor, flaunted royal authority, killed anyone who interfered with him, and became — for all practical purposes — an emperor.

And there was political intrigue and widespread corruption, some of which enveloped Juan Ponce. Ferdinand II of Aragón and Isabela of Castilla were married, but the two kingdoms were ruled separately. For several years after Queen Isabela's death in 1504 there really was no ruler in Castilla, although Ferdinand eventually was to share the Castilian throne with his and Isabela's daughter Juana, "the Crazy One." Christopher Columbus's death in 1506 opened up the whole question of which of his rights and titles to his discoveries in the New World would be inherited by his eldest son, Diego. While Ferdinand's hands were tied by a drawn-out legal battle over

Diego Columbus's claim to his father's titles and privileges, Juan Ponce functioned — at Ferdinand's behest — as *ad hoc* governor of San Juan Bautista (Puerto Rico) with no written contract. Once Diego Columbus won his lawsuit and became viceroy of Española, however, he did everything in his power to stifle Juan Ponce, and there was little Juan Ponce could do but leave San Juan Bautista. Ferdinand suggested that Juan Ponce explore the region to the north of San Juan Bautista and, to encourage this, made Juan Ponce governor of Bimini, a region that included what would later become known as the Bahamas and Florida. Although the Florida voyages undertaken by Juan Ponce were Ferdinand's ideas, they served the interests of both men. Ferdinand was able to limit the power of the Columbus family by naming Juan Ponce governor of Bimini, and Juan Ponce was able to escape from San Juan Bautista — which had almost become a prison for him — while retaining an important administrative position and the prospect of achieving prosperity in his new jurisdiction.

It is, indeed, unfortunate that the true legacy of Juan Ponce de León has never been recognized. On his first voyage to Florida, in 1513, he discovered the Gulf Stream, that river of ocean current that became the marine highway for Spanish ships returning home from the New World. And when Juan Ponce landed on the mainland, he had with him the first European woman and the first black African man to set foot on the Florida peninsula. His second voyage, in 1521, was an attempt to establish the first European colony in what is now the United States. Though his colony failed he did maintain it for about four months, something never accomplished by Pánfilo de Narváez or Hernando de Soto, two other Spaniards who attempted to establish colonies in this same region and had superior resources with which to do so.

Juan Ponce's effort to colonize Florida in 1521 was clearly

overshadowed by Cortés's conquest of Mexico then taking place. At that time everyone in the Indies wanted to go to Mexico — it was a sixteenth-century analogue to the California Gold Rush of 1849 — and no one wanted to go to Florida. Indeed, after the collapse of Juan Ponce's Florida colony and the loss of many lives, including those of Juan Ponce and his nephew, most of the survivors of that colony sailed to Mexico to join Cortés.

Ultimately, in the 1560s, the French planted a substantial settlement in Florida at La Caroline, a short distance upstream from the mouth of the Saint Johns River in what is today the city of Jacksonville. Spain reacted and successfully expelled the French. It is a little more than ironic that Spain finally established a lasting presence on the peninsula after defeating colonists from another European country. Although Juan Ponce's role in the exploration of Florida is largely forgotten, as is the French settlement at La Caroline, we hail as a hero Pedro Menéndez de Avilés, an arch-villain if there ever was one, for his role in expelling the French from their southern reaches and establishing Saint Augustine as an outpost on the Atlantic frontier of Spanish America.

～

Several original documents have been translated as part of the research for this book and some of these translations are included in the pages that follow. Decisions also have been made about the accuracy and acceptability of information in other source material. Perhaps the richest source of unmined documents relevant to the early decades of European colonization in Spanish America is the *Colección de documentos inéditos* (Collection of Unedited Documents), published in Spain between 1864 and 1884. This is a forty-two-volume set of good transcriptions of original documents that are arranged more-or-less (but not always!) in chronological order. However, errors included in the original documents are carried over and there is a probability that some of the transcribed materials contain additional mistakes.

Most of the royal correspondence— decrees, contracts, and similar items — is found in the *Colección*, as are various queries from officials in the New World to the royal authorities in Castilla and, later, Spain. It is here that the contracts between King Ferdinand and Ponce de León for the two voyages to Florida are found. This is also where one would find other letters to or from Juan Ponce, as well as material concerning Juan Ponce but perhaps unknown to him.

Antonio de Herrera y Tordesillas is the primary source for Juan Ponce's first voyage to Florida. His ten-volume *Historia general* (General History) has never been translated and it must be used with care, for Herrera rarely documented his sources and he was a known plagiarist. Nevertheless, Herrera had access to all official Spanish documents while he was Spain's chief historian (1596–1623), and many of his documents are found nowhere else.

The dates referred to in this book are based on the Julian calendar — each is nine days less than, or earlier than, the equivalent date on the Gregorian calendar in use today. When, for example, it is said that Christopher Columbus discovered America on October 12, a Julian date, one would need to add nine days to convert this date to its Gregorian equivalent. Columbus Day really falls on October 21! Pope Gregory XIII made the correction to the calendar in 1582, and Spain and most of the Roman Catholic world accepted the change immediately. Great Britain and its colonies did not adopt the new calendar until 1752.

Geographic names present a special problem in books of this type. Both Indians and Europeans applied names to places. Sometimes Europeans adopted the Indian name of a place, and other times they tried to replace the Indian name with one or more of their own. In this book the contemporary name or names will be used when the place is introduced and the modern name will be given parenthetically. After that the modern name will be used except that, in order to emphasize the details of the principal political and geographic entities central to this drama, the names Castilla (one of the kingdoms that preceded the formation of Spain) and San Juan Bautista (Columbus's name for Puerto Rico) will be used for the periods during which these names were current.

Spanish surnames also require comment. In the fifteenth and sixteenth centuries, there was no fixed rule for the adoption and use of surnames. Coupled with that is the fact that some names have been anglicized to the extent that they are almost unrecognizable in their original form. In a few cases given names have been anglicized. Spanish names of males often include the mother's surname as well as the father's, and sometimes a married woman's maiden name will be retained with the husband's name added at the end.

The following protocols for presenting personal names shall be followed in this book:

1. Well-known anglicized names shall be used with the native name in parentheses at the first occurrence.
2. The first time a Spanish name occurs it will be rendered in its full form. After that, the short form, usually the surname, will be used, but in accordance with contemporary usage during that person's lifetime. This means that for some names the "de" preceding a surname may or may not be employed. For example, Nicolás de Ovando is shortened to Ovando, but Hernando de Soto is given as de Soto.
3. All Iberian royal names will be given in the native language, with the exception of King Ferdinand, Queen Isabela, and Charles V, Emperor of the Holy Roman Empire.

Juan Ponce de León
and the
Spanish Discovery of Puerto Rico and Florida

Prologue

In the year of Juan Ponce de León's birth — 1474 — there was no such thing as "Spain." The country that we know by that name today did not come into existence until 1516. Most of the "Spaniards" who ventured overseas in the late fifteenth and very early sixteenth centuries paid homage to the sovereigns and flag of Castilla. Castilla itself was one of the myriad kingdoms that had evolved on the Iberian Peninsula — kingdoms that incorporated traditions of centuries of human migrations, maritime commerce, and military conflict. Juan Ponce de León happened to live at a time of dramatic change in the history of Iberia and, swept up in those events as much by circumstance as design, he became a significant figure in the rapidly unfolding European exploration and settlement of what became Spanish America. This book is about Juan Ponce de León, but to better understand him it is helpful to know something of the historical background of Iberia that gave character to his place and time.

～

Although the written history of the Iberian Peninsula is long and complex, extending back at least 3000 years, the prehistory of the region covers an incredible span of time. Humanoids such as *Homo neanderthalensis* — Neanderthal man — were present in Iberia as long ago as 200,000 years, and maybe even longer. *Homo sapiens* (modern man) of the Upper Paleolithic and Mesolithic Periods (about 25,000 to 10,000 BC) left paintings on cave walls all over the Iberian Peninsula. The Neolithic

Period (10,000 to 2500 BC) is also well-represented by paintings, and by the end of this time human forms were drawn, giving us some indication of their tools, foods, and clothing. The Neolithic Period in Iberia came to an end about 2500 BC with the arrival of metallurgy and the onset of the Bronze Age.

It is not clear who were the recipients of the first metals that came to Iberia, but the tradition of metal working that developed from these roots made Iberia a center of quality metal armor and weaponry by the onset of European expansion into the Americas. The Basques seem to be the oldest "modern" population in the region, and they or a people like them were probably the first native Iberian metallurgists. Metal usage diffused to Iberia from the eastern Mediterranean and possibly came with the first Phoenician voyagers and, eventually, their trading colonies. Although Cádiz, Spain, and Lisbon, Portugal, have Phoenician roots that go back to 1000 BC or before, Tartessus (also Tartesos) is even older.

Archaeologists have never located Tartessus, but it was a seaport somewhere between the modern border of Spain and Portugal (the Guadiana River) and the Strait of Gibraltar. As was noted by numerous ancient writers, this was the first city on the Iberian Peninsula that had an organized government with a king, a written language, and a far-flung trade network. It is mentioned in the Bible, as Tarshish, in several places, and was known as a source of silver, iron, tin, and lead (Ezekiel 27:12). Tartessus was also the haven to which Jonah was fleeing when he had his encounter with the great fish (Jonah 1:1–17; 2:1–10).

It is possible that the exact location of Tartessus has remained hidden because it lies beneath some other ancient seaport, such as Cádiz, Sanlúcar de Barrameda, or Huelva. The latter is a good choice, for Huelva is not only a mining center (iron and copper, among others), but earthquakes in the eigh-

4

teenth century virtually wiped out everything that had been built before that time. Minerals and mining certainly would have attracted the Phoenicians, and an earthquake might have destroyed any evidence that they had been there.

The Phoenicians were truly one of the enigmatic people of history. No one had ever heard of them before they were subdued by the Egyptians about 1600 BC. By 1200 BC they were once again independent and by 1000 BC the Phoenicians — whose trading empire was centered at Tyre, in what is now southern Lebanon — were sailing westward, beyond the Strait of Gibraltar to England (for tin) and northern Germany (for amber). It was during this time that Phoenecian colonies were founded along the Mediterranean coast of North Africa and in southern Spain on either side of the Strait of Gibraltar. Málaga and Cádiz, for example, are products of this activity, as is Lisbon, on the tin and amber route between the ports of the Mediterranean Sea and northwestern Europe.

The Phoenician homeland was subjected to outside pressure on several fronts, and Tyre fell to the Assyrians in the eighth century BC. The Babylonians, under King Nebuchadrezzar I, laid siege to Tyre between 585–573 BC, and in 538 BC the Persians gained control of the city. After two centuries of Persian domination, Alexander the Great destroyed the Phoenician capital in 322 BC.

No later than 600 BC the Greeks arrived on the shores of southern Spain. As with the Phoenicians, they established trading outposts but there was essentially no attempt to occupy territory beyond the seaport. Two important Greek colonies in Spain were Alonae and Emporiae (Ampurias; Empuries). Alonae has not been positively identified but it may be at Benidorm, twenty-five miles northeast of Alicante, Spain. Emporiae is in Catalonia, about seven miles south of the border of France and Spain.

At about the same time that the Greeks were establishing their trading stations along the northern portion of the Mediterranean Sea, the Celts were moving into the extreme northern portion of the Iberian Peninsula. Because they were primarily farmers and made no serious attempt to form anything resembling a cohesive government, and because they were one of the few European people to choose isolated farmsteads over villages, the Celts threatened no one. They have left very little in Iberia except a few place-names (Galicia is one) and the nasal pronunciation found in spoken Portuguese, Gallego (a form of Portuguese spoken in Galicia, Spain), and even in Castilian Spanish (especially in Asturias).

The Carthaginians were latter-day Phoenicians who emerged from the Phoenician colony of Carthage to challenge Rome for the domination of the western Mediterranean. Carthage was founded in 814 BC on the present site of Tunis, Tunisia, and between 500 BC and 219 BC it conquered most of the Iberian Peninsula. The death knell for Carthage was sounded, however, when Rome won the Second Punic War (218–201 BC). The Romans overran Cádiz in 206 BC and by 201 BC had gained control of the entire Mediterranean littoral of Spain and Portugal. By 133 BC the Romans controlled all of Iberia except Galicia, Asturias, and the Basque region. And by the time of Augustus' death (AD 14) even these northern lands had been conquered — at least in theory. It is more correct to say that the main roads and passes came under Roman control; the remote mountain areas remained as free as they had always been.

The Roman Empire began to decline at the end of the reign of Marcus Aurelius in AD 180. The next one hundred years would witness twenty-seven different emperors and dozens more who claimed the title. The decay of Rome's power was accompanied by massive rebellions, the withdrawal of Roman legions in certain areas, and an explosion of Germanic tribal migrations. By the fifth century AD a number of these Germanic people poured into the Iberian Peninsula. Three of these Germanic tribes (among many) would have a major impact on Iberia.

The Suevi and the Vandals arrived in AD 409; the former, already "Romanized," settled down in the north (mainly in what is now Galicia and Asturias) and created the Kingdom of Galicia (AD 429–585). The Vandals passed through the peninsula and crossed over to Africa in AD 429. The third Germanic group — and in many ways the most significant one — was the Visigoths. They entered Iberia from Italy and southern France in AD 412 and, after first accepting Roman authority, established a kingdom at Tolosa; later the capital was moved to Toledo (southwest of Madrid). By the sixth century the Visigoths had conquered the Kingdom of Galicia and had subjugated the Basques: they had won domination over all of the Iberian Peninsula.

In AD 711 Spanish and Portuguese history made a sudden departure from its long course of European development: the Muslim period began. King Witiza, ruler of the Visigoths, had died in 709. Almost immediately a civil war erupted and a usurper, Roderick, achieved the throne. Witiza's supporters invited the Muslims of North Africa to assist them in overthrowing Roderick, and in 711 a force of about 20,000 Muslims crossed the Strait of Gibraltar. Roderick's army was defeated on July 19, 711, and the Muslims should have returned home. Instead, the Muslims marched to Toledo, the Visigothic capital, to see if there was any truth to the legend that King Solomon's treasures were in that city. To their utter surprise, the Muslims found themselves being treated as heroes, not as a conquering enemy. And so they decided to stay for a while — almost eight hundred years!

7

The remnants of the Visigothic nobility literally "took to the hills," fleeing northward to the mountains of Asturias to escape the invading Muslims. Here, in a region protected on three sides by mountains and by the sea on the north, the Visigoths regrouped. A king— King Pelayo (718–737) — was chosen, and the *Reconquista* (Reconquest) began. A capital was established at Cangas de Onis, then moved to Pravia and later to Oviedo. All of these cities lie north of the Cantabrian Mountains, well within the protected area of Asturias. After Galicia was occupied, the Asturians became bolder and moved their capital south of the mountains into León. Although this was probably a mistake, and certainly premature, the kingdom was to survive until 910, when Asturias became part of the Kingdom of León.

The Kingdom of León existed as an independent kingdom from 910 until 1157, and from 1157 to 1230 it was ruled separately by Castilla. In 1230 León became a part of the Kingdom of Castilla.

Both Castilla and Aragón had become kingdoms in 1035 when Sancho III of Navarra (Navarre) died and left these territories to his sons. It is ironic that the new Kingdom of Aragón annexed Navarra and ruled it from 1076 until 1134. After a long period of independence, Navarra was once again incorporated by Aragón (1458–1479), and in 1512 most of it was again annexed. Castilla expanded by absorbing León (mentioned above) and by slowly advancing southward into Moorish (Muslim) territory. Aragón, on the other hand, federated with Cataluña (Catalonia) in 1140 and expanded into the Mediterranean, eventually bringing a number of islands into the kingdom: the Balearic Islands, Sardinia, and Sicily. Also, the southern part of the Italian Peninsula became part of the kingdom.

Portugal shared much of the Iberian Peninsula's history with the myriad kingdoms that occupied what we now call

Spain. But, having said that, there were several differences. For one thing, there seem to have been few — if any — indigenous peoples within the present Portuguese boundary. For all practical purposes, Portuguese written history began with only one or two Phoenician outposts, and there is even some dispute about them. Secondly, there never were any Greek colonies in Portugal. The Celts in the north seemed to have added no burden to the local farming and fishing population, and Roman control was lax except in the south (Algarve), around Lisbon and its great harbor, and at Porto. Perhaps the lack of any serious Carthaginian threat to Rome spared Portugal from the Second Punic War. The Suevi were mostly in the north — in Galicia — and the Visigoths were mostly to the northeast — in León. The Muslim invasion of 711 never had the impact that it had in the Spanish kingdoms and it did not last as long. By 868 an embryonic Portuguese state existed, and in 1128 the County of Portugal (the northern half of today's Portugal) broke away from the Kingdom of León and joined the evolving kingdom. By 1147 Lisbon had been retaken from the Muslims and by 1185 the southern frontier extended to the Tagus River. The Muslim occupation of Portugal was essentially over by 1252 — two hundred and fifty years before Granada fell to the Castilians.

Portugal became the first true "nation-state" in Europe. By the end of the fifteenth century its various historic peoples (Phoenicians, Celts, Romans, Suevi, Visigoths, Romans, Arab-Berbers) were a well-mixed blend who today we call "Portuguese." They shared (and still share) a common language with no significant dialects, something that modern Spain never achieved. With early cultural unity and with the Atlantic Ocean washing the entire western and southern coasts, it was almost inevitable that Portugal would become a maritime state. But it was a maritime state with a mission.

Beginning in the fourteenth century, Portuguese energy

was expended to achieve three important goals: remove the Muslims from North Africa, locate the legendary Christian kingdom of Prester John (thought to lie south of the Muslims, somewhere in Africa) and enlist its aid in the struggle with the Muslims, and find the source of Muslim wealth — especially its gold — in order to finance the operation. To this end, in 1314, King Dinis began to build a navy.

Although Portugal had five kings during the fourteenth century (with sufficient palace intrigue to go around), the African policy remained firm. The efforts made to acquire the Canary Islands were spinoffs of the African mission, as was the rediscovery of Madeira and Porto Santo islands and the accidental discovery of the Azores Islands. Sailing south along the west coast of Africa — searching for Prester John and Muslim gold — became an obsession with the fourteenth-century Portuguese. One obstacle blocked the way, and it was not Castilla: it was Cape Bojador at 26°21' N latitude, a tongue of land which not only protruded into the Atlantic Ocean for several miles but lay at the latitude where winds and currents carried vessels westward. By borrowing techniques of ship construction from the Arabs, a Portuguese mariner, Gil Eannes, was able to defeat Bojador in 1433. The route to the south was now open and by 1488 Bartolomeu Dias had reached the Cape of Good Hope.

Not only was the West African route a reality but the Indies were just around the corner. The English word "Indies" is an unfortunate synonym for "Indias." The Portuguese (and later the Castilians) were seeking *las Indias*, the Indias (plural), not India (singular). In the fourteenth and fifteenth centuries there were *three* Indias: the country we still know by that name, southeast Asia, and Ethiopia — called the "Third India" until the sixteenth century. The latter was the land of Prester John. It did not extend across Africa as the Portuguese had thought, nor was it rich, but it was Christian: one out of three is not all that bad!

~

Christopher Columbus (Cristóbal Colón) arrived in Lisbon in 1476, just as Portuguese mariners were about to reach the southern tip of Africa. Apparently he was sailing with the Genoese and his vessel was sunk by mistake during the early stages of the Peninsular War (1474–1479) between Portugal and Castilla. History tells us that he literally swam ashore in southern Portugal, immediately went to Lisbon, and was soon sailing with the Portuguese. He married Felipa Monis in 1479 and lived for a period on the islands of Madeira and Porto Santo. During the same year he supposedly went to Genoa for a judicial hearing. His eldest son, Diego, was born on Porto Santo in 1480. Columbus also claimed to have been in Ghana at the Portuguese fort of São Jorge da Mina, now Elmina. Inasmuch as that fort did not exist before the latter part of 1482, it must be assumed that Columbus made at least one trip to Ghana be-

Figure 2. The Ptolemy World Map, 1472, is representative of the European/ Mediterranean view of their known world on the eve of Juan Ponce de León's birth. (Courtesy Biblioteca Apostolica, Vaticana)

tween 1482 and 1485, the year he left Portugal for Castilla.

We may never know why Columbus left Portugal and cast his lot with Castilla. Felipa supposedly died about 1485 but there is no real proof of this. Columbus claimed that his idea to sail west to reach *las Indias* was rejected by João II. Again there is no supporting historical record of this. The rejection is logical, however, for Columbus had miscalculated the earth's circumference and the Portuguese had invested too much time and money in the African voyages to send an exploratory party to the west over a presumed 10,000 miles of ocean. Besides, oceanic exploration was not one of Portugal's high priorities. For whatever reason, Columbus went to Castilla with little Diego and sought royal sponsorship, but that kingdom was not prepared to make any commitments until the Reconquest was a *fait accompli*.

The year of 1474 was a pivotal one in the Iberian Peninsula. As already mentioned, it was the birth year of Juan Ponce de León. It was also the year that Prince João of Portugal (in 1481, João II) was placed in charge of all Portuguese overseas activities, which included colonial policy and exploration. Lastly, it was the year that Isabela ascended to the throne of Castilla.

In 1474 Castilla was in the last few months of the reign of Enrique IV, Isabela's half-brother. The twenty years of Enrique's rule had been a disaster. Castilla was in chaos, politically and economically, and after Enrique's demise the question of succession escalated into a full-blown civil war. The problem of succession involved two women: Isabela (the king's half-sister) and Juana (the king's daughter). Sometime before 1469 while Isabela was still unmarried, her half-brother (Enrique IV) promised her the Castilian throne upon his death. However, Isabela refused to accept anyone's advice and married Ferdinand of Aragón in 1469. Enrique IV had been so angered by Isabela's action that he withdrew the offer of the throne and turned to his daughter, Juana. Juana was to be married to Afonso V of Portugal, and a smooth succession would have meant the merger of the Castilian and Portuguese royal houses.

When Enrique died in 1474, Isabela claimed the throne, becoming Isabela I of Castilla. Her husband became Ferdinand V of Castilla. Afonso V, in support of his wife Juana's claim (and he truly wanted the Castilian throne), invaded Castilla and enjoyed some early successes in León. The invasion, however, bogged down and in 1476, the year Columbus arrived in Portugal, Afonso V went to France where he tried to get Louis XI to invade Aragón and Castilla from the east. The idea was quickly rejected and the Portuguese king became so despon-

Figure 3. Queen Isabela I of Castilla (1474) and Aragón (1479). (From Fiske, 1902)

dent that he abdicated his throne and attempted to make a pilgrimage to the Holy Land. Louis XI prevented Afonso's departure and in the autumn of 1477 sent him back to Lisbon. Crown Prince João was actually declared king in 1476, but when his father returned to Portugal, João stepped aside and allowed Afonso V to reclaim his title. Even so, Prince João functioned as co-ruler until Afonso died in 1481, and then ruled as João II until 1495.

Support for Isabela's claim to the throne was stronger than that for Juana, and the latter lost the throne while her betrothed lost the Peninsular War. Part of Juana's problem lay in the fact that most Castilians did not believe that Enrique IV was capable of having children and, therefore, he could not have been her father. Behind his back he was called "Enrique the Impotent." The war (1475–1479) officially ended with the Treaty of Alcáçovas (September 1479) and was followed by its ratification in Toledo (March 1480). In essence the treaty reaffirmed Castilla's sovereignty over the Canary Islands; Portugal retained the Azores, Madeira and Porto Santo, the Cape Verde Islands, and the lands of northwestern Africa. The Ocean Sea (the Atlantic and Pacific oceans) south of 27^0 N latitude belonged to Portugal, and Castilla had exclusive rights to the Ocean Sea north of that parallel (except for the Portuguese islands named). A careful examination of a world map will show that *every single one* of the islands discovered by Columbus on his First Voyage of Discovery lay in Portuguese territory according to this treaty.

Not only did the Peninsular War end in 1479, but Juan II of Aragón died in the same year. Isabela kept her Castilian throne but also became Isabela I of Aragón. Ferdinand, already Ferdinand V of Castilla, also became Ferdinand II of Aragón. There was a "union of crowns" not a "union of states." Castilla and Aragón were ruled as distinct entities — each with its own institutions, traditions, and even languages — until 1516, at

Figure 4. King Ferdinand V of Castilla (1474) and Ferdinand II of Aragón (1479). (From Prescott, 1904)

which time their merger formed the modern state of Spain.

~

The Muslim kingdom of Granada was the sole surviving territory on the Iberian Peninsula under Muslim control in 1492. Within a decade of the Muslim invasion in 711 the Reconquest had begun. Slowly, but relentlessly, the Muslim-occupied lands had been reclaimed by the Christian Iberians. By the end of the thirteenth century, most of Castilla and Aragón had been re-taken from the invaders: the Balearic Islands (1229–1235),

Figure 5. Olive orchards near Granada, Spain — a typical Castilian land-scape. (Photograph by R. H. Fuson)

Córdoba (1236), Valencia (1238), Múrcia (1243), Sevilla (1248), and Cádiz (1262). By the fourteenth century, Granada had been reduced to little more than a tributary vassal of Castilla, and after Isabela and Ferdinand gained the thrones of Castilla (1474) and Aragón (1479), these Catholic Sovereigns began the drive to finally expel the Muslims from Granada. Málaga was captured in 1487, Almería fell in 1489, and in 1492 the city of Granada surrendered to the forces of Isabela and Ferdinand. The Reconquest was completed after 781 years — the longest war in history.

Somewhere in the midst of the wildly cheering populace that had assembled in Granada on January 2, 1492, were two people whose paths would soon cross. Christopher Columbus was there, still following Queen Isabela about Castilla — still seeking a royal license to sail westward. And Juan Ponce de León, a teen-ager but also a veteran of the Reconquest, was present.

On January 2, 1492, many Castilian and Aragonese soldiers (including knights) became unemployed. And what do soldiers do when a war is over? For many, in this case, the answer to the question would rest with Columbus, to whom Isabela would soon give her blessing and support, and who would discover a New World before the year was out. There were new lands to explore, conquer, and settle, and untold riches to seek and acquire. Iberians, and especially Castilians, would soon sail to the west over the Ocean Sea, for God, Glory, and Gold — but not necessarily in that order.

Almost overnight Castilla became an Atlantic-based maritime state, both thrust and pulled into head-to-head competition with Portugal. Aragón had a long maritime tradition — at least the Catalonian portion did. But it was primarily a Mediterranean-oriented interest, driven mostly by the Catalonians. Trade and cartography were their passions, much more so than exploration. Castilla, however, was a state dominated by the landed aristocracy; its *conquistadores*, soldiers, administrators, clergy, farmers, ranchers, and artisans were mostly from the

Figure 6. The Generalife, part of the Alhambra, in Granada. Both Christopher Columbus and Juan Ponce de León witnessed the surrender of the Moors here on January 2, 1492. (Photograph by R. H. Fuson)

17

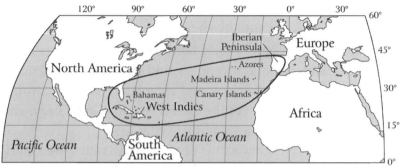

Figure 7. The world of Juan Ponce de León extended from Iberia in the east to the West Indies and Florida in the west.

interior. For over eight centuries they had been in a struggle with another land-based society. Other than a concern for the Canary Islands — prompted more by Portugal's interest than its own — Castilla's most successful maritime endeavor had been piracy.

With the fall of Granada and the completion of the Reconquest, Isabela — monarch of the largest and most powerful kingdom of Iberia — could now give serious attention to the scheme proposed by Columbus of sailing westward in search of Las Indias. Extending Columbus her support, Isabela authorized a voyage to the west, and Columbus departed Palos on August 3, 1492, only seven months after Granada's capitulation. Columbus made his first landfall on the west side of the Atlantic Ocean on October 12, 1492, and opened the door through which Castilla would pass — leading the way into one of the most significant chapters of modern world history. Juan Ponce de León would be an influential participant in the early years of this drama.

Chapter 1
1474–1493

The Early Years
and the Discovery of Puerto Rico

The twenty years from 1474 to 1493 represent the time between the birth of Juan Ponce de León and his presence at the European discovery of Puerto Rico. Among the few glimpses we have of Juan Ponce's early life is information about his birthplace, family, residency in the House of Toral, service during the Moorish wars, and participation in the Second Voyage of Christopher Columbus. Inasmuch as the Second Voyage departed from Cádiz in what was then Castilla, some attention is given to the history of that city (the oldest in the Western World), its magnificent harbor, and neighboring ports. Although both Columbus and Juan Ponce were at Granada for the Muslim surrender in 1492, the men never met at that time and Juan Ponce probably did not know about the First Voyage. But he did know about the impending Second Voyage, and that was what had brought him to Cádiz. Because Juan Ponce sailed with the Second Voyage of Columbus, detail is provided about the fleet itself: size, personnel, provisioning, departure, and management of the entire operation. Also included are portions of a letter written in 1573, describing life at sea on approximately the same route taken by Columbus and under very similar conditions. Columbus's fleet departed Cádiz on September 25, 1493, and traveled south to the Canary Islands, then west across the Atlantic Ocean to Dominica, then north along the Lesser Antilles until, on November 18, 1493, it reached Puerto Rico.

Cádiz, Spain, is a very old city. In fact, it is the oldest city in Western Europe and was already 2500 years old when Juan Ponce de León went there in 1492 or 1493.[1]

Cádiz was established about 1100 BC as a trading colony by Phoenician merchants from Tyre. Gadir, as the Phoenicians called the town that would become Cádiz, was situated on an island that today is named León. This island was separated from the mainland by a maze of creeks and channels — Phoenicians typically chose islands for their settlements that were close to the mainland and approachable only by sea.[2] This was exactly the relationship of the site of the mother city, Tyre, to the mainland, as well as that of the Phoenician settlement at Carthage along the coast of what is today Tunisia.[3]

Figure 8. Cádiz, Spain. Cádiz was the departure port for the Second and Fourth voyages of Christopher Columbus to the New World; the terminus for the Second and Third Columbus voyages; and the port from which Juan Ponce departed for the New World, with Columbus, in 1493. (Courtesy Instituto de Turismo de España — TURESPAÑA)

It was during the waning days of Phoenicia that one of its colonies, Carthage, inherited the Phoenician territories in the western Mediterranean region. Even though older than Carthage, Cádiz became a Carthaginian stronghold in 501 BC and remained such until the city was overrun by the Romans in 206 BC during the Second Punic War.[4]

The Romans changed the city's name to Geddes and, among several physical alterations, constructed a bridge from the island of León to the mainland. This bridge, the Zuazo bridge, is still in use today and was once controlled by the Ponce de León family.[5] For all practical purposes Roman control of Geddes (Cádiz) ended when the Germanic Visigoths destroyed the city in the fifth century AD. Another Germanic tribe, the Vandals, brought the new name Vandalucía, or Andalucía, to southern Castilla at about the same time.[6] Eventually, over the course of several centuries, the Germanic invaders blended with the Romanized native population and thus laid the social foundations for medieval Spain.[7]

When the Moors — North African Arabs and Berbers — crossed the Strait of Gibraltar in AD 711 and captured Cádiz, the name of the city was changed once again. Until Alfonso X — Alfonso the Wise — captured the city for the Castilians in AD 1262, it was called Jazirat Qadis. The modern Spanish name is derived from the Arabic name Qadis.[8]

Cádiz's problems, however, did not end in the thirteenth century. The city was pillaged several times in the sixteenth century by the Barbary pirates, Sir Francis Drake arrived in 1587 and burned the city, the British blockaded the port in 1797 and 1798 and shelled it in 1800, and the French lay siege to it from 1810 to 1812.

～

Juan Ponce de León was only eighteen or nineteen years old when he came to Cádiz. It is unknown if this was Juan

Ponce's first visit to a Castilian port, but he had relatives in the area of Cádiz and this was the best Atlantic harbor that Castilla possessed.

When Juan Ponce arrived at Cádiz something momentous was in the offing. Seventeen ships, including some from the nearby ports of Sevilla, Sanlúcar de Barrameda, Huelva, Palos, and Moguer, were in the harbor being readied for a second voyage across the Atlantic Ocean under the command of Christopher Columbus. There were three *naos*, called carracks by some, each similar to the *Santa María* of Columbus's First Voyage, and fourteen caravels, including the *Niña*, soon to become the first ship to cross the Atlantic and return twice.[9] This voyage would, in fact, be the largest of Columbus's four voyages — more ships would be committed to it than would take part in his other three voyages combined.

Columbus had returned to Castilla from his Discovery Voyage on March 15, 1493, at which time he sent a letter to his friend and sponsor Luis de Santangel.[10] This letter, now known as *La*

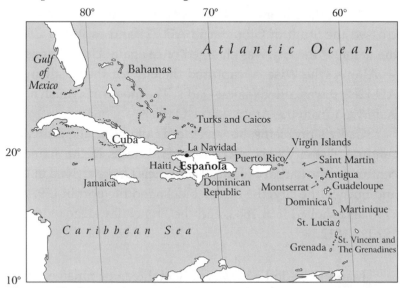

Figure 9. The West Indies, including the site of Columbus's settlement of La Navidad.

Carta de Colón (The Columbus Letter), was published early in April 1493, thereby becoming the first printed notice of the discovery of the New World. It was translated into Latin and published in Rome the next month, and by the end of 1493 ten other editions had appeared. With the original letter to Santangel, Columbus attached a letter to Ferdinand and Isabela, who were in Barcelona at the time. Before the end of March, Columbus had been summoned to the court by the sovereigns in order to provide a detailed report of the Discovery Voyage and plans for a second voyage were finalized.[11]

The Second Voyage was quickly authorized. One reason for haste was the genuine fear that the Portuguese might sail westward themselves and contest the Castilian claims. In fact, João II of Portugal had told Columbus on March 9, 1493, when the latter was in Portugal on his return from the New World, that "he [João] understood that in the agreement between the Castilian sovereigns and himself that the discovery belonged to him [Portugal]."[12] The very next day, March 10, 1493, João II sent an emissary to the Castilian court to clarify the matter, he ordered Francisco de Almeida to sail westward and seize the territories Columbus claimed to have discovered, and he seriously considered arresting Columbus.

There is absolutely no doubt that Columbus had violated the Treaty of Alcáçovas, concluded in 1479 between Portugal and Castilla, which defined the territory over which each would have sovereignty. Every island Columbus touched or saw during the voyage of 1492–1493 was legally Portugal's according to the Treaty of Alcáçovas. Knowing this, the Castilian sovereigns persuaded Pope Alexander VI to relocate the dividing line. In May, 1493, Pope Alexander established the Papal Demarcation Line and thereby "legalized" Castilla's claim to the discoveries Columbus had made on the First Voyage.

Another reason for launching a second expedition quickly

Table 1. The Discovery Voyages of Christopher Columbus

Dates	Port of Departure	Port of Return	Discoveries
1492–1493	Palos	Palos	Bahama Islands, Cuba, Española
1493–1496	Cádiz	Cádiz	Dominica, northern Lesser Antilles, Virgin Islands, Puerto Rico, Jamaica
1498–1500	Sanlúcar de Barrameda	Cádiz	Trinidad, northern South America (Venezuela)
1502–1504	Cádiz	Sanlúcar de Barrameda	Martinique, Honduras, Nicaragua, Costa Rica, western Panama, Cayman Islands

was the belief by Ferdinand and Isabela that, if indeed Columbus had discovered the Indies with their great wealth, a way had been found to finance the liberation of the Holy Land, then occupied by the Muslims. And in addition to the gold, silver, and pearls that might be found, perhaps the East Indian spice trade could be wrested from Arabic-Turkish control. Lastly, if defense of sovereignty and the potential of vast wealth were not sufficient justification for a second voyage, then the clergy had yet another reason: the newly discovered lands held an unlimited supply of souls to be saved.

Given these reasons for haste, the turnaround time between Columbus's return from the First Voyage and the departure of the Second was to have been minimal. The Second Voyage was scheduled to depart on July 15, 1493.[13] But the Catholic Sovereigns made one grave error. They entrusted the outfitting of the fleet to Juan Rodríguez de Fonseca, Archdeacon of Sevilla, later Bishop of Palencia, and still later Bishop of Burgos. By autumn of 1493 Fonseca was Minister of the Indies; eventually, he was to become President of the Council of the Indies.[14]

Bishop Fonseca was an evil man: immoral, ruthless, greedy, and tyrannical. He headed the list of those Castilians who brought chaos to the New World. He despised Columbus and did everything he could to undermine the Admiral, beginning with the Second Voyage. It has been said that Fonseca's hatred of Columbus stemmed from the fact that Columbus, an Italian, was a foreigner in Castilla. Perhaps, but another Italian, Juonato Berardi, was given a contract by Fonseca to furnish many of the supplies, and Berardi's manager was the Florentine, Amerigo Vespucci.[15]

Corruption and graft were cornerstones of Fonseca's organizational skills. Money for the undertaking came from extortion, seizing and selling the properties and personal effects of banished Jews, and from bribes paid by travelers eager to gain passage on one of the seventeen ships of the Second Voyage. By choosing people because they had money, or because they were related to highly placed individuals who also usually had money, Fonseca denied passage to many who possessed skills that were sorely needed on the voyage and in the colony. He also placed 200 "gentlemen volunteers" on the manifest and was responsible for over-crowding every ship. About a thousand people should have made the trip but at least 1200 sailed and it has been argued that 1500 actually went out from Cádiz.[16]

Defective materials were loaded, good food was replaced with bad, and armor and weapons from the armory in Granada were sold to the highest bidder instead of being loaded on the ships for the journey to the New World.[17] Twenty-five fine Arabian horses somehow vanished and were replaced with only twenty nags ready for the glue factory.

～

It is possible that Fonseca's maladroit and malevolent management of the fleet explains how Juan Ponce de León happened to secure a place on board one of the ships. Juan Ponce's name appears on no record that has come down to us. He was too young to have been an officer or an official of any sort. He had little, if any, money and was not in a position to "buy on" as many did. It is possible that he was one of the "gentlemen volunteers."

But Juan Ponce had influential relatives — and noble ones at that — right on the island of León upon which Cádiz was located. Perhaps one of the Cádiz Ponce de Leóns picked up his tab. And there never was a complete list of the "gentlemen volunteers," unlike the normal crew rosters that are mostly intact. If Juan Ponce did not come to the New World in this manner then he could have been one of the hundred or so stowaways, but this is unlikely.

There is neither a complete roster of participants on the Second Voyage nor an official log. Columbus must have kept one but it has never been discovered. For information about this voyage we must rely on letters written by some of the voyagers, verbal accounts of certain participants that were written down by others, and a few histories written by people who had direct access to official documents.

We know, for example, that the flagship of the Second Voyage was a nao, legally named *Santa María la Galante* (Saint Mary the Gallant) but whose name was shortened to *Maríagalante*.[18] This ship was also referred to as *La Capitana* (The Flagship), and the fact that one ship was referred to by three names has introduced some confusion about the composition of the fleet. It is also known that the names of the other two naos were *La Colina* and *La Gallega*. The latter may have been commanded by Juan de la Cosa, whose *La Gallega* had been rechristened *Santa María* before it became Columbus's flagship on the First Voyage.

26

Of the fourteen caravels of all sizes in the fleet, very few are identified in the surviving documents. Only three are positively known to have taken part: the *Niña* (a survivor of the First Voyage and already mentioned), the *Cardera*, and the *San Juan*. These three are specifically named as those involved in the exploration of southern Cuba and the discovery of Jamaica in 1494.[19]

As with the ships, very little can be said about the officers, sailors, and passengers. Only a handful of names has been passed down through the years.[20] We do know that there were no women on the Second Voyage and no Pinzóns — two Pinzóns had been captains on the First Voyage: Martín Alonso on the *Pinta* and Vicente Yáñez on the *Niña*.

Among the noteworthy passengers listed on the ships' rosters were the following:

Diego de Alvarado was a "gentleman volunteer" on the Second Voyage and brother of the future governor of Guatemala who, many years later, would sail from Guatemala to Peru to challenge Francisco Pizarro for control of that country.

Friar Bernardo Buil was a Benedictine monk and apostolic delegate who brought twelve clerics with him and was to say the first mass in the New World.

Dr. Diego Álvarez Chanca was Queen Isabela's personal physician, the medical chief on the Second Voyage, and the author of a detailed written account of the voyage.

Diego Colón was a Taino (Lucayan) Indian who had been with Columbus since his first landfall on Guanahaní (San Salvador) in 1492. Confusing matters is the fact that a second Diego Colón, this one Christopher Columbus's brother, was among the voyagers. These two Diegos, plus the Admiral's elder son, also a Diego, make it necessary to read very carefully whenever the name Diego Colón is mentioned in any document of the period!

Guglielmo (Guillermo) Coma was an Aragonese "gentleman volunteer" on the Second Voyage and the author of a letter to Nicolò Syllacio, a professor at the University of Pavia in Italy, that gives a first-hand account of the Second Voyage.[21] Syllacio published this account late in 1494 or early in 1495, which made it the second printed record of the New World — preceded only by the famous *La Carta de Colón* of 1493.

Juan de la Cosa has already been mentioned as possibly being the captain of *La Gallega*, inasmuch as he once had a ship by that name which became famous as the *Santa María* of Columbus's First Voyage. Not only did de la Cosa own the *Santa María* but he was also one of the ablest pilots of his time. Further, he was an exceptional cartographer and drafted the first map known to show portions of the New World. This famous map, dated to 1500 by most authorities, was made in El Puerto de Santa María, across the bay from the city of Cádiz.

An Italian "gentleman volunteer" on the voyage was Michele de Cuneo, a native of Savona and possibly a boyhood friend of Columbus. His letter of 1495 is one of the primary sources for information concerning the journey.[22]

Francisco de Garay was a notary who served Columbus on the Second Voyage. De Garay later became the governor of Jamaica and an opponent of Hernán Cortés. As governor of Jamaica he authorized the Pineda expedition in 1519 that sailed across the Gulf of Mexico and explored portions of the coast of what is now the United States and Mexico.

Pedro de Las Casas — the father of Bartolomé de Las Casas, an important chronicler of events in Spanish America during the late fifteenth and early sixteenth centuries — was a merchant in Sevilla who had fallen on hard times and joined the Second Voyage in an effort to enhance his poor financial condition.[23] Since there were several prominent members of his family in Sevilla, Pedro probably had little difficulty in securing a billet on one of the ships bound for the New World.

Accompanying Pedro de Las Casas were three of his brothers: Francisco de Peñalosa, choirmaster for the Catholic Sovereigns; Diego de Peñalosa, a notary public and clerk of the court of the king and queen; and Gabriel de Peñalosa. A fourth brother, Juan de Peñalosa, had been sent to Palos in 1492 to recruit seamen for the First Voyage. The surname of the father of these five brothers was Peñalosa; as was the prerogative in fifteenth-century Castilla, Pedro chose to take his mother's surname — Las Casas.

Friar Antonio de Marchena, who had befriended Columbus at the monastery in La Rábida in 1485, found a place on one of the ships, probably aboard the *Maríagalante* with the Admiral.

And last, but certainly not least, there was Alonso de Ojeda. He was a protégé of the Duke of Medina-Celi, the nobleman with whom Christopher Columbus had resided in El Puerto de Santa María from 1489 until 1491. It is more than likely that Columbus and Ojeda had met before 1493. Ojeda was to become the first governor of what is now Venezuela and Colombia.

More than famous, or infamous, people were transported to the New World by the ships of the Second Voyage. The first horses and pigs came to America — and probably the first cattle and goats — and it was this expedition that brought sugarcane, oranges, and lemons to the West Indies. Bananas might have entered the New World at this time but there is no positive documentation of their presence in the region until 1516.

~

The fleet probably assembled at Cádiz because the Bay of Cádiz was the best harbor on Castilla's Atlantic coast and the nearest harbor in Castilla to the Canary Islands, the last landfall before the West Indies. There were, however, other ports

Figure 10. Juan Ponce's Iberia in the late part of the fifteenth century. **Top:** Kingdoms and selected towns and ports of the region. **Bottom:** Principal ports of the Atlantic coast of southwestern Spain. All of Columbus's voyages of discovery and all of Juan Ponce's departures for the New World were from one or another of these ports.

on the bay besides Cádiz from which the fleet could have sailed: Rota (today Spain's largest naval base), El Puerto de Santa María (residence of the Duke of Medina-Celi and Juan de la Cosa), and Puerto Real (built by the Catholic Sovereigns as their "personal port" in 1488). San Fernando (formerly Isla de León) did not exist until 1776.[24] Two other decent ports in Spain west of Cádiz, toward Portugal, were Sanlúcar de Barrameda, which in the fifteenth century included the river city of Sevilla, and the clusterd ports of Huelva, Palos, and Moguer.

Sanlúcar de Barrameda lies about fifteen miles north of Cádiz, at the mouth of the Guadalquivir River. Sevilla is forty-

Figure 11. Sanlúcar de Barrameda, Spain. Christopher Columbus sailed on his Third Voyage from here and returned to this city from his Fourth Voyage. This was also the port from which Nicolás de Ovando, with Juan Ponce as passenger, sailed in 1502. (Courtesy Instituto de Turismo de España — TURESPAÑA)

five miles up the river. Five hundred years ago Sanlúcar de Barrameda and Sevilla were major ports. Every ship that sailed from Sevilla passed through Sanlúcar de Barrameda. When the Casa de Contratación (House of Trade), the institution that ruled the Indies in almost every way, was created and placed in Sevilla in 1503, Sanlúcar de Barrameda and Sevilla eclipsed Cádiz in importance until the Casa was moved to Cádiz in 1717.[25] The original placement of the Casa in Sevilla was a political decision, made by the Crown but with the advice of Fonseca, Archdeacon of Sevilla and Minister of the Indies. Because of its strong orientation to the Indies, Sanlúcar de Barrameda was the port of departure and return for many important voyages to the New

Figure 12. The Torre del Oro, or Golden Tower, was built by the Moors in 1220 to control traffic on the Guadalquivir River at Sevilla, Spain. A similar tower was built on the opposite (right, or west) bank of the river. A chain extended across the river between these towers and was raised and lowered to control traffic. Then, as now, the Guadalquivir River carried more traffic than any other river in Spain. The tower that once existed on the west bank is now gone. (Courtesy Instituto de Turismo de España — TURESPAÑA)

World and beyond at the end of the fifteenth and beginning of the sixteenth centuries. For example, the Third Voyage of Columbus (1498) sailed from here, and the Fourth Voyage of Columbus returned to this port in 1504. The very large fleet of Nicolás de Ovando, the third governor of Española, departed from Sanlúcar de Barrameda in 1502 and headed for Española. In 1514 Pedro Árias Dávila, also known as Pedrarias, sailed from Sanlúcar de Barrameda with seventeen ships to carry 1500 colonists to Darién (now northern Colombia) and to replace Balboa as governor. In 1519 the Magellan fleet of five ships commenced its circumnavigation voyage from Sanlúcar de Barrameda, although it had originated in Sevilla.

Huelva, Palos, and Moguer are three closely spaced cities on the banks of the Tinto and Odiel rivers, about sixty-five miles north of Cádiz. Although this region had served as the point of both departure and return of Columbus's First Voyage, the port facilities were not sufficient to assemble and launch a major enterprise. In fact, Palos was not chosen for the First Voyage because it was such a good port; it was chosen instead because it had been fined two ships for violating the Crown's taxation policy during the Peninsular War of 1474–1479. Today Palos and Moguer are agricultural towns and tourist centers. Most of the maritime heritage of these two towns are either memories or museum attractions, and the monastery at La Rábida, only a mile or so from Palos, is a "must see" site for anyone following the footsteps of Christopher Columbus. Huelva, founded by the Carthaginians, remains an important port.

～

Cádiz, then, was the port of choice for the assembly and departure of Columbus's Second Voyage.[26] The seventeen-boat fleet sailed with the morning tide on September 25, 1493, some two-and-a-half months later than originally scheduled, and steered a course on the well-traveled route to the Canary Is-

Figure 13. La Rábida Monastery, La Rábida, Spain, is the principal symbol of the rapid expansion of the Hispanic world during the fifteenth and sixteenth centuries. Christopher Columbus was befriended by the monks here and their encouragement led to the epic Voyage of Discovery. (Courtesy Patronato Provincial de Turismo, Huelva)

lands. Somewhere on one of those ships, young Juan Ponce probably watched Cádiz fall slowly below the horizon. One of his fellow-passengers, Guglielmo Coma, described the departure this way:[27]

> *Columbus, commander of the royal fleet, and called Admiral by the Spaniards, set out to explore the shores of the Orient, accompanied by a select body of soldiers. On September 25, 1493, with a fair wind, he sailed from the celebrated port of Cádiz, a noble city of Andalucía, outside the Strait of Gibraltar, where the Atlantic Ocean bursts violently into the Mediterranean Sea. In this port a squadron of larger and smaller ships equipped for speed was assembled. Among these were many light vessels which they call Cantabrican barks. The timbers of these were for the most part fastened with wooden pegs, lest the weight of iron should diminish their velocity.*
>
> *There were also many caravels; these also are small vessels, but built strong so as to be fitted for long voyages and heavy seas. Besides*

these there were also vessels specifically designed to explore the islands of the Indies.

Already the religious rites usual on such occasions were performed by the sailors; the last embraces were given by those setting out on the voyage; the ships were hung with banners; streamers were flying from the rigging; the royal standard flew at the stern of every ship. The pipers and harpists held the sea-nymphs and sirens in mute astonishment with their melodic strains. The shores echoed the blare of trumpets and the blasting of horns, and even the sea bottom echoed the canons' roar.

Some Venetian galleys, on their way to the English Channel in search of trade, came into the harbor at Cádiz purely by chance. The crews joined the celebration with zeal and enthusiasm and offered the prayers and blessings which were customary for ships setting sail for the Indies.

When Aurora [ancient Roman goddess of the dawn; the sun], resplendent with her bright trappings, ushered in the next morning [September 25], they sailed with gentle breezes for the Canaries.

The vessels reached Grand Canary a week later — October 2 — and by October 5 the ships sailed into the tiny harbor

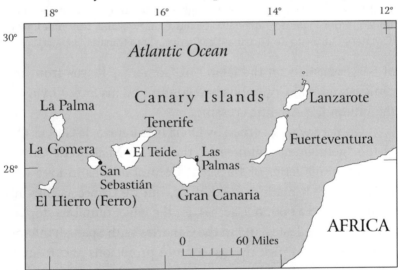

Figure 14. The Canary Islands was a part of Castilla in 1493 and now comprises two provinces of the Spanish State. Typically the Canaries were the last landfall for west-bound ships before beginning the sail across the Atlantic Ocean.

Figure 15. The summit of El Teide volcano on Tenerife in the Canary Islands, at 12,165 feet above sea level, is the highest point in Spain. This view of El Teide is from Pinar de Tamadaba, Grand Canary Island, fifty miles away. (Courtesy Patronato de Turismo, Las Palmas, Gran Canaria, España)

of San Sebastián on the island of Gomera.[28] It was from this same island that Columbus had committed his First Voyage to the unfamiliar Atlantic crossing.

Gomera was governed by Doña Inés Peraza de García. One of the "gentlemen volunteers," the Italian Michele de Cuneo, claimed in his letter of 1495 that Columbus was in love with Doña Inés.[29] It made a good story, but de Cuneo is the only authority, and a poor one at that, for the tale. Columbus stopped at Gomera, the last island in the Canaries with Spanish inhabitants, in order to pick up last-minute provisions and to make any necessary repairs to his vessels before beginning the long crossing of the open Atlantic. Las Casas tells us that the fleet took its departure from Gomera on October 7 and that Hierro,

Figure 16. Terraced fields on the island of Gomera in the Canary Islands. Gomera was visited by Christopher Columbus on all four of his voyages to the New World. It was the last Castilian land to be seen before crossing the open Atlantic Ocean. (Photograph by Eugene Hall)

the most southwesterly of the prominent Canary Islands, faded from view on October 13.

~

During the twenty-two-day crossing of the Atlantic, Juan Ponce de León, the teen-ager from central Castilla, became a sailor. Like so many Castilians from the interior, Juan Ponce had been conditioned by the land-bound struggle with the Muslims; his service during the last five years of this struggle as squire to Don Pedro Núñez de Guzmán, Knight Commander of the Order of Calatrava, had further defined his young life. Now, however, new opportunities had presented themselves and, in response, men from the interior of Castilla were coming to discover the sea for the first time.

Some of Juan Ponce's family, however, were familiar with the sea for, as noted above, a southern branch of the family tree was established on the island of León in the Bay of Cádiz.[30] This southern branch included Rodrigo Ponce de León, Duke and Marquis of Cádiz, who died in August 1492, the same month that Columbus began his First Voyage. Rodrigo was a cousin of Juan Ponce.

Duke Rodrigo was perhaps the most important person in Castilla in bringing defeat to the Muslims of Granada.[31] The Duke was hailed as a "southern El Cid," and the Crown granted the Duke many privileges as a reward for his military service during the Moorish wars. Juan Ponce's brother Luis married Rodrigo's sister (or perhaps his daughter) Francisca, Marquesa de Cádiz — Luis' second cousin.

Aurelio Tió, in *Nuevas fuentes para la historia de Puerto Rico* (1961), makes a very convincing case for the presence of aristocratic blood in Juan Ponce's veins.[32] Juan Ponce's brother Luis was the First Marquis of Zahara and the Fifth Lord of Villagarcía; his nephew, Rodrigo, was the Third Duke of Arcos; another brother, Fray Pedro, was Knight Commander of the Sovereign Military Order of Malta; his father, Pedro, was the Fourth Lord of Villagarcía; his grandfather, Luis, was the Lord of Villagarcía; his grandmother, Teresa de Guzmán, wife of Luis, was the Third Lady of Villagarcía and the House of Toral; and his great grandfather, Pedro, was the Count of Medellín and the First Count of Arcos.

Juan Ponce's mother, Doña Leonor de Figueroa, was the daughter of Lorenzo Suárez de Figueroa and María Manuel. Among other titles held by Lorenzo, the most interesting in this instance is Lord of Salvaleón. Salvaleón is the name Juan Ponce was to give to the town he founded in Española. Juan Ponce's paternal grandmother, Teresa de Guzmán (Doña Teresa Ponce de León y Guzmán), as noted above, was La Señora de la Casa

Toral (the Lady of the House of Toral). This helps to explain the connection between Juan Ponce and the Guzmáns of Toral, which is mentioned specifically by the historiographers Gonzalo Fernández de Oviedo and Bartolomé de Las Casas, twenty years after the Second Voyage occurred.

In *Historia general y natural de las indias,* Oviedo wrote:[33]

> *Juan Ponce was a poor squire when he came here [to Española], and in Spain he had been a servant of Pedro Núñez de Guzmán, brother of Ramírez Núñez, Lord of Toral. This same Pedro Núñez, when Juan Ponce served him as a page, did not have 100,000 maravedís or thereabouts of income, despite the fact that he was of illustrious blood and later the tutor of the Very Serene Lord Prince Don Fernando, who now is king of the Romans.*

And, in a memorial given to Cardinal Cisneros, Las Casas wrote:[34]

> *Juan Ponce was a squire of Don Pedro Núñez de Guzmán, knight commander of the Order of Calatrava; he came to the Indies as a poor foot-soldier with Christopher Columbus, and there he married an innkeeper's daughter in Española.*

Both of these statements are somewhat confused, but Tió has sorted them out. Tió writes:[35]

> *He [Juan Ponce] was a squire without a source of wealth, a veteran of the Conquest of Granada, in search of fame, honor, adventure, and fortune, like the great majority of Conquistadores whether of good lineage or not.*

Also, Tió suggests that Juan Ponce might have been a squire or page in the House of Toral, but he was not a *criado* (servant) as Oviedo states. He had been raised (*avia sido criado*; educated and instructed) by relatives. After all, Juan Ponce's paternal grandmother was not only a Guzmán, she was also the *Señora* (Lady) of the House of Toral.

It should be recalled that understanding and documenting fifteenth-century Spanish genealogy is far from an exact science! First, no rigid rules existed for the selection of the surname. Usually the oldest son chose the father's surname; the others took the mother's surname. But we have seen that this was not the case with Bartolomé de Las Casas and his father and uncles. Nor was it the case with the Ponce de León family, where most members — male and female — tended to use the paternal surname. Nevertheless, there were descendants of Juan Ponce de León y Figueroa (Juan Ponce's complete name) who preferred Figueroa to Ponce de León. Second, there were many illegitimate children, and although most were recognized, some were not. Third, there were marriages involving close relatives. For instance, Juan Ponce's great uncle Juan, the Second Count of Arcos, married a niece; Juan Ponce's brother Luis married a second cousin. Fourth, parochial records were often poorly maintained; some were lost, some damaged by weather and insects, and some were never recorded in the first instance. Fifth, many of the genealogical records maintained in Castilla (and later in Spain) record only those persons married in the country and their descendants who continued to live there. Those Castilians and, later, Spaniards who went to the New World were ignored.

Juan Ponce was born in the village of Santervás (Santhervás) de Campos, approximately thirty-five miles west of Palencia in the northernmost part of what is today the province of Valladolid.[36] This was in the historic province of Castilla la Vieja, or the interior of what is today western Spain. Santervás de Campos is in the district of Villalón de Campos and is situated on the banks of the Valderaduey River. This river, sometimes called the Araduey River, is about 100 miles long and is a tributary of the Duero River, which it joins at Zamora.

We are not certain of the date of Juan Ponce's birth but it was probably in 1474, the same year that marked the birth of Bartolomé de Las Casas and the ascension of Isabela to the throne of Castilla.[37] This was also the year that Prince João, who became João II in 1481, assumed complete charge of all Portuguese exploration and colonial policy.[38]

~

Carla Rahn Phillips has translated a rare description of an early voyage from the Canary Islands to Española. The document is a letter written by Eugenio de Salazar in 1573 to Miranda de Ron, "a friend and fellow bureaucrat back home."[39] Though this letter was written eighty years after Juan Ponce and 1200 others made the westward crossing on Columbus's Second Voyage, very little change had occurred in the conditions of ocean travel during the intervening years. Relative to the Salazar voyage, conditions on the Second Voyage of Columbus were possibly worse, for what was a pioneering journey in 1493 had become a routine journey by 1573. Salazar's letter reads, in part:[40]

> They put us in a tiny chamber that was three palms high and five palms square, in which, as we entered, the force of the sea did such violence to our stomachs and heads, that, parents and children, old and young, we turned the color of corpses, and we commenced to give up our souls (for that is the meaning of being seasick — almadiar) [a play on words], and to say "baac, baac," and after that "bor, bor, bor, bor," together spewing from our mouths all that had entered therein that day and the preceding one, in their turn some cold and sticky phlegm; others burning and bitter choler; and some, earthy and heavy blackbile. In this manner we continued without seeing sun nor moon, nor did we open our eyes, nor change our clothing from when we entered the cabin, nor even more, until the third day at sea, when I, still in that place of darkness and fear, heard a voice that said:
>
>> Blessed be the light, and the Holy True Cross, and the Lord of Truth, and the Holy Trinity; Blessed be the soul, and the Lord who rules it for us; Blessed be the day, and the Lord who sends it to us.
>
> And then this voice said the prayers "Our Father" and "Hail Mary," and after this it said:
>
>> Amen. God give us good days, good voyage, good passage to the ship, sir captain and master and good company, amen;

*So let there be a good voyage, may God grant many good days
to Your Graces, gentlemen, from poop to prow. . . .*

*It [the ship] is an elongated settlement. . . . it has its streets, open
squares and dwellings; it is enclosed by its walls. . . . [It has] a fountain or two called bombas [pumps], whose water neither the tongue
nor the palate would like to taste, not the nostrils to smell, nor even
the eyes to see, because it flows foaming like hell and stinking like the
devil. There are lodgings so closed in, dark and odoriferous that they
seem to be burial vaults. . . .*

*There are trees [masts] in this city, not the kind that exude healthful
gum and aromatic liquors, but those that run continuously with fish
grease and stinking tallow. Also there are ample rivers, not of sweet,
crystalline running water, but of condensed filth; not full of grains of
gold . . . but full of . . . lice, so large that some of them get seasick and
vomit pieces of flesh from apprentice seamen.*

*The terrain of this place is of such a quality that when it rains it is
solid, and when the sunlight is strong it softens to mire and your feet
are stuck to the ground so that you can scarcely lift them. The enclo-
sures inside [the city] have an enormous profusion of . . . cockroaches,
and a great abundance of . . . rats — many of which will turn and
resist their hunters like wild boars. The . . . direction finder . . . is
enclosed at night in the binnacle [compass box], which is a box very
similar to those customarily used to enclose chamber pots in upper-
class bedrooms. In this sad and dark city, it is black outside, and even
blacker inside, with blackish pavements, blackish walls, blackish inhabitants, and blackish officials; in short, it is such that from the bow-
sprit to the counter-mizzen, from stem to stern, from the hawse-holes
to the helm-hole, from the beakhead to the tiller, from the larboard
channel to the starboard mainstays, and from one side of the ship to
the other, there is nothing on board that is good nor seems good. . . .*

*There is in this settlement a body of persons . . . who have their
offices and dignities according to their . . . hierarchies. According to
this hierarchy the pilot has in his charge the governance of the settlement. . . . The captain has charge of defense. . . . The master watches
over household duties; the master's assistant over loading and unloading; the sailors, to sail the ship; the boys and apprentice seamen
to help the sailors; the pages to serve the sailors and apprentice seamen, to sweep and swab, and to say the prayers and keep vigil over
the city. The guardian . . . guards the ship's boat, and he takes account of what is stolen from the passengers and also has water fetched.
The dispenser guards the provisions; and the caulker is the engineer*

who fortifies the city and closes the apertures where the enemy [the sea] could enter. There is in this settlement a barber-doctor to give haircuts to the sailors and bleed them, if necessary. And lastly, [there are] the householders of this city [passengers], who have no more friendliness, faith, or charity than [vicious fish], when you encounter them at sea.

I looked at the pilot . . . and saw him seated with great authority at his tribunal — a wooden easy chair that must have been bought at a barber's auction; and from there made into a Neptune, he pretends to rule the sea and its waves. . . . From there he governs and orders, and all do his bidding. . . . I have not seen a gentleman so well served nor have I seen knaves who serve so well and so well merit their wages as these sailors. . . . And when the pilot has provided . . . orders, it is something to see the diligence and quickness of the sailors in carrying them out, because instantly you will see some on the cross-beam of the topsail; others climbing by the ratlines on the shrouds; other gentlemen on the spars; others clinging to the masthead; others with the topmasts; others clamped on and holding the step of the mast to its cap; others grasping the sheets, hauling and tallying the sail; and others clambering and chasing from one place to another by the rigging, some high and others low, so that they seem to be cats chasing through the trees or spirits of those who fell from heaven and remained in the air. Then, when it is time to raise the sails, it is something to hear the sailors who are working singing shanties, and they raise the sails singing and in the right time [rhythm] of the song. . . .

I was looking at the helmsman as he dispensed orders and at the sailors as they executed them, until, with the sun already on high, I saw two of the pages I mentioned bring from below decks a certain bundle that they called tablecloths, arranging them in the waist of the ship, as clean and white and damask-like as pieces of dark-colored fustian [cotton and linen mixture]. Then they heaped on this table some small mountains of ruined biscuit, so that the biscuits looked like heaps of cow dung in a farmer's field. Then they put three or four large wooden plates on the table, filled with stringy beef joints, dressed with some partly cooked tendons. Once the table was thus finished off, the page called all to the table.

Table, table, sir captain and master and good company, the table is set; the meat laid out; water as usual for sir captain and master and good company. Long live the King of Castile by land and sea. Who says to him war, let them cut off his head; who won't say amen, gets nothing to drink. The table is set in good time, those who don't come won't get to eat.

At the Amen, all the mariners came, sitting on the deck at the table, with the master's assistant at the head and the master gunner on his right. One sailor stuck his legs away from the table, another had his feet forward; this one squatting; that one reclining, and they sat in many other ways as well. And without waiting for grace to be said, these Knights of the Round Table took out their knives big and small of diverse fashions, some made to kill pigs, others to flay lambs, and others to cut purses; and they grabbed in their hands the poor bones, separating them from their nerves and sinews, as if all their lives they had been practicing anatomy studies . . . and in the time it took to say a "Credo," they left the bones as smooth and clean as ivory. Fridays and fast days they dine on broad beans stewed with water and salt. On important holy days they dine on codfish. A page comes by with a container of liquid in his hand and with his cup serves them wine that is less, and worse, and more diluted than they want. And thus dining with the first course last and the last course first and the middle course throughout, they finish their meal without finishing their hunger.

At this same time the captain, master, pilot, and notary of the ship ate apart at their own table; and at the same hour all the passengers . . . also ate. Because in this city it is necessary to cook and dine at the same hour as your neighbors; if not, you will not find light . . . in the stove. So that I with my fastidious tastes have to sup and dine at the same hour as he who has a canine appetite, or dine cold and offended, and sup in the dark. . . . And having asked for a drink, you could die of thirst in the middle of the ocean, because they give you water by the ounce, as in a pharmacy, after too much beef jerky and salted things: for Lady Sea will not tolerate or conserve meat or fish that is not dressed in her salt. Everything else that is eaten is rotten and stinking. And even with the water it is necessary to lose your senses of taste and smell and sight just to drink it and not sense it. That is how one dines and drinks in this agreeable city.

Indeed if in dining and drinking one receives such gratification, what will there be in the rest of the experience? Men, women, youths and old people, the dirty and the clean, all are thrown into a hullaba-loo and a mess, jammed one against the others; and thus jammed together one belches, another vomits, another breaks wind, another discharges his bowels, all while you eat breakfast; and you cannot tell anyone that he is demonstrating bad manners, because the ordinances of this city permit everything. When, on the soil of this city, you set yourself on your feet, a blow of the sea will enter to visit them and leave your shoes or boots whiter than snow from its foamy saliva, and burned with the strength of its salt. . . . And if you would like to relieve yourself . . . it is necessary to hang out over the sea . . . and pay your respects to the sun, to the moon and the other planets, and to summon all of them, and to grasp well the mane of the wooden horse, on penalty that, if you jump up, you will be brought down so hard that you will not be able to ride again. . . .

The music that you hear is that of the winds that come howling, and of the sea and its waves that arrive at the ship roaring. . . . Then if you hit a calm in the middle of the sea, when the ship's supplies are used up, and there is no water to drink, here is your consolation; with the ship pitching night and day, your stomach that was quiet begins to gyrate again, sending to your head the vapors that had settled down, and you see yourself at God's mercy, until, by means of His compassion, the wind begins to blow again.

At times the sails are swollen into a bell shape, which is a pleasure to see; and at times they blow in front and whip the masts, and us even more; because the ship hardly moves at all. Then if the pilot is little schooled in the Indies course, and doesn't know when to be on guard for land, and to take to the open sea to avoid the shallows, shoals, and other dangers, you will think you are on the high sea, and in a trice find yourself high and dry, and then wet, and then they find you drowned. If the ship is a bit of a slow sailer, like the one that carried us, then although it has wind right ahead of the stern, it will scarcely move; oh, how long the voyage is! The other ships each hour lay to, restraining their motion, and it was even necessary to haul our ship along, since it wasn't enough to attach it to a tow line; when there was fair weather, it went rolling along from side to side so that every day we became seasick all over again when we had a bit of weather. . . .

Then the pages go to tend the watch-glass, and say:

> *Blessed be the hour God came to earth, Holy Mary who gave Him birth, and Saint John who saw His worth. The guard is posted; the watch-glass filling; we'll have a good voyage, if God be willing.*

When the sand has finished running through the watch-glass, the page who is tending it says:

> *Good is what's past, and better what comes; one glass is past and the second is filling; more will be filled if God be*

*willing; to keep the right time makes the voyage fine; you at
the prow, be alert and guard well!*

And those at the prow respond with a shout or a grunt, making it
known that they were not asleep. And for each glass that runs out,
which takes half an hour, they start another, until morning. At midnight the page calls those who are on duty for the watch that begins
then and lasts until morning, and says:

*To your watch, to your watch, sir mariners on duty; to
your watch, at the right time for sir pilot's turn, for the hour
is here; arise, arise, arise!*

In this way we sailed alone without other company for six days.
The other . . . ships that left with us as a fleet [from the Canary Is-
lands] quit following the mandates of the Lord Judge of the House of
Trade of the Indies that dispatched us, and each one set off in its own
direction the first night that we sailed. Thus it is that a man finding
himself on a single ship, seeing no land, but only an unquiet sky and
water, travels through those cerulean, greenish-black realms, with
their dark and fearsome terrain, without knowing if he moves at all
from one place nor encountering the wake of a ship, and he seems to
see himself always surrounded by the same horizon, at night seeing
the same thing that he saw in the morning, and today the same as
yesterday, without seeing anything different. What diversion, what
comfort can he have from the voyage? Not even knowing the hour he
will be able to leave the irritations of such a road and lodging place?

Travel on land with a good mount and some money in your pocket
can be quite pleasant; you go for awhile through a plain, then you
climb a mountain, you descend from there to a valley, you pass a cool
river, you traverse a meadow full of diverse cattle, you raise your
eyes, you see diverse birds flying through the air, you encounter diverse people on the road, from whom you ask for news from diverse
parts . . .

If one day you come to a village with nothing much to eat, tomorrow you will find yourself in a city that is copiously and sumptu-
ously provisioned. If one day you dine at an inn with a scar-faced
innkeeper expert in pursuit and practiced in the art of pilfering, and
now a member of an armed unit of the Holy Brotherhood, who sells
you cat for hare, goat for lamb, dried horse meat for beef, and sour
vinegar for pure wine; at night you will sup at the house of a different
sort of host who serves bread for bread and wine for wine. If today
you pass the night in the house of a hostess who is old, dirty, quarrel-
some, wretched, and covetous, tomorrow you will be offered improved

46

luck, and you will fall in with a hostess who is young, clean and cheerful, gracious, generous, of good appearance and much piety; with whom today you will forget the bad hospitality of yesterday. But at sea there is no hope that the road, nor the lodgings, nor the host will improve. Each day everything can only get worse and more annoying with the increasing irritations of the voyage and the lack of ship's stores as they continue diminishing and becoming more offensive. . .

Thus we sailed . . . until even the pilot and the mariners began to sniff the air and conjecture about landfall like donkeys do when they near a pasture. At such times it is something to see the pilot calculate the Pole Star's position, to see him take the fore-staff, set the timbrel, and point it toward the north, and finally to estimate its distance at 3,000 or 4,000 leagues; to see him afterwards at midday take the astrolabe in his hand, raise his eyes to the sun, try to get the sun to shine through the openings in the astrolabe, and then give up without being able to complete his measurements properly; and to see him look at his sailing book; and at last, to throw in his minimal judgments as to the altitude of the sun. At times his estimate rises so high that it is 1,000 degrees over the mark. And other times it falls so low, that one would not arrive there in a thousand years; and above all it made me tired to see how the pilots wanted to keep secret from the passengers the degree or point that they took, and the leagues that it seemed to them the ship had sailed on its course; although afterwards when I understood the cause, which is that they never hit the mark nor understand what they are doing, I had patience seeing that they are correct in not displaying the irregularities of their confused aim-taking; because they take the altitude as a little more or less; and the space the head of a pin on their instrument will cause them to make more than five hundred leagues of error in their estimate.

Spare me this skill. Oh, how God shows His omnipotence in having put this subtle and so important art of navigating among judgments so dull and hands so coarse as those of these pilots! What a thing it is to see them ask one another: "How many degrees has Your Grace taken?" One says: "Sixteen," another: "Just under twenty," and another: "Thirteen and a half." Then they ask each other: "How does Your Grace find himself in relation to the land?" One says: "I find myself forty leagues from land," another: "I one hundred fifty." Another says: "I found myself this morning at ninety-two leagues." And be it three or be it three hundred, not one conforms with another nor with the truth.

We traveled hearing these vain and various judgments of the pilots and masters and of some mariners who presume to be bachelors *in the art of navigation, until, twenty-six days after setting sail, God was served that we saw land. Oh how much better the land seems from the sea than the sea from the land!*

And thus ended Eugenio de Salazar's voyage, at the Antillean island of La Deseada (now La Desirade), a few miles north of Dominica, the site of Juan Ponce's introduction to the New World with Columbus's Second Voyage. The route of Salazar's journey in 1573 followed the one of Juan Ponce in 1493 and, until the Age of Steam arrived in the nineteenth century, this course laid down by Columbus was the usual one taken by ships sailing from the west coast of Europe to the Caribbean and North America. From Europe the sailing directions were simple — sail south 'til the butter melts, then sail west.

The Second Voyage of Columbus sighted land on Sunday, November 3, 1493. [41] The island that came into view was called Caire by the Carib Indians, but the Castilians called it Dominica, Latin for "Sunday," the day of the week upon which it was discovered. Three other islands were also visible that day:

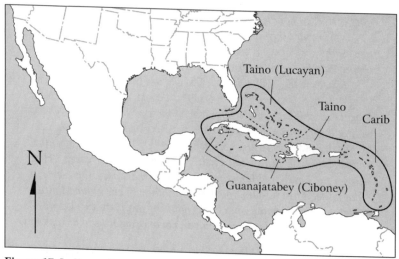

Figure 17. Indian cultures of the West Indies, 1492.

Matinino (now Martinique) was to the south, the smaller Ayay (now María Galante) was to the northeast, and to the northwest was the very large Turuqueira (later Kerkeria and Santa María de Guadalupe, now simply Guadeloupe).

The fleet anchored at Guadeloupe on November 4 and remained there for six days while a search was conducted for an unauthorized and apparently lost landing party.[42] On November 10 the island of Montserrat was named after a mountain near Barcelona. The Caribs had eaten all of the Taino inhabitants of Montserrat, so the island was depopulated when the Castilians first arrived.

After the fleet left Guadeloupe it passed the Carib-inhabited islands of Ocamaniro, which was given the Castilian name Santa María la Redonda, and Yaramaqui, which became Santa María de la Antigua.[43]

Columbus may have named one other island at this time — San Martín — but there is no evidence that this is the island called Saint Martin or Sint Maarten today, and not one of the eyewitnesses on the Second Voyage mentions such an occur-

Table 2. Selected Place-Names and Their Equivalents

Native	Columbus	Colonial	Modern
Guanahaní	San Salvador	Atwoods Cay	Samana Cay
Cuba	Juana	Cuba	Cuba
Bohío	La Isla Española	La Española, Santo Domingo, Saint-Domingue	Española, Hispaniola
Boriquén	San Juan Bautista	San Juan, Puerto Rico	Puerto Rico
Yamaye, Xaymaca	Santiago	Jamaica	Jamaica

rence. After Antigua, the next island that was named with certainty was Santa Cruz (now Saint Croix).[44] After leaving Santa Cruz, Columbus named a large group of islands Las Once Mil Vírgenes (The Eleven Thousand Virgins, now the Virgin Islands). One of them — possibly Saint Thomas — he called Santa Úrsula.[45] By November 18 the fleet was in sight of an island the Taino Indians called Boriquén but which Columbus named San Juan Bautista (Saint John the Baptist, now Puerto Rico).[46] Juan Ponce de León was one of many Castilians who cast the first European eyes on the island that day, and it is possible that he was also among the first Europeans to go ashore when the fleet anchored, possibly at Rincón-Añasco, near Punta Higüey toward the northwestern tip of the island.

The fleet departed San Juan Bautista on the morning of November 22, 1493, and hurried to the settlement of La Navidad which Columbus had left on the island of Española when he had returned to Castilla earlier that year with his two surviving ships.[47]

Chapter 2
1493–1511

Peón, Conquistador, Explorer, Governor

When Christopher Columbus reached the New World the second time, he was anxious to learn the fate of the men who he had left on the north coast of Española. Discovering that the colony had perished, Columbus established his new base several miles to the east. Shortly after this new colony was settled, Juan Ponce de León vanished from the records of the New World for nearly a decade; he either took one of the first ships back to Castilla, went into hiding, or had not, in fact, come to the New World with the Second Voyage of Columbus. Any of these three would have prevented Juan Ponce from participating in a colonial enterprise that was totally out of control. Indeed, Española became so chaotic that in 1499 Isabela and Ferdinand sent a royal commissioner, Francisco de Bobadilla, to straighten things out. His performance, however, was so bad that he was replaced in 1502 by Don Fray Nicolás de Ovando, who sailed from Castilla with thirty-two ships. It is almost certain that Juan Ponce traveled to Española aboard one of these ships.

Juan Ponce distinguished himself in the Indian wars on Española and was rewarded with land and a governorship in the eastern part of the island, where he became a very successful farmer — a rare occupation for a Castilian. Enjoying the confidence and support of Governor Ovando and King Ferdinand, Juan Ponce was named first governor of the Island of San Juan Bautista (later, Puerto Rico) and allowed to establish the first European colony on the island. However, Diego Columbus,

51

Christopher's son, and Juan Ponce became adversaries, and when the courts of Castilla upheld Diego's claim to his father's titles and privileges, including his authority over San Juan Bautista, Diego took steps to weaken Juan Ponce's power and influence on the island.

Juan Ponce de León and the Columbus fleet reached La Navidad on the north coast of what is now Haiti on November 28, 1493.[1] After sailing from San Juan Bautista the fleet had made a couple of stops along the coast of Española, and by the time the ships were anchored at La Navidad the Admiral knew that something had gone terribly wrong on shore.

La Navidad, the first European colony in the New World (discounting any colonies the Vikings might have attempted), had resulted from the loss of the *Santa María* during the First Voyage — the ship had become hopelessly stuck on a nearby sandbar on Christmas Eve, 1492.[2] With only two small ships remaining and insufficient space to carry all of the Castilians, Columbus had been forced to leave either thirty-nine or forty-two men (Columbus gave both numbers) behind in the village of the Taino chief Guacanagarí.[3] This village, reinforced with

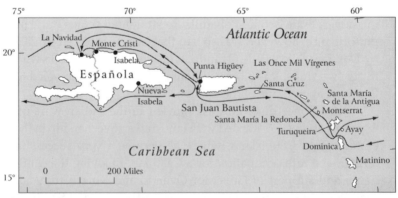

Figure 18. Juan Ponce's West Indies, including the route of Columbus's Second Voyage between Dominica and Española.

Figure 19. The site of La Navidad, the first Spanish colony in the New World, along the north coast of Española in what is now Haiti. (Photograph by M. W. Williams)

timbers, weapons, and supplies salvaged from the *Santa María*, was given the name La Villa de la Navidad (Nativity Town) by the Castilians. It became Castilla's first New World colony by accident. Columbus said it was God's will.

Columbus had sailed from La Navidad for Castilla on January 4, 1493. During his absence, La Navidad had been burned to the ground and not one Castilian was found alive. Columbus's friends, Chief Guacanagarí and his men, had fought valiantly to defend the Castilians and the village, but to no avail. A mountain chief, Caonabó, had attacked and destroyed the colony — the attack brought about by the greed, lust, and cruelty of the Europeans. The Castilians of La Navidad had even fought among themselves — mostly over gold and women. So, if young Juan Ponce did go ashore that November day, he was

Figure 20. A reproduction of the *Santa María*, Sevilla, Spain. The *Santa María*, Columbus's flagship on his Voyage of Discovery, was lost on December 24, 1492, off the north coast of Española. (Photograph by R. H. Fuson)

a witness to the beginning of the destruction of Eden.

Columbus considered, then abandoned, the idea of rebuilding La Navidad, and he turned his vessels to the east. Approximately forty miles east of Monte Cristi, a name that still survives in the town, bay, and province in what is today the Dominican Republic, a new colony was founded and called Isabela.[4] Isabela, named in honor of the queen, was probably established about December 18, 1493, or "a week before Christmas," according to Guillermo Coma, an eyewitness.[5]

Juan Ponce was a participant in the founding of Castilla's first all-European settlement in the New World. Although Isabela survived only a few months, this settlement became the springboard for the conquest of Española. It also became the last settlement many Castilians saw in the New World or, for

Table 3. Castilian and Spanish Exploration and Settlement of Selected Regions in the New World, 1492–1531.

Date	Place	Discoverer	First Permanent Settlement[1]
1492	Bahama Islands	Christopher Columbus	Governors Harbour (1648)
1492	Cuba	Christopher Columbus	Baracoa (1511)
1492	Española	Christopher Columbus	Santo Domingo (1496)
1493	Puerto Rico	Christopher Columbus	San Juan (1521)
1494	Jamaica	Christopher Columbus	Spanish Town (1534)
1499	Colombia	Alonso de Ojeda	Santa Marta (1525)
1501	Panama	Rodrigo de Bastidas	Panama City (1519)
1513	Florida	Juan Ponce de León	Saint Augustine (1565)
1517	Mexico	Francisco Hernández de Córdoba	Veracruz (1519)
1531	Peru	Francisco Pizarro	Lima (1535)

[1] The first permanent settlement was not necessarily established by the discoverer.

that matter, in any other world. Isabela was replaced by Nueva Isabela in 1494 or 1495 and the name of this new settlement was changed to Santo Domingo in 1495 or 1496.

Sometime early in January 1494, Alonso de Ojeda led an expedition of fifteen men into the Cibao, a beautiful valley in the interior of Española.[6] Ojeda was seeking gold, mainly, but he was also on the lookout for Caonabó and the Indians who had sacked La Navidad and killed the colonists. A similar foray, under the command of captain Ginés de Gorbalán, was sent in another direction.[7] Both reconnaissance parties returned within two weeks with the same story: there was gold in the Cibao. The chroniclers do not tell us if Juan Ponce went on either of these expeditions.

～

There is a significant interruption in the historical record of Juan Ponce's life for the period from January 1494 to the summer of 1504. In fact, were it not for the written statements of Oviedo and Las Casas, there would not be one grain of evidence that Juan Ponce came to the New World before 1504. The renowned Spanish historian Manuel Ballesteros Gaibrois does not think it is logical that Juan Ponce was on the west side of the Atlantic Ocean for most of the decade before 1504, but instead he believes that Juan Ponce probably came to America with the new governor of Española, Nicolás de Ovando, in 1502.[8] Ballesteros Gaibrois does not rule out, however, Juan Ponce's passage to America on the Second Voyage of Columbus. But he implies that Juan Ponce returned to Castilla rather quickly, probably on the next boat back, if he had come at all. His reasoning is based on pure logic; not even circumstantial evidence. He reasons that Juan Ponce was not the sort of person to remain unknown during those years of trial and tribulation in Española between 1493 and 1502. One — especially one like Juan Ponce — did not seek fame and fortune in the New World by remaining obscure for ten years!

According to Ballesteros Gaibrois, in 1502 Juan Ponce knew nothing about the people who were discontent with Christopher Columbus or his brothers, he was completely ignorant of the lust for gold among the Castilian residents of Española, and he had little knowledge about the abuses the Castilians were inflicting on the native population.

And why should we take the word of Oviedo and Las Casas that Juan Ponce went to the West Indies in 1493? First, these are the two primary sources for the early Spanish colonial period in the New World. Although these two historiographers often disagreed on social, political, and economic issues, they rarely were at odds with one another on factual details.

Oviedo writes, "I knew him [Juan Ponce de León] very well."[9] Inasmuch as both Juan Ponce and Oviedo were in Spain at the same time (1516–1518), and both in Sevilla, this statement is reasonable, and it is therefore just as reasonable to allow that Juan Ponce actually told Oviedo that he had voyaged with Columbus to Española in 1493.

Bartolomé de Las Casas' father and three uncles were on the Second Voyage of Columbus. They seem like logical sources for placing Juan Ponce on the Second Voyage. Further, Las Casas sailed to Santo Domingo with Ovando's fleet in 1502, and he claimed that Juan Ponce was also on that voyage. Surely, Las Casas was correct in writing that Columbus brought Juan Ponce to Española in 1493. And Ballesteros Gaibrois was probably correct to place him on the Ovando voyage of 1502. But how did Juan Ponce return to Castilla after Columbus's Second Voyage, and when?

~

Antonio de Torres sailed from Isabela on February 2, 1494, and arrived in Cádiz "either on April 8 or 10," according to Las Casas.[10] He returned to Castilla with twelve of the original fleet of seventeen ships, including the *Maríagalante*, the flagship of which he was captain during both the westbound and eastbound segments of the journey. Upon the arrival of the fleet at the new colony of Isabela, de Torres had been named *alcaide* (warden) of the town.[11] He was held in the highest esteem by Columbus, who had absolute trust in him. Likewise, he was also trusted by the Catholic Sovereigns. His sister, Doña Juana de Torres, a close friend of Columbus, was also the governess (often called nurse) of Prince Juan, the son of Ferdinand and Isabela, who died in 1497. In other words, Columbus was very close to both Juana and Antonio de Torres and they, in turn, were favorites in the palace of the Catholic Sovereigns.

One of the main reasons for de Torres's return to Spain in

1494 was for him to hand-deliver a memorandum— the so-called *De Torres Memorandum* — to Ferdinand and Isabela. It had been written by Columbus in the colony of Isabela and dated January 30, 1494. This memorandum was not only a message to the sovereigns but was also an outline for de Torres to follow when he spoke with them face-to-face.[12]

The memorandum details the vast wealth of Española — especially its gold and spices — and it offers many reasons, perhaps excuses, why so little wealth had been forthcoming.[13] Probably the primary reason for so little productivity, according to Columbus, was illness among the Spaniards. He attributed this to "a change in air and water," but he was ill even before the Second Voyage had left Castilla! Illness, said the Admiral, prevented road building, farming, construction, exploration, and other work in general. Not only were half the Castilians in the colony sick, but many who made the journey did not have the kind of skills needed to build a colony in the first place. Columbus expressed his hope that the people who came to Española in the future would pay more attention to why they were sent than to their own selfish interests. In order to rectify some of the problems immediately, Columbus recommended certain adjustments in pay for some of the colonists in Isabela and, apparently, even sent some of the colonists back to Castilla with de Torres.

Columbus also listed a number of items that he thought the colony needed badly, including wheat and barley seed and grape vines. Unknown to the Admiral, however, was the fact that none of these crops would grow in the lowland tropics. Also on the list of needs were wine (much that came on the Second Voyage was ruined because the casks were no good), salted meat (especially bacon), raisins, sugar, almonds, honey, rice, molasses, lambs, calves, mares, donkeys, horses (the ones brought on the Second Voyage were not the ones purchased for that purpose), medicines, weapons, and breastplates.

The local Taino Indians were mentioned in the memorandum, and it is obvious that they were not trusted by Columbus. He indicated that work was proceeding on a wall around Isabela and that guards had been posted.

Columbus also recommended to the Catholic Sovereigns that the sale of Indian slaves could finance Isabela and other colonies in Española. When de Torres returned to Castilla in 1494 he carried an unknown number of Indian slaves — "men and women and male and female children." Columbus claimed that these were cannibals — Carib Indians. But where would Columbus have obtained so many Caribs? There is no evidence that Caribs carried their children with them when they attacked Taino villages, and by 1494 Columbus had encountered Caribs only in the Lesser Antilles and the Virgin Islands. There is a strong suspicion here that some — if not all — of the purported "cannibals" were actually Tainos from Española. A year later — in February 1495 — de Torres transported 500 more Indian slaves to Castilla.[14]

When de Torres returned to Spain in February 1494 he also carried the letters of Guglielmo Coma and Dr. Chanca, documents that since have become primary source materials for the Second Voyage. And he brought a number of disenchanted Castilians returning to Castilla. Some were ill. Some were of the group of 200 or more "gentlemen volunteers." Some had been unwilling to do common labor; their goal had been to get rich quickly and return home — but none had gotten rich.

It is impossible to say with certainty if Juan Ponce was among those who returned to Castilla with de Torres, but he returned with someone and it had to be before the authority of Columbus was disputed by certain colonists — such as Miguel Díaz, Pedro Margarite, Juan Aguado, and Francisco Roldán. Further, we know that Juan Ponce did not accompany Columbus on the voyage that discovered Jamaica in 1494, nor did he march into the forests and savannas of Española with the troops who were seeking gold. He simply vanished from the muster roles and other historical records of this period.

~

Christopher Columbus, and to a lesser extent his brothers Bartholomew (Bartolomé) and Diego, had done a very poor job on Española managing the settlement and turning it into a productive enterprise. Gold production had not sufficiently met expectations. Columbus had been his own worst enemy — by constantly citing the riches of Española, he was expected to produce at a level that corresponded with the claims. If gold production had been high enough it is almost a certainty that any abuse or other failings would have been tolerated. Queen Isabela is, after all, the lady who gave the world the Spanish Inquisition.

By the spring of 1499 the Catholic Sovereigns decided to send a royal commissioner — Francisco de Bobadilla — to Santo Domingo to place things in order. Bobadilla resolved nothing — but he did send Columbus and his brothers back to Castilla in chains.[15] Outraged at the treatment of Columbus, the Catholic Sovereigns recalled the commissioner and restored Columbus's titles and privileges. Columbus, however, would never again have the power he once held, and he was replaced as governor of Española by Don Fray Nicolás de Ovando, Knight Commander of Lares.[16]

Ovando sailed from Sanlúcar de Barrameda on February 13, 1502, with a simple mission: straighten out the mess in Española and return Bobadilla to Castilla. The fleet of thirty-two ships was under the command of captain-general Antonio de Torres.[17] Approximately 2500 people made this trip to the New World, and one passenger among them, probably, was Juan Ponce de León. Other passengers included Pedro de Las

Casas, who had returned to Spain in 1498, and his son, Bartolomé.[18]

When Ovando's fleet was eight days out of Sanlúcar de Barrameda and almost within sight of the Canary Islands, a tremendous storm arose.[19] It was so severe and violent that it caused extreme turbulence in the sea and no one on any of the ships thought that it was possible to escape. One of the largest ships, *La Rábida*, went down and all of the crew and 121 passengers were lost. The remaining thirty-one ships were scattered and everything that was loose — including clothing and casks of wine and water — was thrown overboard to lighten each vessel in hopes that some lives might be saved. A few of the ships went to the coast of Morocco; others sailed to the Canary Islands of Tenerife, Lanzarote, Grand Canary, or Gomera. Each vessel went to whatever land was easiest to reach. Two caravels loaded mostly with sugar had just departed the Canaries and were sunk in the storm. Crates, wood, casks, and other debris floated all the way to Cádiz and other ports in Castilla. Seeing this wreckage, everyone along the coast was certain that all of Ovando's fleet had been consumed by the ferocious sea and the strong wind.

The Catholic Sovereigns were in Granada when they heard the first reports of water-borne debris, almost two weeks after the fleet's departure. The good news — that thirty-one ships had miraculously weathered the tempest — did not reach Granada until the first week in March; news from overseas traveled no faster than the ships carrying it.

Ovando's fleet reassembled in Gomera. A ship from Grand Canary, complete with passengers who wanted to go to the Indies, was added. The fleet was then divided: Knight Commander Ovando took the fifteen or sixteen fastest ships and de Torres led the slower half. Ovando's half reached Santo Domingo on April 15 and de Torres arrived with the "slow sail-

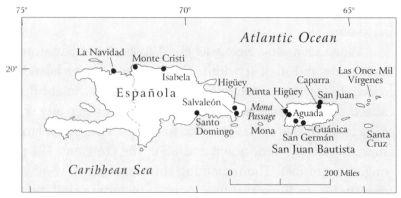

Figure 21. Selected places related to Juan Ponce's activities in Española and San Juan Bautista.

ers" about two weeks later.

Bobadilla relinquished his authority to Ovando and, within two months, had been arrested and placed aboard one of the twenty-eight ships in the harbor.[20] This fleet was also scheduled to carry back to Castilla a large quantity of gold, Roldán and many of his co-conspirators who opposed Columbus and his brothers, and Guarionex, a principal native chief from central Española who had been accused of rebelling against Castilian authority. Columbus's property, seized earlier by Bobadilla, was returned; even gold that belonged to the Admiral was recovered and prepared for shipment to Castilla.

Juan Ponce must have been present when Columbus arrived unexpectedly at Santo Domingo on June 29, 1502.[21] The Admiral was on his Fourth and last voyage and had been forbidden by the Crown to stop in Española as a result of the ongoing legal conflict over rights to explore and establish settlements in the West Indies. Nonetheless, Columbus had stopped at Santo Domingo to replace one of his ships. He also had sensed the onslaught of a tremendous storm and wanted to find shelter in the harbor. His warnings to Governor Ovando concerning the approaching storm went unheeded, and he was denied permission to sail into Santo Domingo harbor.

A hurricane struck the next day, June 30. Columbus and his little squadron of four ships survived, probably anchored at the Bay of Ocoa (now Azua), some fifty miles west of Santo Domingo. Of the twenty-eight vessels that had departed Santo Domingo the day before carrying prisoners and wealth to Castilla, only the ship with Columbus's gold made it across the ocean. Three other ships managed to ride out the storm and returned to Santo Domingo in miserable condition. The other twenty-four ships were lost, along with their crews, passengers, and cargo.

$\sim$

With Bobadilla lost at sea and Columbus sailing westward, Ovando could now turn his attention to increasing gold production and "pacifying," a euphemism for exterminating, the Indians on Española. To accomplish this he turned to the people he could trust; those who came over with him. In light of all of the problems that had befallen Española between 1492 and 1502, Ovando was not going to risk creating additional ones by calling on *los viejos*, "the old ones" of the island.

Higüey, the easternmost region of Española, an area lying in what is now the Dominican Republic, had not been pacified by 1502. Actually, trouble started in Higüey that year when a Castilian's dog killed an Indian.[22] As the story is told, the Indians retaliated for the assault by ambushing and killing eight Castilians in a canoe as they passed to the main island of Española from the tiny island of Saona. This skirmish both angered and delighted the Castilians — it angered them because some of their countrymen had been killed but delighted them because a new war meant more captives — slaves — for sale and for labor.

In 1503, Juan de Esquivel, a cavalier from Sevilla, was chosen by Governor Ovando to conquer Higüey.[23] The Spaniards, with the aid of their dogs, won easily.[24] Even so, the Tainos refused to pay tribute by not supplying cassava bread to Santo Domingo unless the Castilians came to them to get it. And the native chief, Cotubanó (sometimes Cotubanamá), who was not taken captive during the 1503 confrontation, remained a thorn in the Castilians' side for some time to come.

Following the defeat of the Tainos, Esquivel left a token garrison in Higüey, probably at or near the town known today as Santa Cruz del Seibo, or simply El Seibo.[25] Almost as soon as Esquivel departed the small fortress, the Castilian soldiers began brutalizing the Indians and molesting the native women. Then, in 1504, another incident occurred: the fort built by Esquivel was attacked by Indians and burned. Nine Castilians died in the assault. This, to Ovando, was a rebellion. Once again he dispatched Esquivel, along with about 400 men and several lieutenants, to Higüey. One of these lieutenants, Juan Ponce de León, led the force from Santo Domingo. Bartolomé de Las Casas also seems to have been present. The accounts in Las Casas' *Historia* could only have been written by an eye-witness. Though out-numbered four to one, the well-armed Castilians massacred the naked Indians. Chief Cotubanó fled to Saona Island, but he was later captured and taken to Santo Domingo for trial and execution by hanging.

It was this second Indian rebellion in Higüey that catapulted Juan Ponce toward his place in history. Juan Ponce had been a bit-player on history's stage during the first campaign in Higüey, but he became a star during the episode that followed in 1504.

After the successful campaign in Higüey during 1504, Juan Ponce was given an *encomienda* (land grant) on the lower course of the Yuma River, about ten miles from the coast of the Mona Passage and two miles northwest of the town known today as San Rafael del Yuma.[26] He was also assigned a *repartimiento* (a number of Indians to work his land). And Juan Ponce so impressed Governor Ovando during the pacification of Higüey that he was named *adelantado* (frontier governor) of the province.[27]

Simply stated, the encomienda/repartimiento system was a means for the Crown to give land and workers to deserving Castilians, who in turn became *encomenderos*. The grant gave the *encomendero* the right to exact labor or tribute from the hapless resident and generally peaceful natives. In theory, the Indians were to receive rations, housing, protection, wages, and instruction in the Catholic faith. In theory, this was not slavery but rather an expression of sixteenth-century Castilian justice, whereby the Indians were treated as children who could not care for themselves.

In contrast, warring Indians were legally placed in bond-

Figure 22. The Rio Chavón in what is today the Dominican Republic on the island that Juan Ponce knew as Española. Juan Ponce was once governor of Higüey (now La Altagracia) Province, which lies to the east (right) of the river. (Photograph by R. H. Fuson)

age when captured, and Caribs were defined as warring Indians at a very early date. Tainos, however, were taken to Castilla
as slaves as early as 1494 on the return voyage of de Torres;
African slaves were first brought to Santo Domingo in 1502
when Juan Sánchez received permission from the Crown to
bring five caravels of African slaves to Santo Domingo.[28] As the
native Taino population declined — which it did rapidly —
there was greater popular clamor for increasing the number of
African slaves in the colony. The decline of Indians and the
increasing influx of African slaves early in the colonial period
explain the general composition of races seen today in the West
Indies.

The land grant system that developed in Española was
unique. It may have been the only European system of land
distribution based not only on a particular agricultural crop but
also on a specific agricultural technique. For lack of a better
name this was called the *montón* system.[29] A montón was an
artificial mound about eighteen inches high and eight to ten
feet in circumference; it resembled something like a small
pitcher's mound on a baseball diamond. On Española, *yuca*
(manioc) was the main subsistence crop of the people, and it
was grown in *montónes*. Another basic crop, the sweet potato,
also was grown in the same sort of mounds.

Land in Española was granted in two basic units: *caballerías*
and *peonías*.[30] A *caballería* was a grant made to a cavalry soldier,
and a *peonía* was a grant made to a foot soldier. A caballería, by
definition, was an area of land that could hold 200,000 mounds
of yuca — or about ninety acres; a peonía, half that amount.
Under the law, not more than three caballerías (approximately
270 acres) or five peonías (approximately 225 acres) could be
allotted to any one person. As with all laws in the Castilian
colonies, however, there could be — and were — exceptions.

Las Casas writes in his memorial to Cardinal Cisneros,

"Juan Ponce ... pasó á las Indias por peón con Christóbal Colón (Juan Ponce came to the Indies as a foot soldier with Christopher Columbus)."[31] There was absolutely nothing pejorative about the word *peón* in the sixteenth century. To a very large degree, the *caballero* of the Middle Ages began to lose importance as the Moorish wars wound down. There just did not seem to be as much room in the Renaissance for knights as there had been during the feudal period.

When Juan Ponce received his land, he got at least 225 acres, but he might have been given much more. What is known is that he commenced to raise yuca, sweet potatoes, an assortment of other vegetables, pigs, cattle, and horses. From 1504 onward, every Castilian ship departing Santo Domingo for Castilla stopped at the Bay of Yuma for last-minute provisions. Especially important was the cassava — yuca bread — which had a shelf-life that exceeded the time required to cross the Atlantic Ocean. Thus, Juan Ponce the farmer was becoming a rich man without going near a gold mine!

In 1505, Juan Ponce was authorized to establish the sixteenth Castilian town in Española.[32] He chose a site adjacent to his plantation and named it Salvaleón, the name of his maternal grandmother's estate in Castilla. Here he built a massive house of stone which still stands in the Dominican Republic, in the province of La Altagracia, about twenty miles south of Higüey, the provincial capital.

Sometime before Juan Ponce built his house at Salvaleón — but after April 1502, the month of Ovando's arrival — Juan Ponce married Leonor, the Castilian-born daughter of a Santo Domingo innkeeper.[33] The marriage produced three daughters — Juana, Isabel, and María — and one son, Luis.[34] The two oldest children, Juana and Isabel, were probably born in Santo Domingo, but the youngest ones, María and Luis, might have been born at Salvaleón.

Figure 23. Salvaleón, the house built by Juan Ponce around 1505, still stands near San Rafael del Yuma. (Courtesy Fundación Dominicana de Desarrollo, Santo Domingo, Dominican Republic)

During the sixteenth century in the Castilian and, later, Spanish colonies, one's circumstances of birth were paramount. It was not only important who one's parents were but it was equally important where they were born and where their children were born. For five centuries, white Spaniards, born in Spain, were automatically placed at the pinnacle of government, business, education, and the church, a tradition that continues today in some Latin American countries. For many years, it was unthinkable that anyone born in the colonies, regardless of other circumstances such as race, wealth, or even family, could aspire to certain high positions.[35] From a purely sociological perspective, Juan Ponce's career was enhanced — albeit accidentally — more by marrying an innkeeper's daughter *who had been born in Castilla* than it would have been by marrying any woman born in the colony. In the early years of the Spanish Conquest there were no women of marriageable age who were born in

68

the colonies except Indian women. The children of Castilian (Spaniard)-Indian liaisons were to produce a distinct caste — the *mestizo* — but rarely was a mestizo able to break out of the caste system which was becoming established by the end of the fifteenth century.

It was also during this period in Juan Ponce's life that he became friends with Vasco Núñez de Balboa. Balboa had come to Santo Domingo in 1501 from Darién (now northern Colombia), and the friendship established itself after Juan Ponce arrived in 1502. After the pacification of the Tainos, Balboa, like Juan Ponce, became a farmer, but Balboa's encomienda was located at Salvatierra in western Española, in what is now Haiti. Both men apparently shared similar views toward managing their encomiendas, including the relatively fair treatment of their Indian laborers, but the outcome of their efforts was very different. Unlike Juan Ponce, whose farm prospered in great part because it was located along the route ships took when returning to Castilla from Española, Balboa fell into debt and finally, in 1510, left Española and returned to Darién. Ironically, a few years later and on the same day, September 27, 1514, both Juan Ponce and Balboa were named governors of territories they had discovered — Juan Ponce became Governor of Florida and Bimini and Balboa became Governor of the Southern Sea.

~

The period between 1504 and 1507 was somewhat of a chaotic time in Castilian history during which a number of unreported and often illegal actions transpired. This period has even been called the "epoch of secrets."[36] The situation arose following the death of Queen Isabela on November 26, 1504, after which, for a period of two years, the kingdom of Castilla had no king or queen for all practical purposes.[37] When Isabela died the crown of Castilla went to Isabela and Ferdinand's daughter, Juana. Because there was a serious question about

Juana's sanity — she was called *La Loca*, the crazy one — and her husband, Felipe ("the Handsome"), became king consort, not king, Ferdinand ruled Castilla as regent but not as a king after Isabela's death. And Juana never really ruled as queen. In fact, over time her mind drifted further and further from reality. Felipe had become king by the first week of September 1506, but on September 25 he died and Castilla was again without a ruler until Ferdinand was summoned from Naples to resume his reign in 1507. During these years of uncertainty in Castilla from 1504 to 1507, unusual and significant events were also happening in the New World.

At about the time that Juan Ponce was settling in at Salvaleón, the Crown — on April 24, 1505 — named Vicente Yáñez Pinzón captain of San Juan Bautista with the expectation that he would settle the island.[38] This was essentially a bonus for his maritime exploits — he had commanded the *Niña* on Columbus's First Voyage, among other successes. In a symbolic act of taking possession of San Juan Bautista, Pinzón sent García Alonso Casiano to the island with a herd of goats and sheep. No colonization resulted from Pinzón's action, however, and in 1506 he gave his captaincy to Martín García de Salazar. Again no settlement occurred and Salazar's grant expired in 1507.

Christopher Columbus died in 1506, but two governors had served in Santo Domingo before his death and in violation of the agreement between Columbus and the Catholic Sovereigns that he alone would govern the island. Almost immediately after Christopher's death, his elder son, Diego, contested the violation of his father's rights and, temporarily at least, won. Thus the First Admiral's rights and privileges passed to Diego, the Second Admiral. This one decision affected Juan Ponce in a material way, it altered the course of Puerto Rican history, and it probably accelerated the discovery of Florida.

From his vantage point at Salvaleón, Juan Ponce could almost see San Juan Bautista. Cabo Engaño, Española, a few miles east of Salvaleón, is approximately seventy miles from Punta Higüero, San Juan Bautista. Even after the wars of pacification in 1503 and 1504, Indians from Española and San Juan Bautista frequently crossed the Mona Passage going back and forth between the islands, usually by way of Mona Island, which is situated at the southern end of the passage. Not only did Juan Ponce talk with Indians who were canoeing back and forth across the passage but he also had many conversations with Castilians who stopped on the coast of San Juan Bautista to fill their water casks.

Traditional history tells us that Juan Ponce made his first voyage to San Juan Bautista in 1508 and first landed on August 12 near what is today the town of Guánica. There is serious reason to question this fact, and Tió has made a very convincing case for an earlier voyage to the island by Juan Ponce.[39] If Tió is correct — and the evidence weighs heavily in his favor — Juan Ponce reached San Juan Bautista on June 24, 1506, at the identical place where Christopher Columbus landed in 1493.[40] In fact, many Castilian ships had stopped at this location over the years because it was the only good source of fresh water along the entire western side of the island. The Castilians called this place El Aguada, or sometimes La Aguada (the watering hole) and Puerto de los Pozos (the port of the wells).[41]

Higüey, which seems to be derived from the Taino word for water, is rendered in a variety of forms: Higüero, Jagëy, Jagüey, Jigüero, Jigüey, Mayagüez, Yagüey, and Yagüeza. In San Juan Bautista, all of the names were associated with the bay fronting the Añasco (Guaorabo) River and several of them are still in use today. One of those still in use, Mayaqüez, is the name of the third largest city in Puerto Rico; the El Aguada of Juan Ponce's time was located just north of today's Mayaqüez.

Today's towns of Aguada and Aguadilla, north of Punta

71

Higüero, are unrelated to the Aguada of the colonization period, which was located south of Punta Higüero. This similarity of names has caused more than a little confusion over the location of colonial Aguada and at least twenty-five students of the subject have debated the exact location of ancient Aguada for almost three centuries.[42]

~

Oviedo provides at least a partial explanation for why Juan Ponce de León, a successful and wealthy landowner and governor, would abandon the relative security of Salvaleón in eastern Española and look to the wilds of the uncharted Isla de San Juan Bautista. Oviedo writes:[43]

> And since [Juan Ponce de León] had been a captain during the conquest of Higüey he had information from that province and he wanted to know from the Indians who on the island of Boriquén or San Juan [Puerto Rico] had a lot of gold.

It seems as though the governor wished to diversify, and it was apparent from the license given Pinzón that the Crown was interested in having San Juan Bautista settled. Oviedo continues:[44]

> And learning that, he communicated in secret [author's emphasis] with the Knight Commander [Ovando] who at that time resided in Española; who gave him permission [license] to pass to the Island of San Juan [Puerto Rico] to explore and learn what it was like.

There is other evidence that Juan Ponce might have made a voyage to San Juan Bautista in 1506, two years before the traditionally accepted date of August 12, 1508. There are several letters between Ferdinand and Ovando that are dated *before* August 12, 1508, that refer to an earlier voyage to San Juan Bautista by Juan Ponce.[45] Most convincing, however, is a document from the Archivo General de Indias, Audiencia de México, dated June 18, 1532.[46] This is a long document containing evidence presented before a magistrate in Mexico City regarding the merits and services of Juan González Ponce de León, a first cousin of Juan Ponce de León.[47] One of the witnesses to this proceeding was Hernán Cortés, the conqueror of Mexico.

Juan González Ponce de León was the interpreter for Juan Ponce de León, and it was said that he spoke the Taino language with absolute fluency. The testimony of Juan González is crystal clear in stating that five ships, carrying about 100 men, sailed from Santo Domingo to San Juan Bautista in 1506, and landed at El Aguada at the mouth of the Añasco River on June 24. Thus began the Castilian conquest of the Island of San Juan.

Not all members of this expedition stopped at El Aguada. Some of the men under the command of Juan González marched overland to the vicinity of today's city of San Juan, a distance of about eighty-five miles. This party had been directed there after Juan Ponce obtained information from the Tainos about a better port. The Castilians who went to the distant harbor also explored for gold after being shown gold-bearing streams by friendly Indians, and they actually collected a quantity of the metal. The scouting party returned to Juan Ponce's encampment near El Aguada in October or November and, in addition to the gold, they brought maps, data on soundings that were taken in what was to become known as San Juan Bay, and general information about the land and its people.

A skeleton crew took the ships to what is now known as San Juan Bay and the rest of the company, including Juan Ponce and a number of Indians, hiked overland to the newly discovered port. This overland trek took about eight days; the ships had been at the harbor for a week when Juan Ponce's party arrived.

Juan Ponce chose to build his capital about ten miles from what is today the old quarter of San Juan.[48] Settlement of this town, which was later named Caparra, began late in 1506 or early in 1507 with the construction of several buildings of cane and thatch.

According to Oviedo the location of Caparra was terrible.[49] It was situated on a hill in the middle of a swamp. The town was unhealthy and very difficult to reach. Oviedo, who visited the site several years after it was founded, said that the swamp waters were blueish-green and even children turned this color when they quit nursing. In fact, he did not think that children could even grow up in that place. Further, he said, the adults were all sick and discolored and remained that way until they died.

The name Caparra is somewhat intriguing. It appears to be completely coincidental that *caparrosa* (copperas; vitriol) is a synonym for *acije*, the word Oviedo used to describe the color of the water and the people.[50] On the other hand, Murga Sanz stated that Juan Ponce asked Governor Ovando to name the new settlement and that he (Ovando) named the bay and the port in honor of the Roman town of Capera (later Capara, and still later Caparra).[51] But Ovando did not name the settlement because the king had not, at that time, authorized the establishment of a town. Presumably the name was applied once the town became a legal entity.

During the early part of 1507 the Castilians on San Juan Bautista returned to Española, with most of them going to Higüey. Juan Ponce most certainly returned to his wife and four children at Salvaleón. After all, not only did he still maintain a residence there but he also was governor of the province.

But why was this colonization attempt, if that is what is was, made under a veil of secrecy? For one thing, Ferdinand was acting as regent, not king, of Castilla in 1506, and Juana La Loca was too ill to reign. Also, Christopher Columbus had died in 1506 and the question of his elder son's inheritance of titles and privileges was still to be resolved. And, no one wanted to interfere with the concession that had been made in 1505 to

Pinzón to colonize and govern San Juan Bautista, even though the odds were overwhelming that he would not fulfill the conditions of the opportunity.

Governor Ovando, a favorite of Ferdinand, obviously had the Crown's permission to make secret deals with Juan Ponce, a favorite of Ovando. If anyone contested Juan Ponce's clandestine voyage to San Juan Bautista, Ovando or Ferdinand could have said that it was merely a reconnaissance mission, preparatory to the real conquest and colonization.

$\sim$

For all practical purposes, most of 1507 and the first half of 1508 went smoothly for Juan Ponce. He continued to profit from his agricultural and ranching pursuits at Salvaleón, and Governor Ovando allowed him virtually a free rein in governing Higüey. But Juan Ponce may have been restless and he was probably already making plans for a return to the Isla de San Juan.[52]

On May 17, 1508, Juan Ponce asked for royal permission to go to San Juan Bautista, and on June 15 the first official accord was reached between Juan Ponce and the Crown for the expedition.[53] This was not really a *capitulación* (contract) in the strict meaning of that word, but the guarantees were sufficient that Juan Ponce was willing to risk his fortune and his prestige.[54] The agreement was reached primarily on the basis of the gold that had been discovered during Juan Ponce's visit to the island in 1506.

In August of 1508, Juan Ponce, with one ship and fifty men, made his second voyage — but his first *official* voyage — to San Juan Bautista. It is this expedition that most histories treat as the beginning of the Castilian conquest and settlement of the island. In the sense that this voyage marked the beginning of the permanent presence of Castilians on the island the point is accurate.

Juan Ponce and his men sailed from Salvaleón, or what is today the town of San Rafael del Yuma. He sailed first to Mona Island, and from there along the south coast of San Juan Bautista, landing first at Guánica on August 12, 1508. He turned northeastward at the eastern end of the island, and eventually reached the vicinity of today's city of San Juan by sailing west for approximately thirty miles from the northeast corner of the island. He knew exactly where he was going, further evidence that the 1506 excursion had indeed taken place.

Caparra, a few miles inland from the ship's anchorage in San Juan Bay, had been abandoned in early 1507. It was not much then — a few thatched buildings constructed in Taino style. It had all but vanished during the Castilians' absence of a year-and-a-half, but upon their return it was reclaimed and reconstructed. At least one large, whitewashed structure was built that functioned as a barracks, fort, and warehouse. Also, a farm was established with yuca as the main crop, and a bakery was built for making cassava bread from the yuca.[55]

It is obvious that Caparra was situated to facilitate agriculture and mining in the interior of the island, not seafaring. And other than those activities necessary for survival, most of the colonists' energy was directed toward the search for gold.

In April 1509, Juan Ponce went to Santo Domingo.[56] He presented his *relación* (report) to Ovando concerning his August 1508 voyage to San Juan Bautista and the rebuilding of Caparra. On May 2, 1509, a new capitulación was drawn up between Juan Ponce and Ovando in the city of Concepción de la Vega (now La Vega).

As with virtually every agreement between Juan Ponce and Ferdinand, or between Juan Ponce and Ovando, this was at best a private (secret) corporate arrangement involving Juan Ponce, Governor Ovando, the royal treasurer Miguel de Pasamonte, the chief justice Alonso Maldonado, and Ferdinand.

At worst, it was a "gentlemen's agreement."[57] Juan Ponce would return to San Juan Bautista and begin to colonize the island.

~

On July 9, 1509, Diego Columbus, the elder son of Christopher Columbus, arrived in Santo Domingo to assume the recently restored titles and privileges of the First Admiral.[58] Although he had been named "interim viceroy" and governor of all Castilian possessions in the West Indies, Diego was specifically ordered by the courts to leave Juan Ponce alone and told not to interfere with the affairs of the Isla de San Juan even though this island was among those his father had discovered and over which he, Diego, now had legal authority. Accordingly, Diego made Juan Ponce his deputy and, technically, governor of San Juan Bautista — despite the ill feelings he held

Figure 24. Columbus House, Santo Domingo, Dominican Republic. Construction of this house was begun by Diego Columbus, the elder son of Christopher Columbus, at about the time that Juan Ponce made his first voyage to Florida. The statue is a memorial to Queen Isabela I. (Photograph by R. H. Fuson)

toward Juan Ponce as a favorite and agent of his legal adversary Ferdinand. Unknown to Diego and to almost everyone else, including Juan Ponce, Ferdinand appointed Juan Ponce to be governor of San Juan Bautista on August 14, 1509. This was *after* Diego had given Juan Ponce a similar appointment.

If matters were not confusing enough, there was yet a third person on the scene who had, perhaps, a claim to the governorship of San Juan Bautista — Don Cristóbal de Sotomayor. Don Cristóbal de Sotomayor came to Santo Domingo with the same fleet that brought Diego Columbus to that island in 1509. He said that Ferdinand had sent him to be governor of San Juan Bautista, but Las Casas offers half a dozen reasons why this could not have been true.[59] Don Cristóbal, a young man of impeccable upbringing and noble lineage, was perfectly willing to serve Juan Ponce as his lieutenant, and there never was a hint of disappointment in his not receiving the governorship. Thus, Las Casas was probably right: Don Cristóbal de Sotomayor had never been promised the position by Ferdinand.

Ponce de León, acting governor of the island, returned to San Juan Bautista late in the summer of 1509.[60] He had probably finished his stone house in Caparra, similar to the one he had built earlier in Higüey, by that time, and his wife and four children probably accompanied him on this voyage. He also brought supplies, some hogs and calves from Salvaleón, and the wives of at least two men already on San Juan Bautista.

Diego Columbus, upon the advice of his inner circle and with the full realization of the power that flowed his way from his wife's family (María de Toledo was the niece of the Duke of Alba), appointed Juan Cerón to the post of *alcalde mayor* of San Juan Bautista.[61] This was technically the position of chief justice but, for all practical purposes, was synonymous with the governorship. On October 28, 1509, Juan Cerón replaced Juan Ponce as *ad hoc* governor of San Juan Bautista. Juan Ponce stepped aside with grace and dignity, both he and Diego Columbus unaware that Ferdinand had named Juan Ponce governor of San Juan Bautista two months earlier.

Even though acting-Viceroy Columbus had flexed his political and familial muscles by removing Juan Ponce from the acting governorship, the king continued to refer to Juan Ponce as governor during the early months of 1510. Finally, on March 2, 1510, in a double-barreled dispatch — one signed by Queen Juana and one by her father, Ferdinand — Juan Ponce de León was named captain, governor, and judge of San Juan Bautista.[62] This was a clear statement — nothing was uncertain about the posts to which he had been appointed. Juan Ponce did not receive the dispatch containing his appointments until June but, once armed with this new and absolute authority and urged on by Cristóbal de Sotomayor, Juan Ponce ordered the arrest of alcalde mayor Juan Cerón, the *alguacil mayor* (chief constable) Miguel Díaz, and Díaz's deputy Diego de Morales. These men were sent back to Castilla as prisoners in July 1510. Sotomayor, Juan Ponce's close ally in this entire affair, thereafter was named alguacil mayor. Possibly as a reward for loyal service, Juan Ponce gave Sotomayor the Taino village of Guánica, on the southwest coast of the island. The mosquitoes were so bad at that location, however, that Sotomayor moved his town to the old watering site of El Aguada in the northwestern part of the island, which was then called San Germán. Immediately he changed the name to Villa de Sotomayor. Later, in 1511 or 1512, San Germán was rebuilt at Guayanilla, not far from Sotomayor's original grant in the south. The second San Germán was destroyed by French pirates in 1554 and a third San Germán was founded in 1570 — fifteen miles southeast of Mayagüez.

Later in the summer of 1510, Juan Ponce received another royal dispatch, this one naming him *Capitán de mar y tierra y justicia mayor de la isla de San Juan* (Captain of sea and land and chief justice of the Island of San Juan).[63]

During 1509 and 1510, there was a virtual flood of correspondence from Castilla to the West Indies concerning San Juan Bautista, which included royal *cédulas* (decrees) as well as letters. The historian Anthony Devereux has researched this period with great dexterity and careful scholarship, and described it about as succinctly as is humanly possible.[64] Ferdinand not only took a personal interest in San Juan Bautista and Juan Ponce de León, but he was also well aware of the jurisdictional problems caused by the concessions made to Christopher Columbus and the inheritance of these titles and privileges by Christopher's son, Diego.[65] In an attempt to walk on both sides of the street at the same time, Ferdinand often sent his decrees to Santo Domingo only when they pertained to territories under Santo Domingo's jurisdiction, *excluding* San Juan Bautista. And, in order to make this work, the king had to name someone to govern San Juan Bautista who was not really the governor. That someone was Juan Ponce de León, and when he was named "governor" on May 2, 1509, the accord stated: "Por lo presente, entre tanto . . . (For the present, in the interim . . .)."[66] This mind-game continued for almost a year and, if one thinks about it, had been the *modus operandi* of Ferdinand since 1506.

By 1511, Juan Ponce's tenure as the real governor of San Juan Bautista was nearing its conclusion. Whether Juan Ponce was governor or acting governor, he was a good administrator. He was fair, honest, and loyal. In most ways he was a rare man for that time in history and that place in geography. Because he never repeated the mistakes the Castilians had made on Española, he was respected by Castilians and Indians alike. Although the Indians were parceled out according to the repartimiento system, this system did not become truly evil, and for the most part the Tainos were perfectly willing to do some labor in exchange for protection from the Caribs. The lat-

Figure 25. The coat of arms of Puerto Rico was authorized in 1511. The lamb represents San Juan Bautista — Saint John the Baptist — the patron saint of the island. The original coat of arms has been lost. This reconstruction of what the device probably looked like, based on 16th Century documents, is fromTió, *Nuevas fuentes*.

ter were scattered all over the Virgin Islands and apparently had some settlements on the mainland of eastern San Juan Bautista. As for gold, this was of little consequence, for the Tainos of San Juan Bautista placed little value on precious metals. But Juan Ponce could not be everywhere and watch all of the Castilians, and as the Castilian population grew and the Indian population declined — largely because of measles and smallpox — abuses became more numerous. By the early part of 1511 the excesses of the Castilians had become as insufferable to the Tainos as the attacks by the Caribs. The Tainos revolted.

Ponce de León put down the rebellion by the spring of 1511. Cristóbal de Sotomayor and his nephew, Diego de Sotomayor, are sometimes singled out as the individuals who precipitated the Taino uprising.[67] The Taino revolt had com-

81

menced at Sotomayor's village — Villa de Sotomayor — and spread from there. In the process, both Cristóbal de Sotomayor and his nephew were killed and the village was destroyed.

On May 5, 1511, the Council of Castilla found in favor of Diego Columbus in his suit against the Crown and all of the Columbus rights and privileges were permanently restored to Diego. Queen Juana ratified the Council's verdict on June 17, 1511. Ferdinand, however, had written to Juan Ponce on May 31, 1511, and it is probable that Juan Ponce learned of his fate the same month the verdict was ratified.

On November 8, 1511, the Island of San Juan was assigned a coat-of-arms, the first to be granted in America. And on November 28, 1511, Juan Cerón was reinstated as the governor of the Island of San Juan by Diego Columbus. Though Juan Ponce was under constant pressure from Diego Columbus for more than a year thereafter — throughout 1512 — he was somewhat protected because he remained military captain of the island and Ferdinand held him in the highest esteem. In fact, it was Ferdinand who suggested to Juan Ponce that he move on and search for new lands.

Chapter 3
1511–1514

The Discovery of Florida

When Diego Columbus became fully empowered as viceroy, he used every means at his disposal to weaken Juan Ponce's authority in San Juan Bautista. But Ferdinand circumvented Columbus, based on the notion that the viceroy only had authority in the Antilles and particularly in islands discovered by his father, Christopher. Islands lying to the north of Española and Cuba that had not been discovered by Christopher Columbus could be administered by someone appointed by the king and responsible only to the king.

In 1511, Miguel de Pasamonte, Ferdinand's royal commissioner in Santo Domingo, suggested to Juan Ponce that he leave San Juan Bautista and colonize land to the north that was known to the king — land that had been vaguely known since Columbus's First Voyage. Juan Ponce would be governor of this land and any others in the vicinity that were unoccupied by Iberians. Pasamonte guaranteed Juan Ponce that the license would be granted to him, no matter who else applied and no matter how good the plan was. On February 23, 1512, Juan Ponce received his contract from Ferdinand to explore, settle, and govern "Beimeni."

Juan Ponce set sail from San Juan Bautista on March 3, 1513. He reached what he thought was a large island on April 3 — naming it La Florida, "The Flowered One." He sailed the east coast of Florida and, about where today's West Palm Beach is, discovered the Gulf Stream. The voyage continued south past Miami Beach, west through the Florida Keys, and north to the barrier islands near Fort Myers. Backtracking, the ships visited the Dry Tortugas and returned through the Keys and Bahamas to San Juan Bautista, Juan Ponce's ship arriving there on October 19, 1513.

———

Two basic types of voyages occurred within, to, or from Spanish America after 1493. First, there were the authorized voyages, approved and licensed by the Castilian and Spanish crowns. These included trans-Atlantic sailings, expeditions within the newly discovered lands of America, or some combination of the two. The results of many of these licensed expeditions were duly reported to the proper authorities. Second, there were many unauthorized (clandestine) expeditions. Not only did various "Spanish" mariners — Castilians, Andalucians, Aragonese, Catalonians, Gallegos, Basques, etc. — take part in these voyages, but Portuguese (especially Azorean), English, Irish, French, Genoese, Venetian, and sundry other mariners were involved as well. In addition to this — and relevant to both types of voyages — was the tremendous loss of men and ships at sea. Records of these voyages were lost as well — some at sea and others in government and private archives and libraries. For example, Las Casas' abstract of Columbus's journal of the 1492 voyage was misplaced for almost three centuries.[1]

Columbus discovered Cuba in 1492 and had three chances to discover Florida that same year. First, his initial landing would have been in Florida, somewhere near what is today Fort Pierce, if he had not changed course on October 7 to the west-southwest.[2] Second, while anchored at his landfall island in the Bahamas he learned that there was land to the northwest.[3] The log entry for October 12 reads, in part:

> *Many of the men I have seen have scars on their bodies, and when I made signs to them to find out how this happened, they indicated that people from other nearby islands come to San Salvador to cap-*

ture them. . . . I believe that people from the mainland *come here to take them as slaves. [Author's emphasis]*

On the next day, October 13, Columbus wrote:

The natives here [on the landfall island] have indicated to me that not only is there land to the south and southwest, but also to the northwest. . . . Furthermore, if I understand correctly, it is from the northwest that strangers come to fight and capture the people here. [Author's emphasis]

Needless to say, Columbus did not follow up on these clues that a mainland (today's Florida) lay to the northwest. This failure to investigate the presence of a larger land mass seems quite odd if Columbus really was seeking China and the Great Khan. Instead, however, the Admiral set his course for the southwest to look for gold and precious stones.

Columbus's third opportunity to discover Florida came two weeks later. After discovering Cuba on October 28, 1492, he set sail the next day toward the west.[4] On October 31 Columbus entered the following in his journal:

All last night I beat to windward. . . . I saw an inlet or bay where small ships could lie, but I could not reach it because the wind shifted entirely to the north. . . . For this reason, and because the sky indicated a squall brewing, I had to return to Rio de Mares [eastward].

And on November 1 he wrote:

I am certain now that this [Cuba] is the mainland and that I am before Zayto and Quinsay, 300 miles distant, more or less. This is indicated by the sea, which comes in a different manner from how it has come up to now. Yesterday, as I was going northwest, I found that it was becoming cold.

The journal entries of Columbus, while he was on the north coast of Cuba, tell us two things. He documented the presence of a classic cold front in the region between Cuba and the Bahamas, created when the wind shifted to a clockwise direction and brought cooler weather from the north. Columbus could not have sailed to the northwest, toward what is today Florida, under those conditions. Also, his reference to Zayto and Quinsay, names of places brought to the West by Marco Polo, gives us insight into the geographical conceptions of the Admiral. Zayto (also Zayton and Zaitun) is what is known today as Zhao'an, China; Quinsay is modern Hangzhou, which lies 450 miles north of Zhao'an.

Before the Discovery Voyage of Columbus, when most Europeans perceived that only the Ocean Sea separated Africa and Europe from Asia, *mappaemundi* (world maps) and globes depicted a prominent peninsula on the coast of Asia. This region, a part of which was then known as the Indian Province of Mangi, lay south of Cathay (China) and at approximately the same latitude as Florida. Therefore, when Columbus first landed on Cuba on October 28, 1492, he must have thought that Cuba was the island of Japan.[5] Within four days he apparently perceived Cuba to be the Mangi Peninsula. If this were the case, then Española, discovered on December 6, 1492, had to have been Japan.[6]

Columbus should not be faulted for this geographical dilemma, for every map, chart, globe, and book at the end of the fifteenth century overlooked the bifurcation of the Ocean Sea by the American continents. In fact, some cartographers continued to map the newly discovered lands as offshore features of Asia until the middle of the sixteenth century. By that time they had literally run out of room on their mappaemundi for all the new places.[7]

A series of maps and globes dating from 1502 into the 1530s depicted the Mangi Peninsula as being northwest of Cuba. For some this meant that Florida had been discovered at least as early as 1502. It is not at all difficult to understand this arrangement as a geographical concept five centuries ago, but it is inconceivable that some modern "scholars" continue to regard the Mangi Peninsula of east Asia and the Florida Peninsula as

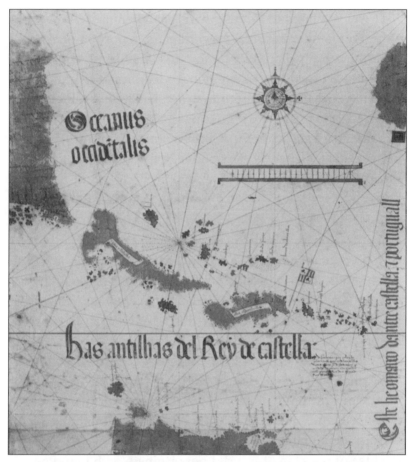

Figure 26. A part of the Cantino World Map, 1502. The two large islands near the center of this section of the map are Cuba and Española. The land to the northwest of Cuba is the Mangi Peninsula of China, not Florida as some interpreters have claimed. Florida had not been visited by Europeans in 1502. (Courtesy Biblioteca Estense, Modeno, Italy)

one and the same.[8]

Florida might have been visited by Castilians before 1511 but we have no record of this having happened, and the peninsula did not appear on any map before that date. Any peninsula located west or northwest of Cuba on a map dating before

87

1511 was intended to represent an Asian peninsula, and probably the Mangi Peninsula. Nevertheless, a portion of Asia — even though misplaced by almost 10,000 miles — could have served as a beacon and thereby have led one navigator or another toward Florida before that peninsula was actually discovered or mapped by Europeans. Perhaps this is how Ferdinand came to hear of Bimini (also Beimini, Benimy, Bimene), that vaguely understood region northwest of Española that included what is now Florida.

~

History tells us that on Thursday, March 3, 1513, Juan Ponce de León led a little squadron of three ships, carrying about sixty-five companions, on a northward voyage from the Isla de San Juan to a land called Bimini. In the process of searching for the mythical Fountain of Youth, he discovered and named the land we today call Florida. But this is, at best, an incomplete history; at worst, it is an incorrect history.

For one thing, Juan Ponce was not the first Castilian to visit what we know today as Florida. Second, the idea to sail northward (actually, northwestward) from San Juan Bautista was not Juan Ponce's. Third, the so-called Fountain of Youth was no more than a secondary motivation for the voyage, and the idea of searching for it did not originate with Juan Ponce.

Florida had been visited by Castilians at least once — and probably several times — before Juan Ponce made his famous "discovery" voyage of 1513.[9] These earlier voyages, for the most part, were slaving expeditions; the Bahama Islands, then called the Lucayos, had been raided systematically by slave hunters after 1494. Despite claims that a large population of Indians inhabited these islands, there were likely to have been no more than 10,000 Tainos (Lucayans) in the Bahamas when Columbus first found them and, by some estimates, the indigenous Bahamian population actually may have been half that number.[10] It is only logical to believe that slavers sought their prey in Florida after the neighboring islands had been emptied. Las Casas tells us:[11]

> At that time [early in 1511] . . . a group came together and fitted out several ships in order to go out and capture the innocent people [Indians] who lived on the small islands [Bahamas]. . . . They sailed from Puerto de Plata [today's Puerto Plata, Dominican Republic] . . . reached the Lucayos [Bahamas], . . . and searched many of them very thoroughly, but found nothing . . . and because it seemed to them that they were going to return empty-handed, not only losing the money that had been invested, plus the danger [endured] and the work [put forth], but facing the embarrassment of returning to this island [Española] without extracting some profit from their voyage, they decided to go toward the north to discover land, as long as the provisions held out, and they found it. . . . It is certain that this was the land and coastline that now we call Florida. . . . They returned to Santo Domingo with their prize [a cargo of Indian slaves].

Las Casas' statement is clear evidence that Florida had been visited by Castilians from Española more than two years *before* Juan Ponce sailed to Florida, and it appears to be the first documentation of the enslavement of Indians by Europeans from any part of what is now the United States.[12] In addition to the written record, a portion of Florida was actually mapped by Andrés de Morales of Sevilla who labeled it Isla de Beimeni.[13] This map was added to some editions of Peter Martyr's *Opera*, first published in 1511, and is the first map printed in Castilla that shows any of the discoveries in the New World.[14]

Peter Martyr said that the Morales map was added "as an afterthought" to his text of 1511.[15] In the same paragraph that refers to the map addendum, Martyr noted that north of Cuba there are "marvelous lands and marvelous countries that have been found."[16]

~

Until the completion of Juan Ponce's voyage in 1513, however, Bimini and Florida were perceived as one and the same.

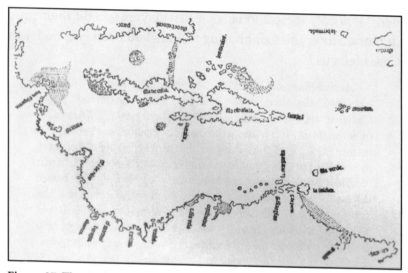

Figure 27. The Andrés Morales Map, 1511, accompanied Peter Martyr's *Opera*. This was the first map printed in Spain that charted some of the early Spanish discoveries in the Americas. Florida is labeled "Isla de Beimeni parte." (From Windsor, 1889)

On the other hand, Ferdinand had authorized a voyage in 1508 by Vicente Yáñez Pinzón, captain of the *Niña* on the First Voyage of Columbus, and Juan Díaz de Solis, who would later, in 1515, discover the Rio de La Plata. The 1508 voyage by Pinzón and Solis along the coast of what is today Brazil, northern South America, and Central America was an attempt to find a passage to the Pacific Ocean. Needless to say, it failed to accomplish this goal. But Pinzón and Solis *might* have visited Bimini (including Florida) during the latter part of this voyage. Whether or not Pinzón and Solis visited Bimini, Miguel de Pasamonte, the royal treasurer and an Aragonese, knew that there was land to the northwest of Española, and during the summer of 1511 he told Juan Ponce about it as a closely guarded secret. Amerigo Vespucci learned of the voyage in his capacity as pilot-major of the Casa de Contratación in Sevilla. He, in turn, passed the information to Bishop Fonseca. Ferdinand heard of the voyage and perhaps of Bimini from one of these people.[17]

On July 25, 1511, Pasamonte received a royal decree from the king asking him to consult with Juan Ponce to determine if he was interested in another adventure.[18] At that time, Juan Ponce only had three months remaining as governor of Puerto Rico. It might have been at this time that Juan Ponce learned of the "secret of Bimini."

In June, Juan Ponce sent a letter and a shipment of gold to King Ferdinand. He received these items on September 8 and responded the next day with a letter to Juan Ponce thanking him for the gold and inquiring if there were any nearby islands that he wanted to conquer.[19]

Pasamonte helped Juan Ponce draw up a contract with complete assurance that it would be accepted. As it turned out, there was competition from Bartholomew Columbus — Christopher's brother and the uncle of Viceroy Diego Columbus — but Juan Ponce received the grant even though his proposal was the weaker of the two. The formal contract between the Crown and Juan Ponce for the discovery and settlement of the Island of Bimini was dispatched from Burgos on February 23, 1512.[20]

Even though Juan Ponce still held several important positions on San Juan Bautista in 1512 — military captain, chief justice, and landowner — he was no longer governor and, in some respects, he felt as though he was living in a prison.[21] He was ready for a change and greeted the opportunity for a new discovery with a great deal of enthusiasm. He also understood immediately that this contract was different from the others; it was not some informal arrangement sealed with a handshake, but a legitimate capitulación signed by the king. Nor was this contract like those made in the first years of colonization. This time there would be time limits, jurisdictional parameters, and financial requirements. Further, the king did not want to am-

plify the jurisdiction of the Columbus family, and it was precisely for this reason that Ferdinand rejected Bartholomew
Columbus's application. But the king told Juan Ponce that the
contract was a reward for his services and proof of the confidence that he, the king, had in him.[22]

⁓

The contract presented by Ferdinand to Juan Ponce for the
exploration and settlement of Bimini is as follows:[23]

> *Whereas you, Juan Ponce de León, have requested that I grant*
> *you the authority to go to discover and settle the Islands of Benimy*
> *[sic], under certain conditions [listed below], in order to bestow my*
> *favor upon you I grant you the authority to discover and settle the*
> *said Island, with the provision that it is not one of those that has*
> *already been discovered, and with the conditions that follow.*
>
> *1. You may go to discover the said Island with the ships you wish*
> *to take at your own cost. To do this you may have three years' time,*
> *reckoned from the day on which this contract is presented to you,*
> *provided that you commence the discovery within the first year of the*
> *said three-year period. On going [to discover the Island] you may*
> *touch any islands or mainland of the Ocean Sea, both discovered or*
> *undiscovered, provided that they are not among the islands and main-*
> *land that belong to the very serene king of Portugal, our very dear*
> *and beloved son.[24] It is understood that you may not take or possess*
> *anything [valuable or otherwise] from these islands or mainland that*
> *lie within the limits stipulated between us [Castilla] and him [Portu-*
> *gal], except the things necessary for your maintenance and provision*
> *of ships and men, and you shall pay for them what they are worth.*
>
> *2. You may take, and are required to take, the ships, supplies,*
> *officers, sailors, and men that you find necessary for the aforesaid*
> *[discovery], in these kingdoms of Castilla or in the said Isla Española.*
> *You are to pay for them in full according to custom in the presence of*
> *our officials of the House of Trade in the Isla Española and [or?] in*
> *the presence of our officials of the House of Trade in Sevilla.*
>
> *3. In order to please you, I order that for a three-year period, no*
> *person may go to discover the said Island of Benimy; and, if anyone*
> *should go to discover it, or discover it by accident, the stipulations of*
> *this contract shall be carried out with you and not with the person*
> *who should discover it. If someone else discovers it [Benimy], you*
> *shall lose none of your rights, provided that, as stated above, you set*

sail to go to discover it within the first year [of the contract], and that it will be of no value in any other way; and provided that it is not one of those that has been reported and is known with certainty.

4. When you find and discover the said Island, in the manner stated above, I grant to you the government and justice of it for all of the days of your life. I grant to you full power and civil and criminal jurisdiction, with all their incidents and dependencies, and annexes and rights.

5. When you find the said Island, you shall be obliged to settle at your cost in the sites and places best suited for same. You may have possession of the houses, farms, settlements, and property that you make there, and any gain derived from the said Island, in accordance with the provisions of this contract.

6. If fortresses have to be built in the said Island, they must and shall be at our cost, and we shall assign wardens, as best fulfill our service. If, while forts are being built, you should build any house or fortified house for protection from the Indians, these shall be yours. If these structures are ever needed for our service, you shall have to turn them over upon being paid their value.

7. I shall give you, for a period of twelve years, reckoned from the day on which you discover the said Island of Benimy, a tenth of all the revenues and profits belonging to us in the said Island, excepting the tenth of our [royal] profits or in any other matter.

8. The repartimiento [allotment] of Indians, who should be on the said Island, shall be made by a person or persons appointed by me, and in no other manner.

9. I order you, that the Indians who ought to be on the said Island, shall be allotted in accordance to the persons who are there [at the time of discovery]. This should be done: the first discoverers shall be provided for before anyone else, and that all the preference that may conveniently be given to them shall be.

10. I grant for a period of ten years that the persons mentioned above who go to discover the said Island, and who settle there, enjoy the gold, and other metals and profitable things which should be on the said Island, do not have to pay any fees or tenths [tithes] the first year; in the second [year], a ninth [part]; in the third, an eighth; in the fourth, a seventh; in the fifth, a sixth; and a fifth for each of the next five years. This is in agreement with the form and manner that exists today on the Isla Española. Other settlers that go later, who are not included among the original discoverers, shall pay the fifth from the first year. For them I shall order exemptions in other things, but not from gold.

11. To show greater benefit and favor to you, the said Juan Ponce de León, it is my will and pleasure that you shall have the government and settlement of all the islands in the neighborhood of the said Island of Benimy, if you should personally discover them and at your cost and expense as stated above. And, the islands must not be among those already known. They must be discovered and settled under the same conditions and in the same manner as the said Island [Benimy], as set forth in this contract.

12. I grant you the title of our Adelantado [Governor] of the said Island and of the other islands you may discover in the aforesaid manner.

13. You shall collect the gold, if there is any, in the same way that it is collected on the Isla Española, or in the form and manner that I shall order.

14. You cannot take in your company, for the aforesaid [Island of Benimy], any person or persons who are foreigners from outside our domains and territories.

15. As a guarantee that you, the said Juan Ponce, and the persons who shall go with you, shall do and comply and pay, and that what is in this contract to be completed and kept shall be so completed and kept, before making the said voyage, must give guaranteed and creditable bonds to the satisfaction of our officials who reside on the Isla Española.

16. You, the said Juan Ponce, and the other persons who shall go and remain there, shall do and comply and pay all that is contained in this contract, and each bit and piece of it. You shall cause no fraud nor deceit, nor shall you give favor, aid, or consent thereto. If you should learn of any, you shall notify us and our officials in our name, under the penalty that you, or whomever should do to the contrary, will lose any favor or office which he might have had from us. Anyone causing fraud or deceit shall pay in his person and goods all the penalties which we may consider fitting and the penalties shall be placed on the person and the person's goods of those who do it, consent to it, or hide it.

17. After you have reached the Island [Benimy] and have learned what is there, send me a relación [report], and another to our officials on the Isla Española, so that we may know what should have been done and make any necessary changes [in the future].

Therefore, if you, the said Juan Ponce carry out all of the aforesaid and each bit and piece of it, and give the said bonds or remain and pay the aforesaid, I promise and assure you that I shall order everything contained in this grant and each bit and piece of it to be kept and *complied with. I shall order our officials, who reside on the Isla Española, that in our name, in accordance with the aforesaid, they should make the said contract and agreement with you and receive the said bonds. For your despatch, I am ordering Don Diego Columbus, our admiral and governor of the said Isla Española, and our appellate judges and treasury officials who reside there, and all the justices of the said Isla Española, that they give you all of the favor and aid that you may find necessary, and that there be no impediments to you in any shape or form.*

   Dated in Burgos, February 23, 1512.

I the King

By command of His Highness, Lope Conchillos
Signed by the Bishop of Palencia

~

Eleven months were to pass before Juan Ponce was able to secure the necessary ships, crews, and supplies for the expedition authorized by Ferdinand. During that time, despite constant support from the Crown, Juan Ponce was harassed, condemned, and intimidated by Cerón, Díaz, and other officials on San Juan Bautista. In fact, Juan Ponce's problems had commenced when Juan Cerón arrived at San Juan Bautista on November 28, 1511, to relieve Juan Ponce of his duties as governor of the island.

On January 20, 1512, before Juan Ponce had received his contract from Ferdinand to seek Bimini, the chief accountant, Francisco de Lizaur, took possession of San Juan Bautista's financial records that Juan Ponce had maintained with great care and impeccable honesty. As Murga Sanz has pointed out, this placed in the hands of Cerón and his associates "all the means necessary to distort information"about Juan Ponce's administration of San Juan Bautista.[25]

Everything that Juan Ponce had done as governor was questioned by Lizaur — including his placement of Indians, management of the royal lands and mines, and payments to the Crown. Juan Ponce's ship was confiscated; a nobleman

95

friend — Juan Bono de Quejo, later to command a ship on the first voyage to Florida — was imprisoned; and Juan Ponce was held as a virtual prisoner on the island. Not only were lies about Juan Ponce broadcast by his rivals, but monetary fraud was committed by none other than the chief accountant. *Cabalgadas*, "hunting parties" euphemistically called *entradas* (entrances), were also allowed to venture deeper into San Juan Bautista in search of Indian slaves.

All of this harassment of Juan Ponce and change in policy was in direct disregard of the king's specific orders, and it was probably carried out with the tacit approval of the viceroy, Don Diego Columbus. Needless to say, the matter was investigated thoroughly by the treasurer Pasamonte, and Lizaur was arrested and returned to Spain as a prisoner in May, 1512.

On June 2, 1512, Rodrigo de Moscoso, still in Castilla at this time, was appointed to replace Juan Cerón as governor of San Juan Bautista and on August 12, Cerón was ordered to return Juan Ponce's confiscated ship.[26] Also on August 12 Juan Ponce was invited to come to Castilla for a personal audience with the king but, apparently, the press of duties in preparing for the voyage to Bimini and Florida prevented Juan Ponce from making this trip to Castilla.

By the end of 1512 Juan Ponce's circumstances had improved. On December 10, Juan Ponce was named *alcaide* (warden) of the fortress that was under construction at Caparra and, in addition, he was named *tesorero* (treasurer) of San Juan Bautista and placed in charge of all royal lands and the distribution of Indian workers. On December 25, Alonso Manso, the first bishop in San Juan Bautista, arrived.[27] Four days later, on December 29, the *Santa María de la Consolación* arrived at San Germán (in the south of the island). This ship was captained by Juan Bono de Quejo, now out of prison, and it carried the new governor, Rodrigo de Moscoso.

Now, free of so many restraints, Juan Ponce was able to leave San Juan Bautista and travel to Santo Domingo and Salvaleón to finalize his plans for the epic voyage of discovery that was about to commence. Article 15 of the contract to discover Bimini required that a bond be posted with officials in Santo Domingo to assure compliance with the terms of the contract. This would have necessitated at least one trip from San Juan Bautista to Española. Article 2 might also have demanded a trip to Santo Domingo, the capital of Castilla's New World colonies, if certain supplies were needed or if certain billets needed to be filled. We may assume, then, that Juan Ponce left San Juan Bautista late in December 1512 or early in January 1513 and went to Santo Domingo. There he acquired the manufactured supplies that he needed. He might have added a couple of crewmen while in Santo Domingo but that is highly doubtful; Juan Ponce had many friends in both Higüey and San Juan Bautista who wanted to make the trip.

Ponce de León returned to his farm at Salvaleón, Higüey, after he left Santo Domingo. Most of the foodstuffs for the voyage, if not all, came from Juan Ponce's own farm. It is also probable that some of the people on the expedition came from the Salvaleón area. Two of the three ships that would sail to Bimini were registered at Yuma (now San Rafael del Yuma), the port for Salvaleón. The *Santiago* was registered for the voyage on January 22, 1513. The second ship, *Santa María de la Consolación*, was registered a week later, on January 29, 1513.[28] Both Devereux and Murga Sanz provide lists of crew and passengers for the two ships, although the two documents are not in complete agreement. Ballesteros does not list the names of all of the crew and passengers but he does offer some information on the regions of Iberia from which some of the participants originated.[29]

The *Santiago* carried at least seventeen and no more than twenty-one people from Yuma, Española, to San Germán, San

Juan Bautista, where it arrived on February 8, 1513. The captain, or master, of the vessel was Diego Bermúdez, and the pilot — perhaps the best in the West Indies — was Antón de Alaminos.[30] In addition to the captain and the pilot, there were six or seven mariners, six to eight cabin boys, one person going only as far as San Juan Bautista, and perhaps three soldiers. The *Santiago* has been called a caravel and a nao. It was probably the former, for not only was it registered as a caravel but the number of passengers suggests that it was about the size of Christopher Columbus's *Pinta*.

The *Santa María de la Consolación* carried twenty-seven to thirty-eight people — including Juan Ponce — on the voyage from Yuma to San Germán, and it arrived on the same day as the *Santiago*, February 8, 1513. At least four of its passengers disembarked in San Juan Bautista. De Quejo was still captain of this ship. One woman, Juana Ruíz (or Jiménez), boarded at Yuma and remained with the expedition for its entirety; she was to become the first European woman known to set foot on the mainland of what is now the United States. There were also two free black Africans on the crew, two Indian slaves, and one white slave. Judging from the number of passengers, the ship was probably a nao, similar in size to the *Santa María* of Christopher Columbus's First Voyage.

Last, a third ship — the *San Cristóbal*, probably a *bergantín* — was added to the little fleet at San Germán. This small craft, a bit smaller than Columbus's *Niña*, was of shallow draft and, with its lateen sails, excellent for sailing close to the wind. Its captain was Juan Pérez de Ortubia. There are no names or numbers available describing the crew, soldiers, or passengers on Ortubia's little ship, but twelve to fifteen people would be expected on a vessel of this type.

Assuming no one joined the expedition in San Germán (which is highly unlikely), the absolute minimum number of people for the three ships would have been forty-nine according to Murga Sanz and fifty-four according to Devereux. But we know that the *San Cristóbal* carried more than one man, the captain. Allowing that another ten or twelve people were aboard the *San Cristóbal*, we can estimate that about sixty-five people made the voyage to Bimini. The group included whites (Andalucians, Gallegos, Basques, Castilians, and probably one Aragonese), Indians, mestizos, and blacks; apparently, there was only one woman in the group.[31]

The fleet departed San Germán on the afternoon of March 3, 1513, a Thursday, and sailed to Aguada on the northwestern coast of San Juan Bautista. This was the same landing site used by Columbus in 1493 and the port-of-entry for Juan Ponce in 1506. The three ships sailed from Aguada on the evening of March 4, 1513, bound for Bimini.

～

Antonio de Herrera y Tordesillas is the man most responsible for assembling the information we have of this "discovery" voyage of 1513. In many respects he is the *only* source of information for the 1513 expedition and his statements have often been accepted as "the last and final word" on the subject.[32]

Herrera was appointed *Cronista Mayor de las Indias* (Chief Historian of the Indies) by Felipe II of Spain in 1596 — eighty-three years *after* Juan Ponce's voyage to Bimini and Florida occurred. During the twenty-five years that Herrera served as the official chronicler for all Spanish activities in the West Indies, he acquired a reputation as one of the greatest plagiarists the scholarly world has ever known — before or since.

Virtually every Spanish scholar, beginning with Antonio González Barcia (1729) and continuing with Juan Bautista Muñoz, Martín Fernández de Navarrete, Marcos Jiménez de Espada, José Torre Revelo, and J. Natalicio González, has indicted Herrera for wholesale literary theft. He lifted whole chapters — verbatim — from Bartolomé de Las Casas, Ferdinand Columbus, Garcilaso de la Vega, and most other important sixteenth-century historians. Modern American scholars — among their numbers Edward Bourne, Lewis Hanke, John and Jeannette Varner, Juan Friede, and Benjamin Keen — have been equally critical of Herrera's methods and products.[33]

Yet, to paraphrase Muñoz (1792), Herrera — by stealing information from so many — has at least preserved many items that otherwise might have disappeared.[34] Muñoz did not say

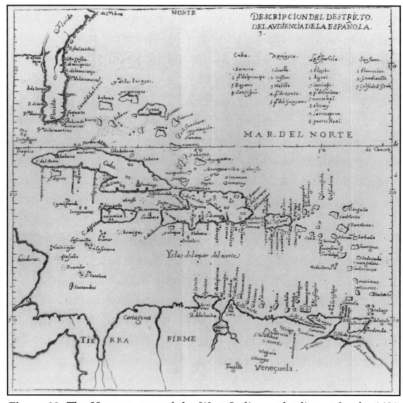

Figure 28. The Herrera map of the West Indies and adjacent lands, 1601. Herrera has moved Cape Canaveral farther north than it was previously placed, and he might have been the first to use the name Tampa Bay on a map. (From Herrera, 1945)

100

how one was to verify material that had no identifiable source, nor did he probe the question of whether Herrera invented or altered information. Is it possible that Herrera tinkered with the facts surrounding the first voyage of Juan Ponce to Bimini?[35]

The Herrera account of Ponce de León's voyage is so detailed that it would appear he extracted his information from a ship's log kept by Juan Ponce or one of his pilots during the 1513 expedition.[36] But we know that this was not the case. Henry Harrisse, in a careful analysis made over a century ago, proved that the latitudes given by Herrera for Juan Ponce's northwestern excursion through the Bahamas were taken from a chart made at least fifteen years *after* the event took place.[37] In addition, this chart was verbally described by Herrera, creating what is known as a "rutter" — sailing directions.[38] The final result was a set of sailing directions that only *appears* to be from a ship's log.

Herrera's rendition of Juan Ponce's voyage to Bimini first appeared in 1601.[39] It is seemingly based on the 1537 work of Alonso de Cháves — a document known as the Cháves rutter.[40] The Cháves rutter, in turn, is largely a verbal rendering of a map made by Alonso de Santa Cruz to accompany a chapter titled "Isla [sic] de los Lucayos" in his book *Islario general de todas las islas del mundo* (General Description of the World's Islands). Although the book by Santa Cruz has been dated to 1541, four years after the Cháves rutter was prepared, it is probable that the portion dealing with the Bahamas dates from the 1530s.[41] Further, it is possible that both Cháves and Santa Cruz used a common source, the Padrón Real (the official Spanish map), which was housed in the Casa de Contratación in Sevilla. Both men were at the Casa de Contratación at the same time; Cháves was the pilot-major and Santa Cruz was the royal cosmographer.[42]

The Casa de Contratación de las Indias had been established by Isabela and Ferdinand on January 20, 1506. It was a

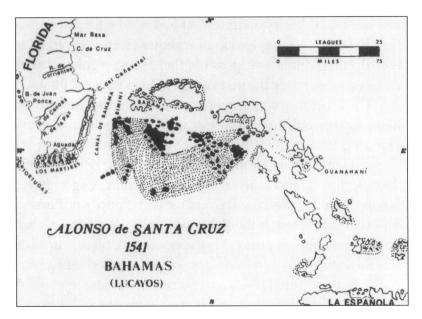

Figure 29. A part of Alonso de Santa Cruz's map of the Bahamas, ca. 1541. This map might be the basis for Herrera's account of Juan Ponce's first trip to Florida. This map also shows Cape Canaveral at its original location; later, this name was moved to the north to another location. (Adapted from the original located in the Osterreiches National Bibliotek, Wien)

large and powerful government enterprise that was involved in every aspect of maritime activity, law, administration, and trade in the New World.[43] The Casa de Contratación had its own pilots, cartographers, and cosmographers (geographers). In an attempt to bring some order to the navigational chaos that followed the momentous discovery by Christopher Columbus, the office of pilot-major was created on March 22, 1508, specifically for Amerigo Vespucci who had emigrated to Castilla in 1492 and become a naturalized citizen in 1505. On August 6, 1508, construction of the Padrón Real was begun under the general supervision of Vespucci. It was hoped that an official map would drive out the many spurious charts that were flooding the country by that time. In theory, every navigator departing Castilla had to be licensed by the Casa and had to utilize the official map. In fact, to use any chart other than the Padrón Real was against the law; offenders were subject to a fine. Further, upon returning to Castilla, all pilots were supposed to be de-briefed by the pilot-major and any new knowledge acquired on the journey was to be added to the map. Unfortunately, poor and incorrect charts continued to be made in every Castilian port, new discoveries were not always added, and old errors were not always stricken. Nevertheless, there were some excellent sections of the official map, especially where information was obtained from Portuguese or Italian sources. Imagine, if you will, an atlas with certain plates out-of-date and crying out for revision while other maps are constantly updated and rank at the very summit of the cartographic art of the time. Much of the navigational knowledge of Castilla as it related to the West Indies was incorporated in the maps and other records of the Casa de Contratación. Not all of this information was equally current or accurate, but it was accessible to government officials and it could easily have been available to Herrera.[44]

Herrera describes Juan Ponce's voyage to Bimini and Florida in 1513 as follows:[45]

> *Juan Ponce de León, finding himself out of office [as governor], because Juan Cerón and Miguel Díaz had been restored to power on the Island of San Juan [Puerto Rico], and seeing himself rich, decided to do something to enhance his self-esteem and to augment his estate. And since he had news that they had found lands to the north, he decided to go and make discoveries in that direction. He armed three ships, well stocked with provisions, people, and sailors, which for carrying out a discovery expedition are absolutely necessary.*
>
> *He departed the island [San Juan] on Thursday afternoon, March 3, sailing from the port of San Germán [Guayanilla]. He went to Aguada [El Aguada del Añasco, south of modern Rincón] in order to plot his course. He left [Aguada] the next night, sailing northwest by north, and the ships covered 8 leagues by sunrise [one league = ap-*

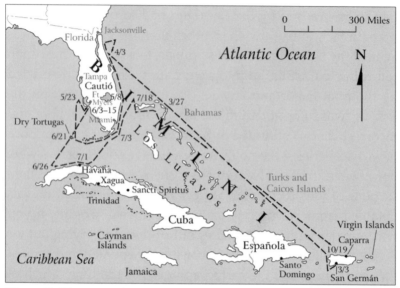

Figure 30. The route of Juan Ponce's first voyage to Florida, March to October, 1513, with dates of visitation given for selected sites.

proximately three nautical miles].

They sailed until March 8 and anchored at an island called El Viejo ["The Old Man," probably Grand Turk], located in the Baxos de Babueca [Mouchoir Bank] at 22⁰ 30' N. On another day [the next day?] they anchored at a Lucayan [Bahamian] islet called Caycós [Caicos]. Then they anchored at another, called La Yagúna [Mayaguna; Mayaguana?], at 24⁰ N.

On March 11 they came to another island, called Amaguáyo [Plana Cays?], where they stopped to make repairs. They then went to the island of Maneguá [Acklin-Crooked?], at 24⁰ 30' N.

On March 14 they reached Guanahaní [Samana Cay, Long Island, Rum Cay, or Watling/San Salvador?], at 25⁰ 40' N. Here they readied a ship to cross the Windward Gulf of the Lucayan Islands. This island of Guanahaní was the first that was discovered by the Admiral Don Christopher Columbus, where during the first voyage he went ashore and named it San Salvador. [Assuming no major course change, the island Herrera referred to as Guanahaní best fits Long Island, not even a serious candidate today in the "landfall debate."]

They departed from here, sailing to the northwest, and on Sunday, March 27, which was Dia de Pascua de Resurrección [Passover of the Resurrection Day; Easter Day], which they commonly called Pascua de Flores *[Passover of Flowers], they saw an island, and did not explore it. [Ponce de León would have seen many islands on any course sailed through the Bahamas. There is simply no way to identify the island seen on March 27].*

On Monday, March 28 they sailed 15 leagues on the same course; and on Wednesday they repeated this. [Nothing is recorded for Tuesday, March 29, unless Wednesday was mistakenly written for Tuesday]. And afterwards, with bad weather, until April 2, sailing westnorthwest, the water depth diminished until it was 9 brazas [1 braza *= 5.5 feet; 9* brazas *= 49.5 feet] 1 league from the land, which was 30⁰ 08' N. They sailed along the coast looking for a harbor, and at night they anchored near the land, in 8 brazas [44 feet] of water.*

And thinking that this land was an island, they called it La Florida, because it presented a beautiful vista of many blossoming trees and was low and flat; and also because they discovered it during the time of Easter [Pascua Florida].⁴⁶ Juan Ponce wanted the name to conform to [agree with] these two aspects [reasons]. They went ashore to gather information and to take possession.

Friday, April 8 they made sail and followed the same course [northward?].

On Saturday [April 9], they turned to the south, going south-byeast and sailed the same course until April 20. They discovered sev-

Figure 31. The Palm Coast of Florida, thirty miles north of Daytona Beach. Juan Ponce landed near here on April 3, 1513. (Photograph by R. H. Fuson)

105

eral Indian houses [on the coast] and anchored. On the next day [Thursday, April 21] they followed the coastline — all three ships — and they encountered a current that they were unable to sail against even though they had a strong wind. [This was the first documented reference to the Gulf Stream — perhaps the most important discovery made on this voyage.] The two ships nearest to the shore anchored but the current was so strong that it made the cables [anchor chains] quiver. [The ships that anchored were the Santiago and the Santa María de la Consolación.] The third ship [the San Cristóbal], which was a brigantine, was farther out to sea and either could not find bottom [to anchor] or did not recognize the current. It was pulled out to sea and they lost sight of it, despite the fact that it was a clear day and the weather was good.

Juan Ponce went ashore here and was called by the Indians who, in turn, tried to take the small boat, the oars, and arms. Because he did not want to start a fight, he had to tolerate their taunts. And, he wanted to establish a good first impression. But because the Indians hit a sailor in the head with a stick, knocking him unconscious, he [Juan Ponce] had to fight with them. The Indians, with their arrows and spears, with points made from sharpened bone or fish spines, wounded two Castilians, and the Indians received little damage. Juan Ponce collected his men, with some difficulty, and they departed during the night.

They left there and went to a river, where they filled their water casks and gathered firewood and waited for the brigantine. They came upon sixty Indians that they stopped, and they took one to serve as their guide and to learn the [Spanish] language. They named this river Rio de la Cruz [River of the Cross; probably Saint Lucie Inlet at the mouth of Saint Lucie River], and erected a stone monument with an inscription. They did not finish taking water because it was brackish.

On Sunday, May 8, they doubled the Cape of Florida [unrelated to the modern Cape Florida] which they called Cabo de Corrientes [Cape of Currents; Jupiter Inlet], because so much water [the Gulf Stream] flowed there, and it had more force than the wind and would not allow ships to proceed even with all of the sails unfurled. They anchored behind a cape, next to a village named Abaióa [near Jupiter, Florida].

All the coast, from Punta de Arrecifes [Reef Point; also called Cabo de la Cruz — Cape of the Cross — until the late 1500s] up to this Cabo de Corrientes runs north and south, and a few degrees to the southeast. It is completely clear [of foul ground] and has a depth

Figure 32. Saint Lucie Inlet, Florida, at the southern end of Hutchinson Island, near the town of Stuart. Juan Ponce called this inlet the River of the Cross on April 22, 1513. (Photograph by R. H. Fuson)

of 6 brazas [33 feet; offshore?]. The Cape [Corrientes] is 28⁰ 15' N.[47]

They sailed until they found two islands to the south at 27⁰ N. One of them, which was at least a league in length, they named Santa Marta [Saint Martha; Key Biscayne]. They took on water there. On Friday, May 13, they sailed along the edge of a bank, and reef of islands, until they came to the location of another island, which they named Pola [Elliott Key], at 26⁰ 30' N. Between the bank and reef of islands and the mainland, stands the great sea, like a bay [Biscayne Bay].

On Sunday, May 15, Whitsuntide [the seventh Sunday after Easter; Dia de Pascua de Espíritu Santo], they ran along the coast of the islands [the Florida Keys] for 10 leagues, up to two white [sandy] islands. And to all of that island reef, and the small islands, they named it Los Mártires [The Martyrs, now the Florida Keys], because seen from a distance the rocks, that stuck up, looked like men who were suffering. And also the name has survived, for the many men who have been lost there since.[48] They [Los Mártires] are at 26⁰ 15' N.

They sailed — sometimes to the north and other times to the northeast — until May 23. On the 24th of May they turned and followed the coast to the south, now carefully examining it to see if it was

Figure 33. The Florida Keys near Key West. To Ponce, these small islands reminded him of the many martyrs who had died for Castilla, hence the name "Los Mártires." (Photograph by R. H. Fuson)

Tierra-Firme [the mainland]. And they came upon several islets that were in the open sea and because it seemed that they had an entrance between them and the coast for the ships, they stopped there [the Gulf of Mexico islands facing Charlotte and Lee counties, Florida] for water and firewood until June 3. They careened one ship, the San Cristóbal, *and Indians in canoes came up to see what the Castilians were doing, for the first time. [The* San Cristóbal *probably was careened on Pine Island, the logical stopping point for the fleet inasmuch as it is the best protected island.]*

    Even though the Indians called to them, the Castilians did not go ashore, wanting to raise the anchor in order to make repairs on it. Thinking that the Castilians were leaving, they [the Indians] put to sea in their canoes and tried to take the big ship by pulling the anchor cable by hand. But the small ship was behind them and it went in to the shore, where the Castilians took four Indian women and smashed up two old canoes. The other times that they [Indians and Castilians] met there was no conflict, but the Indians were not allowed to see any trade goods before they offered either hides [pelts] or gold.

    On Friday, June 4, while waiting for a wind in order to go search for Chief Carlos, who the Indians on board the [Castilian] ships said had gold, a canoe came to the ships, and an Indian who understood the Castilians — who was believed to be a native of Española or some other island inhabited by Castilians — said that they should wait, that the Chief wanted to send gold to trade. And, [while] waiting, there appeared up to twenty canoes — some attached to each other [catamarans?]. Some went to the anchors; others, to the ships. They began to fight from their canoes. Because they were not able to raise the anchors they tried to cut the cables. An armed ship went after them and they fled, abandoning several canoes. They [the Castilians] took five [canoes], killed some Indians, and captured four. Juan Ponce sent two of them to the Chief in order to tell him that although they had killed a Castilian with two arrow-wounds he would make peace with him.

The next day [June 5], the small boat went to take soundings in a nearby harbor, and the crew went ashore [probably near Bokelia, at

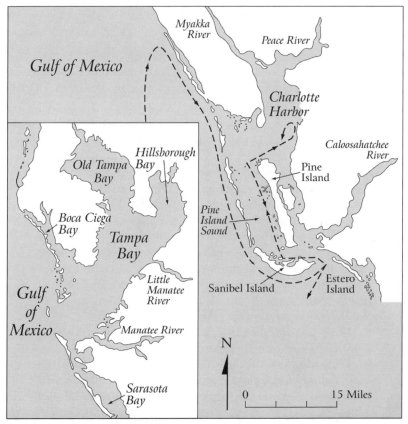

Figure 34. The probable route of Juan Ponce as he explored Charlotte Harbor between June 4 and June 15, 1513. **Inset**: A map of Tampa Bay for comparison with that of Charlotte Harbor. Both maps are at the same scale.

109

Figure 35. Long Cutoff, Pine Island, Florida. This is one of the many "creeks" at Pine Island and might have been the one described by Bernal Díaz in 1517. (Photograph by R. H. Fuson)

the north end of Pine Island]. They encountered Indians who said that the next day the Chief would come to trade [but it was a ruse]. In the meantime, the crew [Castilians] and the canoes [Indians] drew closer together. And so eighty Indians, dressed in breechcloths, attacked the eleven Castilians near the closest ship. They fought from morning till night, without harming the Castilians because the arrows did not reach them. Moreover, the Indians did not dare come near because of the crossbows and artillery shots, and finally the Indians withdrew. After having been there for nine days, the Castilians decided, on Tuesday, June 14, to return to Española and to San Juan [Puerto Rico]. Along the way they wanted to discover some islands that the Indians on board the ships had told them about.

They returned to the island that they called Matanza [Slaughter; Pine Island], because of the Indians they killed, and they took on water. Wednesday, June 15, they went in search of the eleven small islands that they had left to the west. Thursday and Friday they followed the same course. On Tuesday, June 21, they reached the small islands that they named Las Tortugas. [The Tortoises; the Dry Tortugas, and there are seven — not eleven — of them, lying sixty-eight nautical miles west of Key West, Florida. Other than "Florida," "Tortuga" is the oldest European place-name found on modern maps

110

of the United States.] In a short period at night they took, on one of these islands, 170 turtles and could have taken many more if they so desired. They also took fourteen Lobos Marinos [West Indian Monk seals, Monachus tropicalis, *now presumed to be extinct], many pelicans, and at least five thousand other birds.*[49]

Friday, June 24, they sailed southwest-by-south. On Sunday, June 26, they saw land. Monday they sailed along the coast to examine it and on Wednesday [June 29] they made port [on the coast]. They dressed the lateen [triangular] yards and [square] sails, although they were not able to determine what land [country] they were in. Most of the crew thought it was Cuba because they found canoes, dogs, cuttings made by knives and iron tools, but not because anyone knew, individually that it was Cuba, except to say that they had taken that route to Cuba, and that Cuba ran east-west like it, except that they found themselves eighteen long leagues [about sixty miles] off course for this to be Cuba.

They left here on Friday, July 1, to look for Los Mártires [the Florida Keys]; on Sunday [July 3] they reached Isla de Achecambéi [an Indian name; probably Key Largo], and by-passing Santa Pola [Elliott Key][50] *and Santa Marta [Key Biscayne] they arrived at Chequescá [also Tequesta and Tekesta; Miami Beach]. They sailed to several islands that are in the Lucayan Banks [Great Bahama Bank],*

Figure 36. Pine Island and Pine Island Sound, Florida. This might be the island Juan Ponce called Matanza (Slaughter) following his battle with the Calusa Indians on June 4, 1513. (Photograph by R. H. Fuson)

Figure 37. Dry Tortugas, Florida. This westernmost point of Florida was discovered by Juan Ponce on June 21, 1513. (Photograph by F. J. Buchsbaum)

more to the west [sic], *and anchored among them July 18.*

They took on water there and named the island La Vieja ["The Old Woman"], for an old Indian woman they found there all alone. [This was either Memory Rock or Sandy Cay; northwest of Grand Bahama Island, on the edge of Little Bahama Bank.] These islands [sic] are at 28⁰ N.

In the opinion of the discoverers, there was no way to know the pre-European name of Florida. Upon seeing that point of land stick out, they thought it was an island; and for the Indians it was the mainland. They gave the name of each province and the Castilians thought that they were being deceived. Finally, because of their pestering, the Indians said that it was called Cautió. This was a name that the Lucayan [Bahamian] Indians gave to that land because the people of it carried their secret parts covered with palm leaves, woven like a plait [which they called cautió*].*

On July 25, they left the islets to look for Bimini, sailing among some islands that they thought were covered [by water] when the tide was high. After stopping, and not knowing where to go with the ships, Juan Ponce sent the small boat to examine an island which he thought was awash daily. This was the island of Bahama [probably Grand Bahama/Abaco] according to the Old Woman that they had taken aboard [on July 18]. They encountered Diego Miruelo, pilot, with a ship out of Española [dispatched by the viceroy, Diego Columbus, to check on Juan Ponce]. He [Miruelo] had put in at this island — some

112

Figure 38. Fort Jefferson, the largest coastal fort in the United States during the nineteenth century, is a dominant feature of Dry Tortugas National Park. (Photograph by K. F. Buchsbaum)

say by luck — and he went on with his adventures.

They departed from where they had gone on Saturday, August 6, and until finding deep water they sailed northwest-by-west to a small rocky island, just on the edge of the deep water [on the edge of the bank; possibly Moore's Island or near there]. They changed course, running along the edge of the bank to the south. They changed this course the next day, although Bimini was not on this route. And fearing the currents, which on another occasion forced the ships toward the shore of La Florida or Cautió [as they called it then], they turned their course to San Juan [Puerto Rico].

Having sailed until August 18 they found themselves at sunrise 2 leagues from a Lucayan [Bahamian] island, and they sailed 3 leagues up to the cape of this island [possibly Eleuthera]. They anchored there and remained until August 22. From here it took four days to reach the island of Guanimá [probably Cat Island] because there was little wind and the crossing was difficult. They turned back, avoiding the coast of Guanimá, to [go to] the island of Guatáo [possibly Eleuthera]. Because of storms they were detained on it, unable to leave, for twenty-seven days, that is, until September 23. The small ship from Española [Miruelo's ship] that had joined them on or about July 25 was lost but the crew was saved. [The hurricane season was underway.]

Juan Ponce overhauled his ships, and although it seemed to him that he had worked hard he decided to send out a ship to identify the Isla de Bimini even though he did not want to, for he wanted to do this himself. He had an account of the wealth of this island [Bimini] and especially that singular Fuente [fountain or spring] that the Indians spoke of, that turned men from old men to boys. He had not been able to find it because of shoals and currents and contrary weather. He sent, then, Juan Pérez de Ortubia [captain of the San Cristóbal*] as captain of the ship [apparently the* San Cristóbal*] and Antón de Alaminos [from the* Santiago*] as pilot. They took two Indians to guide them over the shoals [banks]. There are so many that it is dangerous to sail through them. This ship left September 17 [sic: the correct date was September 27] and Juan Ponce sailed the next day on his voyage.*

In twenty-one days [on October 19, 1513] he reached the island of San Juan [Puerto Rico] and went to the harbor of La Baía de Puerto Rico [Puerto Rico Bay; today's San Juan Bay]. The other ship [the San Cristóbal*, that had been left behind to find Bimini] arrived [on February 20, 1514] and reported that Bimini [probably Andros Island] had been found, but not the Fountain. It was a large island, cool, and with many lakes and trees.*

And thus ended the discovery of Juan Ponce in La Florida, without knowing if it was the mainland, nor for some years thereafter was this fact certified.

~

The Herrera account leaves a lot to be desired, but it is all we have. Juan Ponce was on his expedition to Bimini and Florida for 230 days, many of which are unaccounted for. Few details of the exploration are given, other than sailing and anchoring. It is not known where Juan Ponce landed in Florida, other than the fact that it was somewhere on the east coast. This as yet undetermined landing place was probably north of what is today Daytona Beach, Florida, and south of the Saint Johns River, probably in the area now known as the Palm Coast. We know that Juan Ponce saw an island on Easter Day, March 27, 1513, but he did not explore it. This was probably Abaco or Grand Bahama, both on the Little Bahama Bank, and about the approximate distance and direction from Florida's Palm Coast.

The actual landing was on the morning of April 3, a Sunday, one week after Easter of 1513.

It is obvious that Juan Ponce never got as far north as the site of modern Saint Augustine, much less even farther north to the mouth of the Saint Johns River. There are two main reasons for believing this. First, Juan Ponce would have paid very strict attention to the hydrology of the region, for he intended to establish a settlement eventually. There is simply no way that he, or the captains and pilots with him, would have neglected to mention the geographic aspects of the area where Saint Augustine was later founded. This area, with several rivers and islands, is unique. The Saint Johns is the largest river in Florida and, as with the Saint Augustine site, it is not something that would have been overlooked or passed by without comment.

Second, there was a large Indian population between the area where Saint Augustine was later settled and the Saint Johns River. Juan Ponce did not report encountering any Indians until April 20, when he saw some native houses just north of what is today Jupiter, Florida. It was here that the first hostile clash between the Indians and Castilians occurred, with no serious injuries on either side. Also, on May 8, Juan Ponce reported seeing an Indian village for the first time, probably at Jupiter Inlet.

It is also apparent from the Herrera account and later information that no one on the Juan Ponce expedition suspected that Florida was part of the North American mainland. On the contrary, Florida was thought to be a large island and its peninsular nature was not understood before 1519 and by many, including Juan Ponce himself, not even then.

~

One of the legacies of Juan Ponce's first voyage to Florida is that many place-names still in use today were first recog-

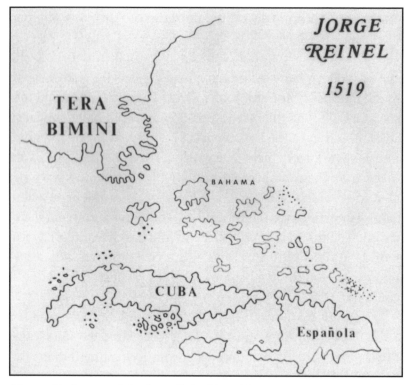

Figure 39. A part of the Jorge Reinel World Map, 1519. Once known as *Kunstmann IV* and erroneously dated 1514, this is the only map to identify Florida as *Tera Bimini*. (Adapted from *Portvgaliae Monvmenta Cartographica*, Volume I, Plate 12)

nized or applied by Europeans during this voyage. Ponce de León named, or borrowed the Indian name for, fourteen different places in or near Florida. Superlative among these is Florida, the oldest European place-name in the United States. Other examples include Matanza, Juan Ponce's name for an island near Fort Myers, Florida, that has been transferred to a nearby strait, and Tortugas, which survives in the form of Dry Tortugas. Tequesta, or Tekesta — derived from the Indian word Chequescá, the Indian name for what is today Miami Beach — is today the name of a city located about ninety miles north of Miami.

116

Table 4. Places Visited and Named by Juan Ponce de León during his First Voyage to Florida, 1513.

Name Used in 1513	Modern Name	Date of Use in 1513	Location
La Florida	Florida	April 2	Southeastern United States
Rio de la Cruz	Saint Lucie Inlet, Saint Lucie River	April 22	27°10'N 80°17'W
Cabo de Corrientes, Cabo de Florida	Jupiter Inlet	May 8	26°57'N 80°04'W
Abaióa (a village)	No longer exists; was near Jupiter	May 8	26°56'N 80°06'W
Punta de Arrecifes (known as Cabo de la Cruz until late in the 1500s)	Cape Canaveral [a]	April 15(?)	28°24'N 80°37'W
Santa Marta	Key Biscayne	May 12	25°42'N 80°10'W
Santa Pola	Elliott Key	May 13	25°27'N 80°11'W
Los Mártires	Florida Keys	May 15	24°45'N 81°00'W
Cacique Carlos (probably *Calos* in the original)	Charlotte (the feminine of *Charles,* the French equivalent of *Carlos)*	June 4	Charlotte County, Charlotte Harbor, Port Charlotte — all in Florida
Matanza	Pine Island	June 6	26°35'N 82°06'W
Las Tortugas	Dry Tortugas	June 21	24°38'N 82°55'W
Achecambéi	Key Largo	July 3	25°16'N 80°19'W
Chequescá	Miami Beach	July 3	25°47'N 80°08'W
La Vieja	Memory Rock or Sandy Cay, Bahamas	July 18	26°52'N 79°07'W 26°47'N 79°02'W
Cautió	Southeastern Florida	July 20	Southeastern Florida

[a] The name Canaveral *(Cañaveral)* does not appear on the earliest maps of Florida. By the 1540s, Canaveral was the name that had been given to the southern end of Jupiter Island; at that time, what is today Cape Canaveral was called Cape of the Cross.

117

It is one of the ironies of history that what is not discovered is often better remembered than what is discovered.[51] This is certainly the case with Juan Ponce's first journey to the land he called La Florida, for when one hears the name Ponce de León, the first thing that comes to mind is the Fountain of Youth.

At best, the quest of the magic fountain was a secondary motive for the exploration, and most likely it was a tertiary one. For Ferdinand, who really wanted to be rejuvenated, the discovery of a mystical fountain was not his highest priority. Instead, he felt a strong moral obligation to repay Juan Ponce for many years of service and loyalty, he wanted to prevent the Columbus family from gaining any additional power, and he always was casting about for a sound investment. As to rejuvenation, Ferdinand had married a French lady — Germaine de Foix, thirty-five years his junior — after Queen Isabela's death in 1504. In 1512, when he was sixty and Germaine was twenty-five, he wanted to father a son to be the future king of Aragón and all of its dominions. Clearly, erasing old age — and in those days sixty years was indeed old age — was possibly an ever-present thought in the king's mind which led him to make inquiries about the "secrets" of all of the newly discovered lands in and around the West Indies.[52] If the search for a magic fountain was motivation for the voyage to Bimini, then it was Ferdinand's idea — not Ponce de León's.

Although Juan Ponce was well-established in both Española and San Juan Bautista, he found exploration to be exhilarating and he probably longed for the opportunity to establish another colony. In addition, he was not opposed to enhancing his estate. But searching for a Fountain of Youth was not his main concern, other than the fact that the king had told him to keep an eye open for it. In fact, Herrera's account does not mention Bimini until July 25 — 144 days into the voyage — and the *Fuente* (Fountain) does not appear in the narration until September 27 — 208 days into the voyage.

Juan Ponce was only thirty-eight years old when he signed the contract to sail for Bimini and he was not yet old enough to need rejuvenation. Also, legends concerning exotic springs and enchanted waters are as old as humankind; the Ganges, Nile, and Jordan rivers as sources of rejuvenation, and the act of baptism, come to mind as examples of the supposed enchanting powers of water. A "Fountain of Youth" legend was associated with the Canary Islands as early as the first century AD.[53] Both T. Frederick Davis and Devereaux devote a great deal of space to the legend and, according to many authorities, the Taino Indians of San Juan Bautista, Española, and especially Cuba believed that a magic fountain and a rejuvenating river existed somewhere to the north of the Greater Antilles.[54] These tales from a wide variety of peoples and places were certainly known to King Ferdinand.

Every significant mineral and thermal spring in Europe has drawn pilgrims and the curious to it for millennia. The same may be said for such localities in the United States and the rest of the world. Sacred waters abound, and in such grottoes as Lourdes, France, miraculous events have been reported. Bath, England, attracted Romans; dozens of counterparts may be found in the German-speaking countries, where *Bad* (Bath) is a common place-name. Even the word *spa* comes from the name of a Belgian town, famous for its mineral springs that are said to have curative powers.

Almost 500 years after Juan Ponce's famous voyage, people are still attracted to Florida's springs, which include seventeen of the seventy-five first-magnitude artesian springs — springs with a flow of at least 100 cubic feet per second (cfs) — in the United States.[55] Florida has fifty second-magnitude springs (10–100 cfs) and over 30,000 lakes. A legend of a magic fountain could not have been applied to a better place!

There is no doubt that Juan Ponce was aware of the legend of the "Fountain of Bimini," as it was usually called. And there is no doubt that he perceived — at least at the outset — that Bimini and the land he would come to call Florida were one and the same. But by July 25, 1513, Juan Ponce had come to realize that Bimini and Florida were two different places. Perhaps the old woman they had picked up on July 18 had told Juan Ponce, through the Indian interpreters traveling with him, that Bimini and Cautió were different localities. Perhaps this is why, near the end of his adventure, Juan Ponce sent Juan Pérez de Ortubia and Antón de Alaminos to find Bimini and its fountain. And Juan Ponce made certain that he took Diego Miruelo — Diego Columbus's shipwrecked spy — back to San Juan Bautista, just in case there was a fountain and credit for its discovery might go to someone else. Even so, the discovery of new lands was the real motivation for the voyage.

In the process of sailing to Bimini and Florida, Ponce de León also found the Gulf Stream, perhaps the single most important Castilian discovery since the First Voyage of Christopher Columbus. This vast river within the ocean moves as much as four billion tons of water a minute at speeds up to five miles per hour near Palm Beach, Florida. The volume of its flow at this point is a thousand times greater than that of the Mississippi River.[56]

Columbus discovered the route to the west, where the northeast trade winds consistently propel a sailing craft forward. Ponce de León discovered the best way back. Both of these discoveries strongly influenced traffic on the North Atlantic Ocean until the advent of steam in the nineteenth century, and both still play a vital role today for any ship that is able to ply their courses. Almost immediately after Juan Ponce's voyage of 1513, the Castilians came to realize the value of the Gulf Stream, the great *corriente*, that flowed eastward along the

Florida Keys and then northward along Florida's east coast and beyond. It was the presence and importance of the Gulf Stream that soon would make Havana, Cuba, the preeminent city of Hispanic America, and it played an important role later in determining the location of Saint Augustine, the oldest city in the United States founded by Europeans.

Juan Ponce had been away from San Juan Bautista and his family for almost eight months while exploring Bimini and Florida, and during this time some significant events had transpired on the island.[57] On June 2, Diego Columbus arrived at the port of San Germán with a collection of people he had named to various positions for the governance of the island. On that very day the Caribs attacked Caparra and burned the town to the ground. Juan Ponce's house was destroyed and his wife and children barely escaped with their lives. Also, the residence of bishop Alonso Manso was consumed.[58] Several Castilians died in this attack, and Diego Columbus blamed Ponce de León

Figure 40. The ruins of Juan Ponce's house at Caparra, Puerto Rico. (Photograph by George Barford)

Figure 41. The monument at the ruins of Juan Ponce's house at Caparra, Puerto Rico. The ruins of this structure, which was built around 1508 and was similar to Salvaleón in Higüey, lie about ten miles from the center of Old San Juan, Puerto Rico. (Photograph by R. H. Fuson)

RUINAS DE LA CASA DE JUAN PONCE DE LEON

RESIDENCIA DEL CONQUISTADOR. CASA-FUERTE Y SEDE DE GOBIERNO. SUS MUROS FUERON EL AMPARO DE LOS PRIMEROS POBLADORES CONTRA LOS ATAQUES DE LOS INDIOS. LA ESTRUCTURA. DE MAMPOSTERIA Y PIEDRA. SE COMENZO EN 1508. EL PROPIO JUAN PONCE DE LEON LA DESCRIBE ASI:

"FICE UNA CASA MEDIANA CON SU TERRADO. E PETRIL (SIC). E ALMENAS. E SU BARRERA DELANTE DE LA PUERTA. E TODA ENCALADA DE DENTRO E DE PUERA. DE ALTOR (SIC). DE SIETE TAPIAS EN ALTO CON EL PRETIL E ALMENAS"

EL INSTITUTO DE CULTURA PUERTORRIQUEÑA

RUINS OF THE HOUSE OF JUAN PONCE DE LEON

RESIDENCE OF THE CONQUEROR. FORTIFIED HOUSE AND SEAT OF GOVERNMENT. ITS WALLS WERE THE REFUGE OF THE FIRST INHABITANTS AGAINST THE INDIAN ATTACKS. THE STRUCTURE. OF MASONRY AND STONE. ITS (CONSTRUCTION) BEGAN IN 1508. JUAN PONCE DE LEON HIMSELF DESCRIBED IT THUSLY:

"I BUILT AN AVERAGE HOUSE WITH A FLAT ROOF. AND PARAPET. AND BATTLEMENTS. AND ITS BARRICADE IN FRONT OF THE DOOR. AND EVERYTHING WHITEWASHED INSIDE AND OUT. THE UPSTAIRS. (WAS) SEVEN ADOBE BRICKS HIGH WITH PARAPET AND BATTLEMENTS"

THE INSTITUTE OF PUERTO RICAN CULTURE

Figure 42. The monument in Caparra, Puerto Rico, near the site where the first cathedral in the Americas was established sometime after 1512. The cathedral was abandoned in 1521, the year that a new cathedral was built in San Juan. (Photograph by R. H. Fuson)

PRIMERA CATEDRAL DE AMERICA

EN ALGUN PUNTO DE ESTOS CONTORNOS SE LEVANTA LA PRIMERA IGLESIA EN PUERTO RICO. CON LA LLEGADA DEL OBISPO ALONSO MANSO EN EL 1512. PRIMERO EN PISAR TIERRA AMERICANA. LA HUMILDE ESTRUCTURA DE MADERA Y PAJA SE CONVIRTIO EN LA PRIMERA CATEDRAL DEL NUEVO MUNDO.

EN ELLA EJERCIO SU APOSTOLADO EL OBISPO MANSO HASTA EL TRASLADO DE LA CIUDAD A LA ISLETA DE SAN JUAN DONDE SE CONSTRUYO LA NUEVA CATEDRAL.

EL INSTITUTO DE CULTURA PUERTORRIQUEÑA

AMERICA'S FIRST CATHEDRAL

SOMEWHERE IN THIS VICINITY WAS BUILT THE FIRST CHURCH IN PUERTO RICO. WITH THE ARRIVAL OF BISHOP ALONSO MANSO IN 1512. FIRST TO WALK ON AMERICAN SOIL. THE HUMBLE STRUCTURE OF WOOD AND STRAW WAS CONVERTED INTO THE FIRST CATHEDRAL OF THE NEW WORLD.

IN IT BISHOP MANSO EXERCISED HIS APOSTOLATE UNTIL HE MOVED TO THE CITY OF THE LITTLE ISLAND OF SAN JUAN WHERE A NEW CATHEDRAL WAS CONSTRUCTED.

THE INSTITUTE OF PUERTO RICAN CULTURE

---

for placing Caparra in such a vulnerable location.

In response to the Indian attack, Juan Enríquez had been sent after the Caribs by Diego Columbus. Although the attacking Indians did not live on San Juan Bautista, and no Caribs were ever found, Columbus's people had been allowed to renew their advances into Taino territory. Once Juan Ponce returned to San Juan Bautista and became aware of these developments, he saw Diego's policy as simply a means — an excuse — for taking more Indian land — Carib or Taino — and establishing more Castilian control over the Caribbean region.

Although Juan Ponce realized that Caparra had been poorly situated, he also saw a plot developing among Diego Columbus and his allies to depopulate Caparra, discredit him, move the capital to San Germán, seize Indian lands in San Juan Bautista, and arm a fleet to go to the home islands of the Caribs (the Lesser Antilles) and seize them to become slaves. In Juan Ponce's mind, waging war on the Caribs was quite different than attacking the Tainos; after all, the Caribs had burned his beloved Caparra, destroyed his home, and very nearly killed his family. He was certainly determined to punish the Caribs, but at the same time, he was not willing to link every problem in San Juan Bautista with a brief invasion of about 200 Caribs. He came to the conclusion that it was pointless to discuss this with the viceroy. Juan Ponce de León would take his complaints directly to King Ferdinand.

Chapter 4
1514–1521

The Years Between the Florida Voyages

When Juan Ponce returned to San Juan Bautista after his first voyage to "Bemeni" he discovered that hostilities had broken out on the island between the Castilians and the Indians. Realizing that complaints to the local authorities would be useless in dealing with the problem, Juan Ponce went directly to the king in April 1514. Ferdinand, in Valladolid at the time, received Juan Ponce as an old friend and trusted subject. As matters unfolded during their discussions, Juan Ponce was given many honors and titles and a second contract to return to Florida and Bimini. He was also given command of a fleet that was to operate out of San Juan Bautista to find and pacify the hostile Carib Indians.

After Ferdinand died in January 1516 and Carlos I ascended to the throne, Juan Ponce returned with his fleet to the now-unified kingdom of Spain to protect his rights and privileges. He was in Spain from November 1516 until May 1518, during which time there were at least two voyages from the Antilles to Florida, both of which were unauthorized. After Juan Ponce went back to San Juan Bautista in 1518, events occurred that affected him personally and the direction and pulse of Spanish colonization in general. It became apparent to Juan Ponce that he had to act now, or never, on his plans to settle Florida.

In April of 1514, Juan Ponce de León was prepared to do something that no other conquistador had ever done — he was

125

going to return to Castilla and go directly to the court of Ferdinand II to speak with the king. Ballesteros has called this "a new adventure, the most dangerous of his [Juan Ponce's] life."[1] It was dangerous in the sense that he knew almost everything there was to know about the Indies — the officials involved in the conquest and settlement; their greed, avarice, and excesses; and their treatment of the Indians. Juan Ponce was, therefore, in a position to become one of American history's first "whistle blowers."

Juan Ponce departed San Juan Bautista, accompanied by Juan Pérez de Ortubia, captain of the *San Cristóbal*, in April, 1514. They arrived in Bayona, Castilla's large port in the province of Galicia, later that month. They did not, however, sail on the *San Cristóbal*, but rather on a small caravel owned by Diego Corral.[2] And Ortubia went as a passenger, not as Juan Ponce's personal captain. Juan Ponce carried with him 5000 pesos in gold for the royal treasury — a sizeable sum, but its value to Castilla was nothing compared to his knowledge of lands to the north of Española and the promise of other as-yet-undiscovered lands lying beyond those.

From Bayona, Juan Ponce traveled to Sevilla to report to Juan Díaz de Solis, who was now pilot-major of the Casa de Contratación, on the voyage to Bimini and Florida during the previous year. It is not known when Juan Ponce reached Sevilla, nor the route he took to get there, but he had reported to the Casa no later than September.[3]

Some who have studied Juan Ponce's life have made much over the fact that he and Ortubia sailed to Bayona rather than to Sevilla, the usual port-of-entry for ships coming from the Indies.[4] We may never learn the real reason or reasons for this, but several possibilities come to mind. The *Pinta* had reached Bayona on its return from the Discovery Voyage of Christopher Columbus because of the weather. Does anyone know what the weather was like over the North Atlantic Ocean during April 1514? Perhaps atmospheric and maritime conditions made a landing at Bayona more feasible than one at Sevilla. Or maybe Juan Ponce wanted to go first to the Court in Valladolid. Or perhaps he wished to see his childhood home and relatives a few miles northwest of Valladolid. And, he may have sailed from Bayona to Sevilla, as the *Pinta* once had done, and did not travel overland at all. We simply do not know if Juan Ponce saw Ferdinand before or after he visited the Casa.

It is known that Juan Ponce was warmly received by Ferdinand whenever it was that he was in Valladolid. For one thing, Pedro Núñez de Guzmán, Juan Ponce's tutor almost a quarter-century earlier, was now the tutor of Ferdinand's favorite grandson and namesake, Prince Ferdinand.[5] Further, Guzmán was Knight Commander of the Military Order of Calatrava and brother of Ramírez Núñez de Guzmán, Lord of Toral. Juan Ponce's paternal grandmother — a Guzmán — was Lady of Toral before Pedro and Ramírez were born.

While at Valladolid, Ponce de León was knighted and given a personal coat-of-arms — the first conquistador to receive these honors — and from that moment on he was properly known as Don Juan Ponce de León, "Don" being the Spanish equivalent of the English "Sir."

Once he reached the Casa de Contratación, Juan Ponce met with Solis, Juan Vespucci (nephew of Amerigo), Sebastián Cabot, and Vicente Yáñez Pinzón. Not only were Juan Ponce's discoveries — Florida, the Florida Keys, the Tortugas, Bimini, and other islands of the Bahamas — added to the Padrón Real, but Vasco Núñez de Balboa's discovery of the South Sea (Pacific Ocean) had recently been reported to the Casa and was being hailed as a momentous achievement. It is indeed unfortunate that no transcripts of these conversations were made.

On September 27, 1514, a flurry of documents emanated

Figure 43. The coat of arms awarded to Juan Ponce de León in 1514. (From Sarramía Roncero, 1993)

from the Court at Valladolid. One must assume that Juan Ponce had his audience(s) with the king before that date, and it is probable that Juan Ponce carried some of these royal encyclicals from Valladolid to Sevilla. This may or may not have been Juan Ponce's first trip from Bayona to Sevilla, via Valladolid. Although we are mostly interested here in those royal documents that pertain to Juan Ponce, it is worth noting that one of the decrees he carried to the Casa was the appointment of Vasco Núñez de Balboa to be "Governor of the Southern Sea."[6]

Ballesteros has summarized the significance of the documents that came from the king in September 1514, as far as they concerned Juan Ponce.[7] These documents included:

1. Agreements between Ferdinand and Juan Ponce, some of which were also signed by Queen Juana, concerning the settlement of Bimini and Florida.

2. Designation of Juan Ponce as Governor and Chief Justice of Bimini and Florida.

3. Regulations concerning the settlement of these territories.

4. Appointment of Juan Ponce as Captain of the Armada to subdue the Caribs; the Armada was to be organized in and to sail from Castilla.

5. Instructions for the implementation of the campaign against the Caribs.

The contract between Ferdinand and Juan Ponce for a second voyage to Florida is of particular concern here. This document reads as follows: [8]

> *The agreement that was made by our command with you, Juan Ponce de León, to go and settle the Island of Bimini and the Island of Florida, which you discovered by our command, in addition to the contract and agreement that was made with you when you went to discover, is the following:*
>
> *1. Whereas in the said contract and agreement that was made with you by our command, concerning the discovery and settlement of the said Islands, I gave you license and authority for the time and term of three years, which commenced the day that you received the said contract. You could take, at your cost and expense, the ships that*

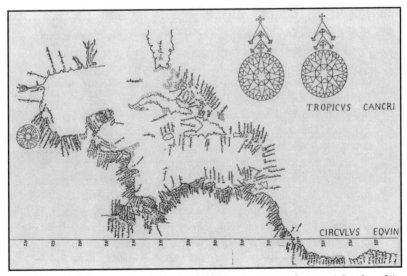

Figure 44. The Turin Map, ca. 1523. Florida is depicted as an island and is labeled *Isla Florida*. The anonymous cartographer apparently was unaware of the voyages of Garay and Ponce de León. (From Harrisse, 1892)

you desired, provided that you were obligated to begin discovery within the first year, and because until now you have been busy with matters in our service and have not had time to pursue it, it is my pleasure and will that the said three years will commence and be counted from the day that you embark for the said Islands.

2. As soon as you reach the said Islands and go ashore you shall notify the chiefs and Indians there by whatever means it takes to make them understand what is to be said to them about conforming to El Requerimiento [The Requirement] that has been ordered by many learned men, which will be given to you, signed by the Very Reverend Father in Christ, the Bishop of Burgos, Archbishop of Rosario, our head chaplain and one of our Council, and by Lope de Conchillos, our secretary and one of our Council, and by several cleric-proctors.[9] By every way and means that you can devise you are to bring them [the Indians] to understand our Catholic Faith, and to obey and serve it as they are obliged to. And you are to record in writing, before two or three notaries, if you have them, and before the most creditable witnesses that are present in order to serve as our justification and you will send the said written records and requirements that are made one and two and three times.

3. If after the aforesaid they do not want to obey what is contained in the said Requirement, in such case you may make war and seize them and take them away as slaves. But if they do obey, give them the best treatment possible and try, as it is stated, by every means at your disposal to convert them to our Holy Catholic Faith. And, if by chance, after having once obeyed the said Requirement, they again rebel, in such case I command that you again make the said Requirement before making war or doing harm or causing damage.

4. Moreover, that no trader or other person may go armed or send to the said Islands for slaves or for any other people, and if they should have to go it shall be with the consent of the said Juan Ponce and not in any other way, provided that they pay us the fifth and other fees that we have to have for the armadas and aforesaid things that pertain to us.

5. Moreover, inasmuch as in the said contract and agreement that I commanded to be made with you at the time you were going to discover the said Island, I made a grant to the persons that were going [with you] to discover the said Island that they would pay no fees on any gold, other metals, or profitable items discovered the first year [they would pay no "tenth"]. The second year they would pay a ninth, the third an eighth, the fourth a seventh, and the fifth a sixth part. The following years a fifth [is to be paid], as is the custom on Española.

130

Therefore, for the present, I confirm and approve the aforesaid and it is my wish that it have effect for the time of the said twelve years, which shall begin as soon as the settlement of the said Island begins.

6. Moreover, I shall give license and I hereby give it to the said Juan Ponce de León to make and build houses on the said Island and settlements of residences in the manner that they are made and built in these realms, with the provision that the foundations be adobe and gravel and the walls be adobe. Likewise, he may establish whatever farmland [is necessary] for bread and wine and plant whatever fruit trees or non-fruitbearing trees and other things that are suitable for the said land.

7. After you have made war on the said Caribs, or have protected the chiefs and Indians and pacified them, you may go or send the ships and the people of the said armada to visit the said Islands of Bimini and the Florida Island, when there is no need for your presence, and do what seems best to suit our service.

8. As a guarantee that you, the said Juan Ponce and the persons that may go with you, do and comply and will be discharged, provided for, and paid according to the terms of this contract, that pertains to you to take care of and complete, before making the said voyage you shall give a full and creditable bond to the satisfaction of our officials that reside on the said Island of San Juan [Puerto Rico].

Lastly, the said Juan Ponce, completing everything that is said and every part and parcel of it, and giving the said bonds, and taking care of and paying the aforementioned things, I hearby promise you and swear to you to command, provide for, and fulfill everything that is contained in this contract and every part and parcel of it. And I order our officials who reside on the Island of San Juan that, in our name, they conform to the aforesaid and take with you the said agreement and contract and receive the said bonds. And for your expedition I command Don Diego Columbus, our Admiral, Viceroy [and] Governor of the Island of Española, and our appellate judges who reside on it [Española], and to our officials who reside on the said Island of San Juan, and all the justices, that they give you all of the favor and assistance that you might need, without impeding you in any manner whatsoever.

Dated in Valladolid, September 27, 1514.[10]

I the King

Countersigned by Conchillos
Signed by the Bishop

⌇

The only item in Juan Ponce's contract to undertake a second voyage to Florida that was really new to contracts between the Crown and authorized explorers was Article 2: *El Requerimiento*. This document was unique — even for the sixteenth century — and caused so much laughter and so many tears that it merits a close inspection.

Dr. Juan López de Palacio Rubios, one of sixteenth-century Castilla's most respected jurists, is usually credited with drafting The Requirement, though as chief jurist for the Crown he was only one member of the Royal Council who collectively created the document. In addition to Palacio Rubios, four other members of the Royal Council signed the final draft.[11]

The Requirement — which in 1513 was added to the Laws of Burgos, 1512 — was intended to bring some relief to the Indians.[12] As early as 1494, Queen Isabela had formed a commission of leading jurists and theologians to determine if the Indians could be enslaved. The commission reported that the Indians were free and could not be reduced to slavery.[13] Palacio Rubios, studying the question for Ferdinand, agreed with the earlier commission, but argued that the Conquest of the Indies canceled all preexisting political arrangements. In effect, according to this interpretation, the Indians lost their various sovereignties and the right to govern themselves.

All of this simply meant that Castilla had the right of governance in lands that it was occupying in the Americas. If there was resistence from the Indians, then — according to the Castilian reasoning — a war that ensued was just. If the war was just, then it was also just to make slaves of any hostile captives. Essentially, this is what The Requirement said.

Several scholars have offered their own observations about The Requirement. To quote the American historian Juan Friede:[14]

> *Whether the long, official text of the* requerimiento *was read to the Indians, or whether the Indian slaves had been warlike, was another question, but the conscience of the king and his counselors were set at rest because the legal formalities had been complied with. The eventual failure to comply with the conditions burdened the conscience of the slave hunter, not the king.*

Anderson has pointed out that even Spanish grave-robbers in the sixteenth century followed the law to the letter.[15] He went on to say that The Requirement was a "curious and presumptuous document" that was used "as a sop for . . . massacre and pillage of the natives."[16]

In the nineteenth century, the great British scholar, Sir Arthur Helps, wrote:[17]

> *If our own age did not abound in things as remote from all common sense as this Requisition [Requirement], we should wonder how much a folly could ever have been put forward, or even acquiesced in, by persons of such intelligence as those who surrounded the Spanish Court.*

Oviedo may have been at one of the first readings of The Requirement, and he was certainly the first to publish what was read.[18] On June 13, 1514, he landed at Santa Marta, in what is today Colombia, with Pedrarias, who was slated to replace Balboa as governor of Castilla del Oro (today's Panama and extreme northwestern Colombia). When confronted by several hundred Indians, all armed with poisoned arrows, Governor Pedrarias read The Requirement, after which he handed the hand-written copy to Oviedo, who wrote in his *Historia*:[19]

> *. . . to read it, as if I understood the Indians, or if we had someone there who could make them understand, wanting them to hear; then to show them the paper upon which it was written to make the case — but because it is a good idea to know ahead of time what is required of them, I want to state it here to the letter.*

Oviedo then published the entire Requirement.[20]

The next day, June 14, the landing party occupied an empty

village and, in the presence of all of the captains and senior officials, Oviedo said to the bishop there:[21]

> Sir, it seems to me that these Indians do not want to listen to the theology of this Requirement, nor do you have anyone who can make them understand it. Would Your Honor keep it until we have one of these Indians in a cage in order for him to learn it leisurely and then the Lord Bishop can make him understand it?

Oviedo then added, "And he took The Requirement and laughed, and everyone who heard it laughed."

The Requirement of 1514 reads as follows:[22]

> On the part of the King, Don Fernando, and of Doña Juana, his daughter, Queen of Castilla and León, subduers of the barbarous nations, we their servants notify and make known to you, as best we can, that the Lord our God, Living and Eternal, created the Heaven and the Earth, and one man and one woman, of whom you and we, and all the men of the world, were and are descendants, and all of those who come after us. But, on account of the multitude which has sprung from this man and woman in the five thousand years since the world was created, it was necessary that some men should go one way and some another, and that they should be divided into many kingdoms and provinces, for in one alone they could not be sustained.
>
> Of all of these nations God our Lord gave charge to one man, called Saint Peter, that he should be Lord and Superior of all the men in the world, that all should obey him, and that he should be the head of the whole human race, wherever men should live, and under whatever law, sect, or belief they should be; and he gave him the world for his kingdom and jurisdiction.
>
> And he commanded him to place his seat in Rome, as the spot most fitting to rule the world from; but also he permitted him to have his seat in any other part of the world, and to judge and govern all Christians, Moors, Jews, Gentiles, and all other sects. This man was called Pope, as if to say, Admirable Great Father and Governor of men. The men who lived in that time obeyed that Saint Peter, and took him for Lord, King, and Superior of the universe; so also they have regarded the others who after him have been elected to the pontificate, and so has it been continued even till now, and will continue till the end of the world.
>
> One of these Pontiffs, who succeeded that Saint Peter as Lord of

the world, in the dignity and seat which I have before mentioned, made donation of these isles and Tierra-firme [mainland] to the aforesaid King and Queen and to their successors, our lords, with all that there are in these territories, as is contained in certain writings which passed upon the subject as aforesaid, which you can see if you wish.

So their Highnesses are kings and lords of these islands and land of Tierra-firme by virtue of this donation: and some [inhabitants of] islands, and indeed almost all those to whom this has been notified, have received and served their Highnesses, as lords and kings, in the way that subjects ought to do, with good will, without any resistance, immediately, without delay, when they were informed of the aforesaid facts. And also they received and obeyed the priests whom their Highnesses sent to preach to them and to teach them our Holy Faith; and all these, of their own free will, without any reward or condition, have become Christians, and are so, and their Highnesses have joyfully and benignantly received them, and also have commanded them to be treated as subjects and vassals; and you too are held and obliged to do the same. Wherefore, as best we can, we ask and require you that you consider what we have said to you, and that you take the time that shall be necessary to understand and deliberate upon it, and that you acknowledge the Church as the Ruler and Superior of the whole world, and the high priest called Pope, and in his name the King and Queen Doña Juana our lords, in his place, as superiors and lords and kings of these islands and this Tierra-firme by virtue of the said donation, and that you consent and give place that these religious fathers should declare and preach to you the aforesaid.

If you do so, you will do well, and that which you are obliged to do to their Highnesses, and we in their name shall receive you in all love and charity, and shall leave you your wives, and your children, and your lands, free without servitude, that you may do with them and with yourselves freely that which you like and think best, and they shall not compel you to turn Christians, unless you yourselves, when informed of the truth, should wish to be converted to our Holy Catholic Faith, as almost all the inhabitants of the rest of the islands have done. And, besides this, their Highnesses award you many privileges and exemptions and will grant you many benefits.

But, if you do not do this, and maliciously make delay in it, I certify to you that, with the help of God, we shall powerfully enter into your country, and shall make war against you in all ways and manners that we can, and shall subject you to the yoke and obedience of the Church and of their Highnesses; we shall take you and your wives and your children, and shall make slaves of them, and as such shall sell and dispose of them as their Highnesses may command; and we shall take away your goods, and shall do you all the mischief and damage that we can, as to vassals who do not obey, and refuse to receive their lord, and resist and contradict him; and we protest that the deaths and losses which shall accrue from this are your fault, and not of their Highnesses, or ours, nor of these cavaliers who come with us. And that we have said this to you and made this Requisition [Requirement], we request the notary here present to give us his testimony in writing, and we ask the rest who are present that they should be witnesses of this Requisition.

～

By September 30, 1514, Juan Ponce de León was ready to leave the royal court in Valladolid and head south for Sevilla. He was loaded down with documents from the king which were to be delivered to officials at the Casa de Contratación. Among the more than a dozen items Juan Ponce carried with him was the new capitulación that authorized him to settle Bimini and Florida, certain *ordenanzas* (laws) for the people of Bimini and Florida (the first European laws ever promulgated for those lands), and the Royal Provision that named Juan Ponce governor of Bimini and Florida. In addition, Juan Ponce's former titles on San Juan Bautista were ratified: captain-general of San Juan Bautista for life, perpetual member of the city council (later called the city of San Juan), and chief justice of San Juan Bautista. Juan Ponce was also reimbursed for his earlier expenses, awarded an annual salary of 50,000 *maravedís*, made captain of the armada to fight the Caribs, and given civil and criminal jurisdiction over the Windward Islands.[23]

But Juan Ponce was not to leave Castilla until his three-ship armada for fighting the Caribs was readied. Although it took about six months to outfit the ships for the voyage, it was not as long as some scholars have perceived, and it was not due to bureaucratic bungling. The Casa de Contratación was in charge of the operation and, for all practical purposes, was almost broke. The Casa was in no position to even consider new

136

ships, so it purchased three older caravels which were left over from the Pedrarias expedition to Darién in 1514. All three ships were in port at Sanlúcar de Barrameda. They were the flagship *Barbola*, the *Santa María*, and the *Santiago*. None exceeded 100 tons in weight.[24]

These caravels carried a total crew of about fifty men, but they were not seaworthy at the time of purchase, which was early in September and *before* Juan Ponce received his command. If they had been fit to sail, it is almost a certainty that Pedrarias would have taken them with him to Darién in April. After they were acquired by the Casa, carpenters, caulkers, and other artisans worked on them in an overtime mode. This form of labor allocation may have delayed completion of the repairs, but it was cheaper than having a full crew of refurbishers working full-time.

The ships were repaired, armed, and provisioned by May 14, 1515, at which time Juan Ponce set sail once again for the New World — but this time he was *Capitán de la Armada*. The traditional route across the Atlantic was followed: sail south to the Canary Islands and the trade winds, then ride the easterly trade winds west to the Indies. Like Columbus and others who crossed the Atlantic after him, Juan Ponce stopped in the Canaries and topped off his supplies before entering the open ocean. From the Canaries, he sailed directly for Guadeloupe, a Carib stronghold.

It is at Guadeloupe that the records fail us, but two versions emerge from secondary sources about an incident that transpired there. One version of events was promulgated by Peter Martyr, who said that Juan Ponce "lost his honor" on Guadeloupe.[25] This is the same Peter Martyr who, while claiming a close friendship with Christopher Columbus, did not even mention the First Admiral's death until ten years after it occurred![26] And this is also the same Peter Martyr who believed so completely in the myth of the Fountain of Youth that he wrote a letter to Pope Leo X in support of the truth of the notion.[27]

According to Martyr, Juan Ponce anchored at Guadeloupe, probably the principal Carib island in 1515, and sent a party of women ashore to wash clothes and linens. Accompanying the washerwomen were a few soldiers, sent to obtain water. Without warning, the Castilians were attacked by Caribs using poisoned arrows. The women were captured, a number of soldiers were killed, and Juan Ponce abandoned the lot of them, literally fleeing for his life.[28]

The other version of this incident comes from Ballesteros[29] and Murga Sanz[30] who agree with Martyr that Juan Ponce made his New World landfall at Guadeloupe, concluding a remarkable piece of sixteenth-century navigation. Their version also confirms the Carib attack. But Guadeloupe was a heavily forested island and Juan Ponce had no idea of how many Caribs lay in wait in the jungles. A precipitous rescue attempt might well have cost the lives of more men and possibly could have resulted in damage to or loss of the three caravels. There is some doubt as to whether there were any women with the tiny armada, and there are no official records concerning casualties.

Ballesteros dismisses the incident on Guadeloupe as a minor one and concludes that the stopover was not part of the anti-Carib campaign. Murga Sanz mentions no loss of life in this encounter and states that all of the wounded Castilians were retrieved.

Juan Ponce reached San Juan Bautista on July 15, 1515. He then appointed Captain Iñigo de Zúñiga to command the fleet and sent him to the Lesser Antilles and possibly, in 1516, to the coast of Central America. It is this latter — and highly speculative — voyage that is sometimes thought to have been commanded by Juan Ponce himself. Tió and others have claimed that, on this voyage, Juan Ponce discovered the Yucatan Peninsula and the site of the Mexican port of San Juan de Ulúa, soon to become Veracruz, after which he sailed eastward across the Gulf of Mexico to reach Cuba and, eventually, San Juan Bautista.[31]

Juan Ponce's efforts to protect the Tainos of San Juan Bautista were hindered at every step of the way by those who preferred to enslave the Indians. This opposition occurred in spite of specific royal instructions to the contrary. The new governor of San Juan Bautista, Sáncho Velázquez, had arrived on November 22, 1514, and served until 1519.[32] During his entire administration he saw Juan Ponce as a threat to his control of the island's affairs. It was probably a welcome relief to Juan Ponce when Velázquez was imprisoned by his successor, Antonio de la Gama, who was married to Isabel, one of Juan Ponce's daughters.

~

On January 23, 1516, six months after Juan Ponce returned to San Juan Bautista, Ferdinand died and left the throne to his grandson, Carlos. Carlos became Carlos I of Spain in 1516 and later, in 1519, became Charles V, Emperor of the Holy Roman Empire. Carlos' mother, Queen Juana, had not been an active ruler for some time, though she often cosigned letters and royal documents. Upon Ferdinand's death, because of Juana's inability to rule and Carlos' being king of the Netherlands at the time, a regency was established, as prescribed by Ferdinand before his death, to rule until Carlos could return to Spain.[33] The regent chosen to rule Castilla was Cardinal Francisco Ximénez (Jiménez) de Cisneros, while Aragón was to be under the regency of Archbishop Alonso of Zaragosa, Ferdinand's illegitimate son born before his marriage to Isabela.

It now became imperative that Juan Ponce return to Spain to assure that his titles and privileges be preserved, for Ferdinand had been his firm supporter for many years. He arrived in Spain on November 16, 1516, where he remained until the spring of 1518.[34] Juan Ponce's loyalty to the Crown was beyond question. He was an experienced governor and had served Ferdinand and Juana faithfully as a soldier, explorer, settler, town planner, judge, council member, farmer, rancher, and even jailer. His rapport with the Indians was unusually good for this period of history and, though many colonists disapproved of Juan Ponce's methods for winning the goodwill of the Indians, most Spaniards were highly supportive of the adelantado. It would have been sheer folly for anyone in Spain involved with the Indies — be his or her interest religious, political, or whatever — not to take advantage of Juan Ponce's knowledge of and experience in the New World.

Ballesteros has suggested that Juan Ponce spoke with both Cardinal Cisneros and the Jeronymite Fathers about political and economic matters in San Juan Bautista *before* he sailed to Guadeloupe in 1515 with his tiny armada.[35] In fact, Ballesteros is of the opinion that Juan Ponce believed that an official armada was not necessary to punish the Caribs but that the presence of an armada in the Antilles might help to stop the Castilians from taking Indian slaves. Consequently, Juan Ponce never oppressed the Indians when his fleet was out, even though he ostensibly directed at least three campaigns against the Caribs. This was one of the reasons why he returned to Spain with the fleet as soon as he learned of the death of Ferdinand; he seems to have had prior knowledge that the armada's official mission to find and punish the Indians would be carried out by the new administration. Juan Ponce also might have had a prior commitment from Cisneros for a speedy liquidation of the fleet in order to prevent unnecessarily harsh measures being taken against the Caribs under a new sovereign.[36]

From all outward appearances, it seemed as though the anti-Carib armada had returned to Sevilla and all accounts were cleared to the satisfaction of the officials at the Casa de Contratación. A document to that effect was issued on November 27, 1516,[37] but this was not a finality — officials at the Casa came up with one trivial thing after the other to prolong the process of dissolving the fleet. Eventually — on April 6, 1517 — Cardinal Cisneros demanded that the fleet's liquidation be finalized. With great bureaucratic haste, Juan Ponce's accounts were satisfied and the fleet was dissolved on November 27, 1517 — exactly one year after Cisneros had first ordered the termination.[38]

~

While Juan Ponce was whiling away most of 1517 in Spain, events in the Indies were moving apace. Earlier in the year — maybe even late in 1516 — Diego de Velázquez, the governor of Cuba, had sent a slave-hunting expedition to Florida. This came to the attention of Cardinal Cisneros in the summer of 1517. On July 22, a royal *cédula* was issued castigating Velázquez for his incursion into territory governed by Juan Ponce and his capture of at least 300 Indians, probably Matacumbes, who lived in the Florida Keys.[39]

In April, 1517, yet another voyage from Cuba reached Florida, albeit indirectly, and it was documented by Bernal Díaz del Castillo who later would provide an important eye-witness account of Cortés's conquest of Mexico.[40]

Bernal Díaz, twenty-two years old, had left Castilla in 1514 with the Pedrarias voyage to Darién but, after several months, more than a few disputes, and at least one epidemic, he went to Cuba, which at that time was governed by his relative, Diego de Velázquez. After three years in Cuba where, in his own words, he "did nothing worthy of record," Díaz joined with 110 others to seek his fortune in Yucatan.[41] The three-ship expedition under the command of Francisco Hernández de Córdoba and piloted by Antón de Alaminos departed the Cuban port of Ajaruco (near what is today Havana) on February 8, 1517, and set a course for Cape Catoche at the northeastern tip of the Yucatan Peninsula. In addition to the relatively slow rate of travel — the fleet averaged fourteen miles per day, about 300 miles in twenty-one days — and the terrible storm they encountered in the Yucatan Channel, serious difficulties began to appear at Cape Catoche, where a pitched battle with Indians left at least fifteen Spaniards wounded. Farther down the coast, at Champotón, the Mayas killed forty-eight Spaniards and captured two. Only one man was not wounded at Champotón — and he was captured and probably killed later in Florida. Captain Hernández de Córdoba received ten arrow wounds, and Díaz received three. Battered and discouraged, the expedition set sail for home.

For the pilot Alaminos, having been to Florida four years

Figure 45. Rio de San Pedro and San Paulo, Mexico. Today, this river forms the boundary between the Mexican states of Campeche and Tabasco; in 1519 it marked the boundary between the discoveries of Garay (to the north and west) and Velázquez (to the south and east, beyond the river in this photograph). (Photograph by R. H. Fuson)

earlier, the best way to Cuba was by way of southwest Florida: fresh water was available there for the survivors who were perishing of thirst. Alaminos consulted with the pilots of the other two vessels, and they agreed to follow Alaminos inasmuch as he knew the route. With the captain mortally wounded — he was to die later from the arrow injuries — Alaminos, for all practical purposes, became the fleet's commander. They reached Florida sometime during the middle part of April 1517.

According to Bernal Díaz, Florida came into view four days after Hernández de Córdoba's fleet departed the Yucatan coast.[42] Upon landing near a creek, Alaminos announced that this was the precise location he had visited with Juan Ponce in 1513. And it was also at this place that they had been attacked by the Caloosa Indians. Díaz, Alaminos, and twenty soldiers landed to get water. Fearing an Indian ambush, Alaminos posted two soldiers as guards. Good water was found but, despite a hasty warning by one of the guards, a large war party of Caloosas arrived before the Spaniards could return to their ships. Some came on foot and others by canoe. All were big men, wearing deerskins. Without hesitation, they let their arrows fly, and six Spaniards — including Díaz and Alaminos — were wounded at the outset. The landing party was successful in driving off the attacking force, but the latter waded out into the water to help their comrades who had already captured one of the Spanish vessels. The Indians were towing it up the creek and fighting hand-to-hand with the sailors still on board.

The landing party rushed to the aid of the struggling sailors and, fighting in waist-deep water, was able to free the ship. Díaz estimated that twenty Indians were killed and three were captured. The three who were captured had been wounded, and they died aboard ship. One of the two guards who had been posted, the only man not wounded at Champotón, was carried off by the Caloosas and presumably killed. Díaz and his men searched for the abducted guard, but to no avail. Another Spaniard on one of the ships drank so much water that, according to Díaz, he died within two days.[43]

The trip from Florida to Cuba was itself almost a disaster. As soon as the fresh water was brought aboard, sails were raised and the vessels sailed for Havana. In the Florida Keys, the flagship ran aground and started taking on water. With everyone manning the pumps, and with the sails trimmed, the survivors managed to reach the port where Havana is now situated. After reaching Cuba, Captain Hernández de Córdoba was taken to Sancti Spíritus, where he died within ten days.

In spite of all the agony of this ill-fated venture, the expedition provided the Spaniards their first contact with the Yucatan Peninsula and the Mayan Indians who lived there.[44]

~

The year 1517 was also eventful in Spain. Oviedo, Las Casas, and Ponce de León were in Sevilla at the same time. Oviedo had returned to Spain in October or November, 1515, and remained there for five years.[45] Las Casas arrived in Sevilla on June 7, 1517, and was in Spain until December 1520.[46] Ponce de León did not depart Spain for San Juan Bautista until April 1518.

Murga Sanz declares, and Devereux agrees, that Juan Ponce married Juana de Pineda in Sevilla in late 1517 or early 1518.[47] This presupposes that Leonor, Juan Ponce's wife of many years, was deceased. There is no record of this. On the contrary, every other source cites 1519 as the year of Leonor's death, and that date is repeated over and over by Juan Ponce's children and grandchildren. Further, Leonor was alive and well when Juan Ponce returned to San Juan Bautista in May, 1518. It is virtually impossible to ascertain where Murga Sanz got such a notion, but he writes that Leonor was an Indian "because her name does not appear in any document."[48] Tió has thoroughly de-

144

bunked this idea.[49] Murga Sanz has somehow twisted Juan Ponce's genealogy and, apparently, commingled different generations and similar names. For example, there were several descendants of Don Juan Ponce de León named "Juan," and there were a few "Juanas."[50] Juan Ponce's grandson also was named "Juan," and Juan Ponce's daughter was named "Juana." Juan Ponce's daughter Juana named her daughter "Leonor," after her mother. *This* Leonor, Juan Ponce's granddaughter, named her daughter "Leonor." This lineage with so many shared names is confusing and is likely the basis for Murga Sanz's and Devereux's apparent error.

Juan Ponce came home to the island of San Juan in May 1518 and found that a number of changes had occurred while he was in Spain.[51] For one thing, a new governor — Antonio de la Gama, soon to become Juan Ponce's son-in-law — was to arrive in September. Also, the name that Christopher Columbus had given to the island, San Juan Bautista, was being replaced by a new name, Puerto Rico. This came about in part because the citizens of Caparra were moving to the little island in the harbor, where Old San Juan is today, but they had not brought the name of Caparra with them. The settlement with no name became *el puerto rico de San Juan*, the rich port of San Juan. The town was destined to be named San Juan in 1521, and the island became known as Puerto Rico.

Juan Ponce opposed the move of his settlement from Caparra to this little island, citing lack of water and poor soil at the new site as two of the most important reasons for not relocating.[52] To him, farming, livestock, and mining took precedence over trade. The maritime trading interests, however, won; Juan Ponce was out-voted eight to one on the *cabildo* and in 1521 the move became official. Bridges were built to the island and that is where most tourists go today to see the oldest city that flies the American flag. Old San Germán, founded in 1506, and the ruins of Caparra, which date from late in 1506 or 1507, are now forgotten by most people.

~

Juan Ponce's desire to return to Florida was heightened not only by events in San Juan Bautista but by two personal tragedies that occurred in 1519. Juan Ponce's close friend, Vasco Núñez de Balboa, died in Panama in January of that year. Not only were they friends, and about the same age, but each had been named governor on the same day. Later in 1519, sometime after July, Ponce's beloved Leonor passed on.[53]

Also in 1519, exploration of the lands bordering the Gulf of Mexico was carried out by agents of the governors of both Cuba and Jamaica. Under the authority of Governor Velázquez of Cuba, Hernán Cortés led an expedition to Mexico in 1519 with a large force of over 350 men.[54] In that same year, Francisco de Garay, the governor of Jamaica, sent four ships under the leadership of Alonso Álvarez Pineda into the Gulf of Mexico. Additional expeditions were sent to the north and west by both governors in 1520, and the combined effects of these efforts led to, among many consequences, a refined image of Florida and the first representations of this region on maps.[55]

The fleet that Governor Garay of Jamaica authorized to explore the Gulf of Mexico and its northern borderlands in 1519 was to explore the province of Amichel, Garay's name for that part of the mainland extending from what is today northeastern Mexico to western Florida — a region Garay was licensed to settle.[56] Pineda was also instructed to search for a strait that might link the Atlantic and Pacific oceans.

Pineda's voyage of 1519 lasted "eight or nine months," during which time the fleet explored the coast of the Gulf of Mexico from Apalachee Bay, off of what is today western Florida, to the Pánuco River, about seven miles south of Tampico, Mexico. One of the important discoveries made during this voyage was a large river which Pineda named Rio del Spíritu Sancto (Rio del Espíritu Santo; River of the Holy Ghost), today's Mississippi River. Pineda actually sailed some distance up the Rio del Spíritu Sancto, hoping that it was the passage to Balboa's South Sea, beyond which would lie the East Indies.[57]

Pineda made a sketch map of the region he was exploring and included on this map, among other features, the great river he had investigated. Relevant to the emerging image of Florida is the fact that he also added the name *La Florida* to this map.[58] Two notes were appended to his rough chart of the Florida peninsula, both of which pertained to Juan Ponce's first voyage to Florida. The note in south Florida reads: "Florida, which they call Bimini, that Juan Ponce discovered." In north Florida, near Apalachee Bay, another note reads: "Juan Ponce discovered up to here." This latter annotation by Pineda contradicts almost all of the other evidence that places the northern limit of Juan Ponce's first voyage at no more than 27° N latitude, approximately at the northern part of Charlotte Harbor.[59]

Pineda's first voyage ended no later than December 24, 1519.[60]

～

While Pineda was exploring the coast of Amichel for Governor Garay, Hernán Cortés was launching his own adventure in Mexico under the authority of Governor de Velázquez of Cuba.[61] Cortés's mission was to establish a colony in Mexico — nothing more, nothing less. The coast of Mexico had been explored the year before by Juan de Grijalva, a nephew of Diego de Velázquez, but no colony had been founded. Cortés, who had gone to Cuba in 1511 with Velázquez, was initially selected to lead the expedition to Mexico in 1519. Governor Velázquez thereafter changed his mind about putting Cortés in charge of the expedition, but Cortés hurriedly put together a fleet and sailed before Velázquez could stop him. Cortés's fleet of eleven

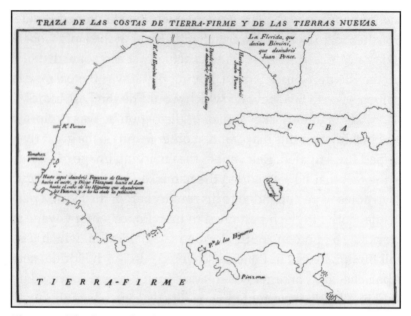

Figure 46. The Garay sketch of the Gulf of Mexico, 1519, the first use of the name Florida on a map. The original map, now in the Archivo General de Indias, was made by Alonso Álvarez Pineda who had been sent to explore the Gulf and, in the process of sailing from Florida to Mexico, became the first European to report seeing the Mississippi River. The original of the copy reproduced here was made by Juan Bautista Muñoz in 1792. (From Navarrete, 1945, Volume 3)

ships, piloted by Antón de Alaminos, departed the western tip of Cuba and set sail for Yucatan on February 18, 1519. On Holy Thursday, April 21, 1519, this fleet reached the site of what is today Veracruz, and here Cortés established La Villa de la Vera Cruz, Spain's first colony in Mexico.[62] Then, insubordinate and acting upon his own agenda, Cortés moved inland and commenced the conquest of Mexico.

The celebrated *First Letter* of Cortés, an important document describing the events of his first months in Mexico, was dispatched to King Carlos on July 16, 1519.[63] This document, which has been lost since the sixteenth century, was carried to the king by Alaminos. Alaminos also carried another letter, this one from Cortés's men at Veracruz, which expressed not only their submission to the Crown but pleaded that Cortés remain their leader and asked that all of his actions be sanctioned.[64] Shortly after Alaminos's departure, Cortés made one of the boldest moves ever made by a military commander by destroying every Spanish ship in Mexico, save one. This solved once and for all the threat that anyone in his expedition would leave.[65]

Accompanying Alaminos to Spain were Francisco de Montejo, once a supporter of Diego de Velázquez and later the conqueror of Yucatan and the founder of Mérida, and Alonso Hernández de Puertocarrero, a close relative of the Count of Medellín and a man with many connections at the Court. By sheer coincidence, Benito Martín, chaplain to the governor of Cuba, was in Sevilla, and upon hearing of Cortés's actions in Mexico he made a formal complaint on behalf of Velázquez to the Casa de Contratación. The authority of Cortés was challenged, but the king — also Emperor of the Holy Roman Empire — left Spain without resolving the dispute.[66]

The door was left open for Diego de Velázquez to send an armada to Mexico to thwart the aspirations of Cortés. To this end, Velázquez organized the largest fleet ever assembled in the New World — an armada of eighteen ships that carried 900 Spaniards and about a thousand Taino Indians.[67] Only the Ovando fleet of 1502, which contained thirty-two ships and had sailed from Castilla to Española, had been larger. Velázquez considered personally leading the expedition to unseat Cortés, but then selected Pánfilo de Narváez as his commander.[68] Prescott described Narváez as:[69]

> *A man of some military capacity, though negligent and lax in his discipline. He possessed undoubted courage, but it was mingled with an arrogance, or rather overweening confidence in his own powers, which made him deaf to the suggestions of others more sagacious than himself. He was altogether deficient in that prudence and calculating foresight demanded in a leader who was to cope with an antagonist like Cortés.*

149

Diego de Velázquez began to outfit his armada and seek recruits as early as October 1519. Within a few months, the *Audiencia* in Santo Domingo began to take notice and, fearing that Spaniard was about to be pitted against Spaniard, sent Lucas Vázquez de Ayllón to Cuba in an attempt to diplomatically resolve the differences between Velázquez and Cortés.[70] Vázquez de Ayllón, however, was unable to dissuade Velázquez from his mission to Mexico. But still determined to prevent a war between the forces of Velázquez and Cortés, Vázquez de Ayllón sailed with Narváez in March 1520 and arrived at Veracruz on April 23, 1520.[71] Once in Mexico, at the Narváez encampment just outside Veracruz, Vázquez de Ayllón realized that Narváez was determined to attack Cortés and punish him — perhaps execute him — for his rebellion. Vázquez de Ayllón was seized and placed on a ship for Cuba,[72] but he persuaded the captain to take him to Santo Domingo where he immediately filed a report against Narváez and his governor, Velázquez.[73]

Meanwhile, Narváez's emissary to Cortés — a padre named Guevara — had been taken to Mexico City and, through a bit of deceit, was shown only the positive side of the Mexican conquest. The padre's report to Narváez was met with great excitement; of particular interest to Narváez was every word mentioned by the padre of gold and other wealth.[74] Cortés's campaign to eliminate Narváez had already begun.

Narváez moved his troops to Cempoala, on the road to Mexico City, and here the battle was joined. Cortés defeated Narváez in extremely short order, took him prisoner, dismantled his fleet, assimilated Narváez's forces into his own, and immediately got back to the business of conquering Mexico.

The only serious impact that the Narváez landing had — and it was extremely serious — was the introduction of smallpox into Mexico by an infected member of the Narváez party.[75]

Thousands of Mexicans, from the lowlands to the central plateau, died during the great smallpox epidemic of 1520–1521. Narváez was allowed to return to Spain after the Aztecs capitulated on August 13, 1521. Seven years later he would die in the Florida panhandle.

After the Narváez incident every ship that arrived at Veracruz was thoroughly stripped and most of the men on board were "recruited." A supply ship from Velázquez, who was certain that Cortés had been deposed by Narváez, became instead a relief ship for Cortés. This ship's captain also carried an order from Bishop Fonseca to return Cortés to Spain in irons![76] Needless to say, the order was ignored. Velázquez even sent a second ship to Narváez; as soon as it was unloaded, its crew joined the Cortés contingent. Cortés was to have no additional significant challenges, either from within Mexico or without.

~

In 1520, Pineda made a second voyage to the coast of Amichel for Garay.[77] There were perhaps three ships in this expedition and possibly 150 men, but there is some disagreement between the primary sources on this matter. One thing which all of the sources agree on, however, is that the voyage was a disaster for Pineda and a windfall for Cortés.

Pineda, operating as an agent for Garay, attempted to establish a colony on the banks of the Pánuco River, a few miles south of the modern city of Tampico, Mexico, some 370 miles north of Cortés's colony at Veracruz. During his first foray into the Gulf of Mexico, Pineda and his party had had a rather easy time of it when they were ashore between Florida and southwestern Louisiana. The Indians in this region had been mostly Muskogean, and Pineda's long stay in the lower Mississippi Valley was among the Choctaws and Chitimachas, two Muskogean tribes who were not particularly unfriendly toward the Spaniards.[78] But once the expedition had moved west of the

151

Figure 47. The house of Hernán Cortés in Mexico City. This structure was built about the same time that Juan Ponce's Casa Blanca was being built in San Juan, Puerto Rico. (Photograph by R. H. Fuson)

Sabine River, which separates what are today Louisiana and Texas, they encountered different Indians.[79] The Karankawa and the Tamaulipec people were not as willing as were the Muskogeans to accept the Spaniards as transient guests, and during Pineda's second expedition several bloody skirmishes between the Indians and Spaniards ensued along the coast of Texas and northeastern Mexico.[80] This obviously took its toll on Pineda and his men, but a real catastrophe struck when they encountered the Huastecs, north of the Pánuco River and not far from what is today the city of Tampico. Although the Huastecs are sometimes confused with the Aztecs, or thought of as an Aztecan subculture, they were actually a Mayan-speaking group who had become separated from the principal Mayan culture before AD 300.[81] Certain pre-Aztec influences, notably of Téotihuacano and Toltec origin, had filtered into the area

152

from central Mexico by the time Pineda arrived, perhaps most important of which was their ability and willingness to go to war. Thus, Pineda lost his life, some of his men, and possibly two of his ships to the Huastecs.[82] At least one ship, with wounded, sick, and starving survivors, managed to reach Veracruz.[83]

Prescott says that the second survey of the Gulf of Mexico by Pineda included three ships, and that one of these was lost in a storm. He writes nothing about the fate of its crew. Pineda, and apparently some others, were killed at Pánuco, but some ships (Prescott says "others") managed to make it to Veracruz with some 150 men and twenty horses surviving.[84] If one ship was lost in a storm and "others" made it to Veracruz — and there were three to start with — then it is clear that two vessels reached the Cortés colony. Further, if there were 150 survivors, it would seem to indicate that most crewmen of the storm-tossed ships were rescued. These survivors joined Cortés at Segura de la Frontera, today's Tepeaca, about twenty miles east of Puebla, sometime in the middle of May 1520.

At least one other ship reached Veracruz during this time. It was a ship from the Canary Islands that had stopped briefly in Cuba, where the captain learned of Cortés's Mexican adventure. The captain sailed to Veracruz whereupon Cortés bought all of the supplies and the ship, and enrolled the entire crew in his entourage. Something similar probably happened on numerous (but unreported) occasions, and for a while it looked as if the entire Spanish population of the New World would be drawn to Mexico and to Cortés.

Bernal Díaz del Castillo, the prime source for Prescott, tells a somewhat different story of the second Pineda voyage.[85] For one thing, Díaz states that all of Pineda's soldiers (and sailors?) died with their captain, that all of the horses were killed, and that all of the ships were burned. Then Díaz contradicts himself and claims that one ship, with Diego de Camargo as captain, reached Veracruz with sixty thin, swollen, yellowed survivors. Even though sick, they made the long, uphill march to Cortés at Tepeaca.

Díaz also mentions two additional supply ships that were sent to Pineda — who was supposed to be at Pánuco — by Garay. One, commanded by Miguel Díaz de Auz, carried fifty soldiers and seven horses. The other vessel was commanded by an "old man named Ramírez," but nothing is known about the number of soldiers and sailors on board that ship.

It is possible that about 150 men did reach Veracruz— including survivors from the Pineda expedition and crew and passengers of the two ships sent to Pánuco by Garay. This is the figure given by Prescott, and 110 men were reported on two of the four ships cited by Díaz. Also, there is no proof that all of the ships in the second Pineda voyage sailed at the same time. In other words, the so-called supply ships may have been part of the original armada. The last ship listed by Díaz, the one with Ramírez as captain, may have been a supply ship sent as an afterthought by Garay. That would mean there had been a three-vessel flotilla, with ships commanded by Pineda, Camargo, and Díaz de Auz, with Ramírez bringing up the rear in a fourth ship. Perhaps Pineda's ship was burned and some of the crew lost; these survivors added to the number of men on the other two ships would approximate the figure given by Prescott. If Díaz de Auz arrived at Pánuco late, it would explain why his men were so healthy compared to the men aboard the vessels of Pineda and Camargo. And lastly, Díaz de Auz and Ramírez may have sailed together from Jamaica to Pánuco, arriving perhaps a month later, just in time to rescue the starving survivors.

Francisco de Garay personally led a third voyage from Jamaica to Pánuco.[86] He probably wondered what was happening to all of his ships and crews, for after Pineda's first voyage there had been virtually no communication with Mexico. On June 24, 1523, Garay set out with a major expedition of eleven ships, some 600 men, and about 150 horses for what he thought was his colony on the Rio de Pánuco. Diego Miruelo, whom Juan Ponce had encountered in the Bahamas during the latter's first trip to Florida, was pilot-major of this armada. Upon arriving at Pánuco, Garay must have been stunned to find a new settlement, Santistében del Puerto, just established by Cortés. And, as had happened so many times before, the newly arrived ships were seized, the men were assimilated into Cortés's forces, and Garay was "invited" to be Cortés's guest in Mexico City. Sometime in December 1523, Garay died of pleurisy, pneumonia, or poisoning — and would never again challenge the authority of Hernán Cortés.

⁓

Several events associated with the explorations of Pineda and Cortés's conquest of Mexico overlapped and fused. One of the byproducts of this union of people and experience was the emergence of a revised perception of the geography of lands bordering the Gulf of Mexico. Both Pineda and Cortés contributed to the new image of the region which, in turn, inspired and facilitated subsequent exploration of the Gulf coast and the lands that bordered it.

A part of Garay's authorization for Pineda's second voyage, which was dated 1521 but probably was written in 1520, reads as follows:[87]

> *They [Pineda's fleet, in 1519] sailed eight or nine months, and never found it [the strait], but in the midst of other low and sterile land that they discovered they came across the land of Florida,which Juan Ponce de León discovered, and having noticed and sighted it tried to skirt its coast but were unable to. The land to the east stuck out, blocking the prows, and because of that and the wind that was always variable, and because of a strong current that they found, they*

*were forced to turn, and skirt the coast toward the west. Along this
coast they were able to carefully examine the land, harbors, rivers,
and people, and everything else that should be seen. And they sailed
so far that they came across Hernán Cortés and the Spaniards that
were with him on the same coast they were on. And when they got
there they marked the boundary up to the point where they had discovered, and altogether they had discovered more than 300 leagues
[about 1000 miles] and took possession in our [the Sovereigns'] name.
And having done that, they turned back with the said ships and entered a river that they found; one that was very large and carried a
great deal of water. They found a large town near the entrance and
were there more than forty days careening the ships. The natives were
very friendly with the Spaniards that went there with the said armada, trading with them and giving them what they had, as far as 6
leagues [about 20 miles] up-river. The said ships [crews] found forty
towns on one side or the other [of the river] and the said pilots sailed
by these and discovered them thus. The pilots of the armada examined
very thoroughly, the land, the harbors, and the rivers, and a map [of
the region] was made [by the pilots] and brought to us [the Sover-
eigns].*

The document discusses the nature of the land and recog-
nizes that Florida is, indeed, part of the mainland and that it
connected with Mexico. And the territories discovered by Juan
Ponce de León, Francisco de Garay (by Pineda), and Diego de
Velázquez (by Hernán Cortés) are delineated. Pineda's map,
produced during his voyage of 1519, clearly belongs with this
document even though it antedates the authorization by at least
one year and maybe two. And just where was this map?

By 1520, the map — either the original or a copy — had
fallen into the hands of Cortés. The sketch must have come to
Cortés after his *First Letter* was dispatched in July 1519, or else
he would have mentioned this important document in the letter and probably would have forwarded it to Spain.

Through pure luck, some of Cortés's men had appre-
hended six crewmen from Pineda's first expedition in August
1519 near Veracruz. The map could have been in their possession, and they could have turned it over to Cortés following

their capture. Or, it might have fallen into Cortés's hands after members of Pineda's second expedition reached Veracruz sometime in May 1520. The map that Cortés had could have been the original, or it could have been a copy of the 1519 original, made between July 16, 1519, when Cortés dispatched his *First Letter* to Charles V, and October 30, 1520, when he prepared his *Second Letter* to the king.

Cortés's famous and oft-quoted *Second Letter* was written at Segura de la Frontera on October 30, 1520, but because no ship was available it was not sent to Spain until 1521.[88] Pineda's sketch of the Gulf of Mexico, made in 1519, was sent to Spain along with Cortés's *Letter*.[89]

Also taken to Spain in 1521 with the *Second Letter* was what has become known as the *Cortés Map of the Gulf of Mexico*.[90] This map was printed in Nürnberg, Germany, in 1524, and became the first *printed* map that displayed the name *La Florida*. It is highly possible that this is a "cleaned up" version of Pineda's 1519 map, with some additional place-names included. Accompanying the map was a plan of Mexico City, which also was published in 1524 and on the same plate as the map of the Gulf of Mexico.[91] Because the original is lost, there is no way to tell precisely when the map that was published in 1524 actually was made. But there is at least one place — Rio de las Palmas in Mexico — that was not named until 1523 and could not have been on Cortés's map that was sent to Europe in 1521.[92] Obviously, this name was not derived from Pineda's map of 1519. In any event, we have an unpublished sketch of the Gulf of Mexico made in 1519 which shows Florida as a peninsula before Juan Ponce made his second voyage to the mainland, and a map that was published in 1524, after Juan Ponce's untimely death, that also depicts Florida as a peninsula of the North American mainland.[93]

Juan Ponce may have heard vague reports of Pineda's voyage in 1519, but he obviously was unaware of its scope. For one thing, the expedition had sailed dangerously close to western Florida and to Juan Ponce's jurisdiction, perhaps even trespassing on it, so that information would likely be kept secret by Pineda and Garay. In addition, Juan Ponce never saw Pineda's map which, for the first time, showed Florida by name and depicted its articulation with the mainland. Instead, Juan Ponce still perceived Florida to be an island and he died with that image in his mind. In fact, one of Juan Ponce's objectives for the second voyage was to determine whether Florida was an island or a peninsula.

The escalation of interest in the lands bordering the Gulf of Mexico that took place in 1519 and 1520 meant that the time was rapidly approaching when Juan Ponce de León would have to make his move to colonize Florida or face the possibility of losing it to other adventurers. Juan Ponce could either let the aspirations, actions, and successes of the governors of Cuba and Jamaica, or perhaps others, challenge his legitimate claim to Florida and drive him into despair, or he could rekindle the flame that had driven him to seek new lands and adventure in the first place. The old order of Hispanic colonization in the New World was changing rapidly, and his legal jurisdiction over Florida offered him the opportunity to effect some changes of his own. He had little choice but to act now on his opportunity to colonize Florida, so the year 1520 was one of feverish activity for Juan Ponce as he planned and organized his second voyage to Florida.

Chapter 5
1521

The Second Voyage to Florida

Juan Ponce de León sailed from San Juan, Puerto Rico, for Florida on February 20, 1521, with two ships and no more than one hundred people. The primary purpose of this venture was to found a colony, and the appropriate implements, seed, and animals were carried aboard the two ships. There is little evidence about Juan Ponce's second attempt to settle Florida — indeed, there is almost no evidence. All we have had passed down to us are three letters, a fourth letter that was seen but is now missing, a few very brief mentions by sixteenth-century chroniclers, and an error-ridden piece by Oviedo. Juan Ponce's second voyage to Florida was a total failure that ended in tragedy. None of the goals was achieved. During the first week of July 1521, Florida's first governor died in Cuba of a wound received in Florida, his nephew was buried at sea, a number of the colonists died in Florida at the hands of the Indians, and others died in Cuba of infections. Those who escaped misfortune went directly to Mexico and joined Cortés.

Early in January 1521, Juan Ponce de León left Puerto Rico and journeyed to Santo Domingo, Española. Accompanying him was his close friend and confidant, Pedro de la Mata.[1] Although Juan Ponce had 6000 pesos of gold from his own resources to help defray the cost of a second expedition to Florida, he needed some financial assistance from de la Mata. It may be recalled that, according to the agreement between Juan Ponce and the Crown, none of the money for this second voyage to Florida was to be supplied by the government. The Crown had authorized the voyage and set forth certain rules, but Juan Ponce had to pay for the ships, supplies, wages, and other incidental expenses. Pedro de la Mata either invested money in the undertaking or raised additional money for that purpose in Española, or both. Sometime in January, de la Mata returned to Puerto Rico, and by February Juan Ponce also had gone back, probably to the city we now call San Juan.

Regrettably, very little was written by the leading chroniclers of that time concerning Juan Ponce's second voyage to Florida. Not only is the event scarcely mentioned by the historiographers but the information that is available is convoluted and universally incorrect. Not one of the chroniclers reported the expedition with a high degree of accuracy, and the analysis made by Henry Harrisse over a century ago is probably the closest thing we have to a true account of the voyage.[2]

The facts about this voyage that we do know for certain are the date of departure from Puerto Rico, the number of ships involved, and the general objectives of the voyage.[3] This information is derived from three letters that have survived, two of which were written by Juan Ponce and one by Antonio de la Gama.

The first of these letters, dated February 10, 1521, is from Ponce de León to Adrian, the Cardinal of Tortosa, who became Pope Adrian VI in 1522. The letter in full reads:[4]

> *Illustrious and Extremely Reverend Lord. I have served the Royal Crown a great deal in these parts of the Indies, by order of the Catholic King, and until now my services have been suspended, therefore, here in the continuation that I shall reveal [I trust] that you will recall the favors granted to me in the past. For this reason I also believe that the time spent and the difficulties that have befallen me are*

160

thereby [related to] having become a widower and left with daughters that I did not wish to leave nor abandon until they were married. And now they are married, may it please God.

I well know that there has been no lack of trials and tribulations for His Majesty as well as for Your Lordship, but I hope to God that everything will turn out well and the Estate and dominions of His Majesty will be greatly augmented and that favors will be granted to me. I have decided, because of my present impoverished position, to serve His Majesty and go to the Florida Island and its environs, and settle if possible and discover everything I am able to [discover]. I am leaving to go there in five or six days, with two ships and with the people that I am able to carry.

I shall make a report about the place and what is done there to His Majesty and to Your Lordship and I hope that one remembers how I have served [in the past] and how I serve [now], and how I have spent whatever I had in order to serve, and now the cupboard is bare.

To Your Lordship I pray that through your hand I shall receive His Majesty's rewards for being able to serve. To tell the truth, I do not want rewards given to me to be treasured [hoarded] nor in order to get through this miserable life, but for serving His Majesty with them and with my person and that which I might have; and to settle that land that I discovered, and God and His Majesty may be served by the agricultural production there; and it is my intention of serving and, in order to help me [serve], I ask favors from His Majesty. But if I have to retire with what I have, I have much more from God than I deserve.

I pray to Your Lordship to judge my intention and learn who I am and that which I have served, and see how I serve, and conforming to that help me and cause favors to be given to me in order that I am able to serve.

My Lord: my services are known to everyone, but I offer as witnesses the Lord Bishop of Burgos, and Secretary [Lope de] Conchillo, and the Lord Knight Commander of the Order of Knighthood of Calatrava [Pedro Núñez de Guzmán, Juan Ponce's relative and childhood tutor], and [Juan de] Samano. They will tell you [about me] and all that has been said, and they are available.

May Our Lord keep the Illustrious and Extremely Reverend person of Your Lordship with increase of much prosperity and greater estate as Your Lordship desires.

From this Island of San Juan and City of Puerto Rico, which is in the Indies of the Ocean Sea. Ten days of February of one thousand fifteen hundred twenty-one years [February 10, 1521].

Servant and Server of Your Very Illustrious and Very Reverend
Lordship. Juan Ponce de León [signature].

This letter, in addition to being an appeal from Juan Ponce
for favors from the Crown, provides us with some information
about Juan Ponce's second expedition to Florida. For one thing,
it clearly places Juan Ponce in the settlement of San Juan on the
island of Puerto Rico. It also provides an approximate date of
Juan Ponce's planned departure for Florida — "five or six days"
after the date on the letter, or about February 15 or 16, 1521. We
also learn that the expedition would consist of "two ships" and
would include "the people who I am able to carry." Apparently, the ships were to carry as many people as either Juan
Ponce could recruit or could physically fit aboard the ships, or
both. And, lastly, we are informed about the two objectives of
the voyage — to establish a colony and explore the region. Logically, the first would take the higher priority, because an exploratory expedition would not have been practical with ships
crowded with colonists, their supplies, and livestock. It has been
noted that Juan Ponce still regarded Florida as an island, and
one of the reasons for exploration after the colony was planted
was to determine whether or not Florida really was an island.

Also on February 10, 1521, Juan Ponce wrote the following letter to his king, Charles V.[5]

> *Very powerful Lord: Since my habit and custom has been to serve*
> *in these parts [lands] of the Royal Crown, and in the growth of Your*
> *[Majesty's] Yields and Dominions, by command of the Catholic King,*
> *now, although impoverished, I have wanted to continue the service of*
> *Your Majesty, and to wait for favors as I hope for them. Among the*
> *services that I have mentioned, I discovered at my expense and mis-*
> *sion the Florida Island and others in its region. [The latter, seemingly*
> *the Bahama Islands which Juan Ponce visited in 1513,] are not worth*
> *[another] mission because they are small and useless. And now I am*
> *returning to that Island [Florida], if it pleases the will of God, to*
> *settle [it], being able to carry enough people to be able to do it, because*
> *there the name of Jesus Christ may be spoken, and Your Majesty may*

be served by the agricultural production of that land.

And also, I intend to discover more of the coast of the said Island, and to learn if it is connected with the land where Diego de Velázquez is [Mexico] or with some other land, and I will try to ascertain everything that I am able to. I shall leave here in five or six days to continue my voyage. That which is made or seen in those places where I shall go will be reported to Your Majesty upon my return, and I shall ask for favors. And from now on I pray they are brought to me, because I cannot imagine undertaking such a grand thing [as settling Florida]. Neither the many costs nor the ability to emerge from them [can be managed] except by means of favors and rewards from Your Imperial Majesty. Up until now I have not asked for favors because I have seen that Your Majesty has had little rest and a lot of work, which I honestly feel as though I had passed through it.

May Our Lord keep Your Very Royal person with an increased long life and many other Kingdoms and Dominions, as is wished for Your Majesty.

From this Island of San Juan and City of Puerto Rico, which is in the Indies of the Ocean Sea. Ten days of the month of February of one thousand fifteen hundred twenty-one years [February 10, 1521].

From Your Majesty's slave and servant who kisses His Very Royal feet and hands. Juan Ponce de León [signature].

The third known surviving letter relevant to Juan Ponce's Florida expedition was written by Antonio de la Gama, Juan Ponce's son-in-law and governor of Puerto Rico until January 15, 1521, when he was succeeded as governor by Pedro Moreno. De la Gama's letter was written to King Carlos and dated February 15, 1521.[6] In it he discusses many items not related to the second voyage of Juan Ponce. However, in the next-to-the last paragraph, he writes:

The Governor Juan Ponce de León departs from this Island [Puerto Rico] on the 20th of this month [February], with another armed fleet, to settle the Florida Island, and to make discoveries in the neighboring regions.

This letter establishes a firm date for the departure of Juan Ponce's second voyage to Florida, and it also clearly states that the departure was to be from Puerto Rico. Inasmuch as de la

Gama's letter was dispatched from "the City of Puerto Rico," today's city of San Juan, as were the two previous letters from Juan Ponce, it seems appropriate to infer that the two ships sailed from the city of San Juan. Nevertheless, there are some scholars who believe that the second voyage departed from San Germán and followed the same itinerary as the first voyage.[7] If this was the case — and there is absolutely no evidence for it — there was a departure from the city of San Juan on February 20, a cruise to San Germán (Guayanilla), and a final sailing for Florida on February 26. Such a detour would seem redundant in 1521 and the reasons for following such a route in 1513 no longer existed in 1521.

Apparently there was a fourth letter, this one written by Ponce de León and sent to Juan de Samano, the king's secretary.[8] This letter — the third written by Juan Ponce — was seen by Antonio de Herrera but has since disappeared.[9]

~

One of the earliest — and maybe the first — of the sixteenth-century historiographers to write about Juan Ponce's second expedition to Florida was Gonzalo Fernández de Oviedo y Valdés.[10] Oviedo, who probably met Juan Ponce in Spain in 1516, wrote the following:[11]

> He [Juan Ponce] turned to outfitting certain ships that he had acquired [for the second voyage] with more attention and at greater cost [than the ships of the first voyage]. He intended to reach the coast of the northern mainland at the tip of that mainland that extends into the sea 100 leagues long and 50 leagues wide, more or less. . . . And it seemed to him [Juan Ponce] that the others [Indians] he could catch would know about the islands that are there and those on the mainland would know other secrets [the Fountain of Youth?] and important things. And to convert those people to God would be of great benefit to him in particular and to those who went with him in general. . . .
>
> There were two hundred men and fifty horses aboard the [two] ships, as already said. And, in order to outfit this armada, a lot [of

*money] was spent. And he sailed to that land during the month of . .
. [a blank space in the text], in the year of one thousand and five
hundred and twenty [sic] years. And as a good colonist, he carried
mares and heifers and pigs and sheep and goats and all sorts of useful, domestic animals to serve the people. And also, for agriculture
and farming all sorts of seeds were provided, as if the business of his
settlement was no more than arriving and cultivating the land and
grazing his livestock.*

*But the temperature of the region was very disagreeable and dif-
ferent from what he had imagined, and the natives of the land [were]
very surly and very savage and bellicose and ferocious and uncon-
trollable and not accustomed to tranquility nor to easily give up their
liberty at the will or discretion of foreigners, nor at the option of those
friars and clerics who accompanied him to offer the devine rites and
services of the church. Although they preached as much as they wished,
they could not be understood in as brief a time as they imagined or
was imagined by the one [Juan Ponce] that brought them there. Certainly, God, with his absolute power, did not make them understood
by those barbarous people and idolatrous savages [who] were filled
with wickedness and vices. I want to say, that although, as in truth
all that seems difficult is easy for God to do when it pleases Him, it is
well for us to think that we do not deserve that straightforwardness,
nor are trout caught without any effort. And first, He wants the fish-
ermen to reform, in order that those who hear and follow them may
come to know the truth. Notwithstanding that religious persons of
sound doctrine went with this captain, but inasmuch as everything
went wrong, and the fleet and the captain and the time and [the]
money were lost simultaneously, and in a few days, it is to be thought
that God was not served nor had the time arrived for the conversion
of that land and province to our Holy Catholic faith, since He still
permits the Devil to deceive those Indians and keep them for his own,
and the population of Hell is augmented with their souls.*

*This fleet reached that land the year already mentioned, and then
the governor, Juan Ponce, when he disembarked gave an order, as a
man would issue a decree, that the people of his fleet should rest. And
when it seemed to him [that they had rested], he moved with his people
and went ashore and in a skirmish or battle that he had with the Indians, since he was a courageous captain and at the front, and not as
skillful [as a soldier] in that land as in the islands, so many enemies
and such enemies charged that his people and his efforts were not
sufficient to resist. And in the end they defeated him and killed some
of the Christians, and twice as many Indians died. And he [Juan Ponce]*

escaped, badly wounded by an arrow, and he decided to go to Cuba to be cured, if it was possible, and to return to that conquest with more people and greater vigor. And so he embarked and arrived at the island [Cuba] and the port of Havana, where after he arrived he lived a short time. But he died as a Catholic and received the sacraments. And others who were wounded also died, and others [died] of illnesses.

Oviedo knew very little about Juan Ponce's second voyage to Florida. Like so many others, Oviedo was probably preoccupied with Cortés and his adventures in Mexico at the time all of this was happening. He was clearly wrong about the number of people on the ships; half as many — about 100 — would have been a crowd, and there was no way that those two ships could have carried a hundred people and all of those animals. Instead of fifty horses, ten would have been more likely. Oviedo did not know the month Juan Ponce sailed for Florida and he was incorrect about the year. It is not clear what significance may be attached to the statement about the weather. Even the winters are mild in southwestern Florida and Juan Ponce arrived in March. He should have experienced no cold weather and the rainy season had not yet begun. And lastly, Oviedo apparently believed that Juan Ponce sailed to Florida, had a fight with the Indians almost upon reaching that peninsula, and then sailed away. Actually, Juan Ponce was in Florida for at least four months before the disastrous battle with the Indians, which is discussed more fully below. Oviedo mentions the death of Ponce de León in one other place in his *Historia*, but it adds nothing to the account given above.[12]

Bartolomé de Las Casas offers even less about this expedition than does Oviedo.[13] Las Casas gives 1512 as the date of the second voyage to Florida — an error of nine years — and he has Juan Ponce setting sail from the port of Santo Domingo, not San Juan. And, Las Casas is the only historian who cites Puerto Príncipe, Cuba, as the town where Juan Ponce drew his last breath. In his defense, though, Las Casas used words such as "I think" and "If I have not forgotten." But he wrote many years after the event and did, indeed, forget some critical facts. Of all the early historiographers, only Herrera provides an additional fact about the second voyage: Juan Ponce's wound was in his thigh.[14]

Juan Ponce's second voyage to Florida was ignored by almost all of the chroniclers for many reasons. The obvious one, their preoccupation with Cortés and the Aztecs, has already been mentioned. Cortés's conquest of Mexico had begun in 1519 and was winding down just as Juan Ponce sailed for Florida in 1521. In fact, the Aztec leader, Cuauhtémoc (Guatémoc), surrendered to Cortés on August 13, 1521 — about two or three weeks after Juan Ponce died.[15] Also in 1519, Magellan had departed Spain, and by 1520 he had sailed into Balboa's "South Sea," renaming it the "Pacific Ocean" and forever reshaping mankind's comprehension of Earth's geography.[16] Although Magellan died on the Philippine island of Mactan a few weeks before Juan Ponce's fatal encounter with the Florida Indians, nineteen of his original contingent of 227 men completed the circumnavigation and returned to Spain in 1522, survivors of a saga that was almost as gripping as Cortés's conquest of Mexico. Unfortunately, it did not take these or other momentous events to overshadow Juan Ponce's second voyage to Florida — for Juan Ponce's voyage produced absolutely nothing of immediate significance: no gold, no colony, no map or chart, no diary or log. That Florida was a part of the mainland had already been determined by Pineda *before* Juan Ponce's second voyage, and Juan Ponce's only significant discovery during his voyages to Florida — the Gulf Stream — had been made during his first voyage!

～

In some ways, Ponce de León was facing one of the same problems Christopher Columbus had encountered on his last voyage. There was a need for something spectacular to come out of the voyage if support for it was to be sustained. He had to find gold, or a strait, or both. Juan Ponce had to outdo Cortés. Knowing full well that this was a "do or die" adventure, Juan Ponce set sail for his new dominion, presumably headed for Charlotte Harbor on Florida's Gulf coast.

The paucity of written records has kept information about Juan Ponce's course from Puerto Rico to Florida well-hidden. Almost anything we say about the events between departure and landing can be little more than speculation. The sail to Florida may have taken two or three weeks; it may have been longer, depending on many, many variables. Nothing is known about the winds, weather, or currents they encountered. We also do not know if there were mechanical problems, stop-overs, or any among a host of other possible problems. It is even possible that there was interference from unauthorized or competing Spanish ships, similar to Velázquez's illegal slaving expedition to Florida in 1517 or Miruelo's spying operation during Juan Ponce's first voyage to Florida.[17]

Juan Ponce would have been wise to stay as far north of Cuba as was practical. Velázquez was not only unpredictable, he had also become obsessed with the destruction of Cortés, whom he regarded as a rebel. Although there was probably some merit in this belief — after all, Cortés supposedly was working for Velázquez — Velázquez was beginning to view the Gulf of Mexico as his own personal lake. He had sent out patrol ships in the past and, while they might have been seeking one of Cortés's lieutenants, they also might have interfered with authorized voyages such as Juan Ponce's.

There are many places where the two small vessels might have left the Atlantic Ocean and crossed into the Gulf of Mexico. Inasmuch as Juan Ponce had some first-hand knowledge of the region, it is reasonable to think that he would logically have tried to pass through Los Mártires into Florida Bay, and then take aim on Florida's west coast. Despite Juan Ponce's fight with the Caloosa Indians eight years before, it seems as though the little flotilla headed for the same general area of Charlotte Harbor in which the encounter had taken place. If Charlotte Harbor was, indeed, the destination this time, then Juan Ponce and his fleet probably arrived there about the middle of March 1521.

As with most aspects of this voyage, very little can be said about the crew, soldiers, settlers, or priests who went along. Of the hundred-or-so people with the fleet, only four names other than Juan Ponce de León have survived the erosion of time.[18] Juan Ponce's nephew, Hernán Ponce de León, was one of the voyagers. The other three included Juan Garrido, a free black man; Alonso Martín de Jérez; and Pedro Jiménez.

As with the personnel, not much is known about the ships, other than that they were small and not much larger than the *Pinta* of the Columbus discovery fleet — about seventy feet long with a twenty-two-foot beam and a draft of about seven feet. If one of the ships was a nao, it would have been about seventy-eight feet long. Even if both vessels were naos, they would have been very crowded with 100 people, a few animals, the implements needed for starting a colony, and the other necessary provisions on board. We do know that the ships were armed, but the type and quantity of the arms is another mystery.

One may reasonably assume that the colonists and most of the soldiers and priests would have been left at a suitable location before any serious exploration began. That location is also unknown, but Juan Ponce's experience on Puerto Rico suggests a few of his rules for colonization. For one thing — perhaps the paramount requirement — good potable water was a must. Coupled with the need for a good water supply was Juan Ponce's personal dislike of insular locations for settlements. His struggle to prevent the relocation of Caparra to San Juan Bay clearly established his feelings on this matter.[19] Added to this is the fact that most small islands are poorly endowed with water. The barrier islands of Florida, and many islands in the Bahamas, are classic examples of this circumstance, and Juan Ponce had first-hand familiarity with both types of islands. Also, and this is certainly worthy of consideration, Juan Ponce had a terrible experience with the Caloosa Indians during his first voyage to Florida, probably at Pine Island in Charlotte Harbor. He may have returned to the general area of Charlotte Harbor in 1521 but it is highly unlikely that he would have chosen Pine Island or any other of the nearby islands — today's Sanibel, Captiva, Estero, or others — for the site of his colony. He would most likely have tried to establish his colony on the mainland, in an area of fertile soil, near the mouth of a river, or along a navigable river. Salvaleón, his plantation in Española, would have been the perfect model for the agricultural colony he envisaged. Juan Ponce was, more than anything else, a farmer. Unlike almost any other Spanish conquistador, he had become a wealthy man largely because of his successful livestock and farming operations.

Juan Ponce selected a site for his colony at an undisclosed location on the west coast of Florida. Taking into consideration the many factors that might have influenced the selection of a site, Juan Ponce most likely would have tried to place his colony somewhere between Charlotte Harbor and the Caloosahatchee River on the south, what is today the Fort Myers area, and Apalachee Bay on the north, where the Florida coast turns toward the west. Beyond these southern and northern extremes, other good sites could have included Estero Bay between what are today Fort Myers and Naples, Sarasota Bay, Tampa Bay, Chassahowitzka Bay, Homosassa Bay, Crystal Bay, Waccasassa Bay, Suwannee Sound, Horseshoe Cove, and Deadman Bay. On some maps drawn a century after Juan Ponce's second voy-

Figure 48. Sarasota Bay, Florida, one of several possible locations of Juan Ponce's Florida colony in 1521. This is also one of the possible locations of the "Bay of Juan Ponce" shown on some seventeenth-century maps. (Photograph by R. H. Fuson)

age, Tampa Bay is labeled "The Bay of Juan Ponce." This has caused a number of people to jump immediately to the conclusion that Juan Ponce's colony was somewhere on the shore of Tampa Bay. The label, however, at best is weak evidence for such a conclusion, and it is probably not evidence at all.

Oviedo's comment that the temperature of the region was very disagreeable and somewhat unexpected by Juan Ponce has already been mentioned, but it deserves a little more explanation.[20] It is possible that Oviedo was reporting something he had heard from a participant on the expedition. If this is true, and there is no way to establish its veracity, then it could only mean that Juan Ponce took his colonists as far north as Apalachee Bay. North Florida *could* have experienced a cold snap in March. There is no way that Juan Ponce would have regarded warm weather as unusual and disagreeable. If the weather was truly disagreeable, then it had to have meant that it was cold, and this could only have occurred at the northern extremity of Juan Ponce's domain — in the vicinity of Apalachee Bay.

There is also no way of knowing if the colony remained in one location for the entire time Juan Ponce was in west Florida. It may have been relocated one or more times during the few months following the first landfall as the party evaluated the water, soil, timber, and Indians at or near any given site.[21]

About July 1, 1521, there was a deadly confrontation between the Spaniards and the Indians. This fight seems to have involved Caloosa Indians, but the evidence supporting this conclusion is not firm. If the Indians were Caloosas, however, this indicates that the fight most likely took place south of Tampa Bay.

Inasmuch as there are no written records by or from an eye-witness to the final encounter with the Indians, we are again left to speculate about what exactly transpired. Were all of the colonists, ships' crews, soldiers, and priests in one place when the final battle was fought? Or was one ship somewhere else? Maybe both ships were at sea. No one knows.

Although the details are lacking, it is obvious that the Spaniards were overwhelmed and overrun. Not only does the number of Spanish dead remain a secret, but the names of only two of those killed have been passed along to us. Juan Ponce de León died from an arrow wound to the thigh, but only after his comrades had taken him to Havana, Cuba. Juan Ponce's nephew, Hernán, was buried at sea; the place and exact cause of his death are unknown. From all accounts — and there are not many — several other Spaniards died in Havana.

It is assumed that there was a rapid and immediate withdrawal of the colonists from Florida after their defeat by the Indians. The ship carrying the gravely wounded governor went to Havana, arriving there during the first week of July. The other ship went to Veracruz, where it arrived no later than July 15,

1521, the date that Cortés sent his *Third Letter* to Charles V. In the *Letter* Cortés mentioned the arrival:[22]

> *By now the Spaniards who had been wounded at the time of our defeat [the defeat of Cortés and his men by the Aztecs] had recovered. Moreover, a vessel belonging to Ponce de León arrived at Veracruz, and the people of the town sent me some powder and crossbows, of which we had great need.*

From Cortés's letter we learn two things about the waning gasps of Juan Ponce's attempt to settle Florida. First, Juan Ponce was mortally wounded in a battle that took place *before* July 15. If a ship left west Florida and headed for Veracruz immediately after such a battle, and experienced good weather and no countercurrents, it would have taken about a week or ten days to sail to Veracruz. Second, the ship that reached Veracruz still had a supply of powder and a number of crossbows. Beyond the facts, one wonders why one ship went to Veracruz in the first place? Did all of the wounded sail to Ha-

Figure 49. San Juan Cathedral, San Juan, Puerto Rico. Juan Ponce is entombed inside this cathedral. (Photograph by R. H. Fuson)

Figure 50. The tomb of Juan Ponce inside the San Juan Cathedral, San Juan, Puerto Rico. The inscription on his tomb is shown in detail in Figure 51 and is transcribed below this figure and Figure 51. (Photograph by George Barford)

I. N. D.

BAJO EL PONTIFICADO DE SU SANTIDAD PÍO X Y OCUPANDO LA SEDE EPISCOPAL DE PUERTO RICO

MONSEÑOR GUILLERMO JONES, SE TRASLADARON Á ÉSTA IGLESIA CATEDRAL, DESDE LA

CONVENTUAL DE S^{TO} TOMÁS DE AQUINO (HOY DE SAN JOSÉ) DONDE SE HALLABAN

DEPOSITADOS DESDE 1559, LOS DESPOJOS MORTALES DE

JUAN PONCE DE LEÓN

(NATURAL DE LA TIERRA DE CAMPOS) DE CUYO LINAJE HIDALGO PUERON LIMPIA EJECUTORIA

SUS BIZARROS HECHOS. SOLDADO EN GRANADA, CAPITÁN EN LA ESPAÑOLA, CONQUISTADOR

Y GOBERNADOR DE SAN JUAN DEL BORIQUÉN. DESCUBRIDOR Y PRIMER ADELANTADO DE LA

FLORIDA: MILITÉ VALEROSO, DIESTRO CAUDILLO VASALLO LEAL. PROBO ADMINISTRADOR,

PADRE AMANTISIMO Y COLONO LABORIOSO Y CONSECUENTE. RINDIÓ EL ALMA Á DIOS Y EL

CUERPO Á LA TIERRA EN LA HABANA (JUNIO DE 1521). Á SU MEMORIA VENERANDA Y EN

HONOR Á LA CIVILIZACIÓN CRISTIANA POR SU IMPULSO INTRODUCIDA. POR SU BRAVURA

CIMENTADA, Y POR SU DILIGENTE COOPERACIÓN DIFUNDIDA EN ÉSTA FECUNDA TIERRA

PORTORRIQUEÑA, CONSACRA PIADOSO HOMENAJE.

EL CASINO ESPAÑOL DE SAN JUAN

A. D. 1909

Figure 51. The inscription on the tomb of Juan Ponce. (Photograph by R. H. Fuson)

IN THE NAME OF GOD

UNDER THE PONTIFICATE OF HIS HOLINESS PIUS X AND OCCUPYING THE EPISCOPAL SEAT OF PUERTO RICO MONSIGNOR GUILLERMO JONES. MOVED TO THIS CATHEDRAL CHURCH, FROM THE CONVENTUAL OF SANTO TOMÁS DE AQUINO (TODAY SAN JOSÉ) WHERE THEY HAD BEEN INTERRED SINCE 1559, THE MORTAL REMAINS OF

JUAN PONCE DE LEÓN

(A NATIVE OF TIERRA DE CAMPOS) WHOSE GALLANT DEEDS WERE EVIDENCE OF HIS NOBLE AND PURE LINEAGE. SOLDIER IN GRANADA, CAPTAIN IN ESPAÑOLA, CONQUEROR AND GOVERNOR OF SAN JUAN DEL BORIQUÉN. DISCOVERER AND FIRST GOVERNOR OF FLORIDA: VALIANT MILITARY MAN, SKILLFUL LEADER, LOYAL SUBJECT. HONEST ADMINISTRATOR, LOVING FATHER AND INDUSTRIOUS AND CONSISTENT COLONIST. HE SURRENDERED HIS SOUL TO GOD AND HIS BODY TO THE EARTH IN HAVANA (JUNE 1521). TO HIS VENERABLE MEMORY AND IN HONOR OF THE CHRISTIAN CIVILIZATION INTRODUCED THROUGH HIS IMPETUS, FOUNDED BY HIS BRAVERY, AND SPREAD BY HIS DILIGENT COOPERATION IN THIS BOUNTIFUL PUERTO RICAN LAND, A DEVOUT TRIBUTE IS CONSECRATED.

THE SPANISH CLUB OF SAN JUAN

A. D. 1909

---

vana and the nearest hospital while the unscathed went to Veracruz to join up with Cortés and seek the fortune that Juan Ponce had failed to provide?

~

The death of forty-seven-year-old Juan Ponce de León was barely mentioned by the chroniclers of the sixteenth century. Many years passed before his remains were taken in 1559 from Havana to San Juan, where they are now at rest in San Juan Cathedral. Perhaps no better epitaph was ever written for Florida's first governor than the one found in Manuel Ballesteros Gaibrois' book, *La idea colonial de Ponce de León.*[23]

> *And a final conclusion, homage is owed to the memory of the great Castilian: he is without doubt the first Puerto Rican who founded a lasting house on the island, who carried his family to it, who buried his wife in it, and who saw his daughters married in it, planting the most beautiful and perennial of all the plants: that of his ancestry. . .*
>
> *The originality of the colonial idea of Ponce de León consisted precisely of its lack of originality, since at a time when many others lost their heads in careers of excessive personal enrichment, [the era] nevertheless produced the ideological storm of [Fray Reginaldo] Montesinos, Las Casas, and the moralists. He [Juan Ponce] proceeded according to Christian logic, and surely would have been greatly astonished if someone had said to him that doing something normal — settling, peacefully governing the Indians, raising livestock, importing plants, building houses, etc. — was something that the others were not contemplating as their ultimate goal. Perhaps one of the most difficult human undertakings is to conduct oneself simply as a man, without excesses or smallness, because the Latin saying still makes sense:* in medio virtus *[virtue is in the middle].*

Chapter 6
1521–1565

From the Dream of Juan Ponce
to the Reality of Saint Augustine

After Juan Ponce de León's disastrous trip to Florida in 1521, forty-three years were to pass before a permanent European presence was established on the peninsula. During this time, there were at least five authorized Spanish expeditions to Florida, one questionable and probably unauthorized Spanish venture, and two French landings. The second French expedition, in 1564, marked the beginning of a permanent European presence in the region. The Spanish decimation of the French colonists in 1565 and their planting a colony at Saint Augustine that same year reestablished Spanish supremacy on the Atlantic coast of what is today the southeastern United States. Although Spanish control over this region was progressively weakened, most of what is today the state of Florida remained a colony of Spain, except for a brief period, until it was acquired in two units by the United States in 1812 and 1817.

When Juan Ponce de León met his unfortunate end in 1521, the land that was only then coming to be known as Florida was essentially the peninsula that is today's state of Florida, along with the northward continuation of the Atlantic coast as far as the Carolinas. By the time that Saint Augustine was settled, the entire Atlantic coast of North America, from today's Florida to southern Canada, was known as La Florida, or to the French, La Floride. The exploration, conquest, and settlement of eastern North America by French, British, and other European nations during the ensuing two centuries, however, resulted in other names being applied to the east coast of the continent. Consequently, the name La Florida applied to an increasingly smaller area and, by early in the eighteenth century, essentially included only today's state of Florida, plus an extension of the modern Florida panhandle westward to the Mississippi River. In the eighteenth century, the region from the Apalachicola River to the Mississippi River was known as West Florida and was claimed by both Spain and Great Britain. The western boundary of modern Florida dates from 1813, when Andrew Jackson captured Pensacola from the British and established the boundary in its current location.

The first Spanish foray to Florida after 1521 may have been one led by Diego Miruelo — the same Diego Miruelo who Juan Ponce had encountered in the Bahamas during the 1513 voyage.[1] Sometime after 1521, but before 1524, Miruelo claimed that he had been blown by a storm to the Florida coast, where he traded successfully and peacefully with the Indians. Unfortunately, he did not bother to record the latitude nor did he even make a sketch map of the location. In other words, Miruelo did not know where he had been, and he might not have been in Florida at all.

At about the same time, a slave-hunting mission from Santo Domingo discovered and named Santa Elena at what is today Parris Island, South Carolina. The men on this voyage lost one of their two ships and all of its human cargo, but those who returned to Santo Domingo added their exaggerated claims of new-found wealth to the tales circulating around town concerning the voyage of Diego Miruelo. This was sufficient evidence for Lucas Vázquez de Ayllón, one of the major investors in the slaving enterprise, to seek royal authorization for a voyage of discovery.

The patent was granted, and in 1524 Vázquez de Ayllón sailed with three ships, firm in his belief that Miruelo's discovery was richer than the one in South Carolina.[2] Miruelo was even named pilot-major of Vázquez de Ayllón's fleet. There was, however, one small problem: Miruelo did not know where he had been in Florida, and he was unable to find the place where he claimed he had obtained gold and silver from the Indians. The chronicler Garcilaso de la Vega stated that Miruelo became so despondent over his inability to locate the site that he "fell into such a melancholia that in a few days he lost his reason and expired." Surely Vázquez de Ayllón saw the Florida peninsula, but there is no evidence that he landed there.

After Miruelo's death, Vázquez de Ayllón sailed northward from Florida, toward a region he called Chicoria — now Georgia and the Carolinas. On a river he called the Jordan — probably the Cape Fear River near what is today Wilmington, North Carolina — Vázquez de Ayllón lost one of his three ships. From here he sailed along the North Carolina coast, possibly to the vicinity of Jacksonville, North Carolina, and landed with 200 men. After three or four days of peaceful relations between the Indians and Spaniards, the Indians attacked and killed most of the Spaniards. Vázquez de Ayllón, however, managed to escape and returned to Santo Domingo, a broken and disheartened man.

~

The first major attempt to found a colony in Florida was made by Pánfilo de Narváez in 1528.[3] Narváez was born about 1470 and, when he undertook the colonization of Florida at the age of fifty-eight, he was older than the typical conquistador of his time.

Narváez received his capitulación from the king on De-

Figure 52. Rio de las Palmas, Mexico. During most of the sixteenth century this river was considered to be the western boundary of Florida. (Photograph by R. H. Fuson)

cember 11, 1526, but he did not sail from Spain until June 17, 1527. His contract with the king authorized "the discovery, conquest, and settlement" of Florida from "the Rio de las Palmas up to the Island of Florida and all of the said coast from one sea to the other."[4] The Rio de las Palmas is known today as Laguna Madre; it is located in northeastern Mexico, just south of Brownsville, Texas. It is interesting to note that Florida was still being referred to as an island in 1526 even though its correct geography had been mapped as early as 1519. Narváez's contract also called for the establishment of at least two towns, with no fewer than 100 persons in each, and three forts. All of this, of course, was to be paid for by Narváez.

Narváez departed Spain from Sanlúcar de Barrameda with five ships and about 600 men. Among those making the voyage was Álvar Núñez Cabeza de Vaca, the fleet's treasurer and high sheriff and, as one of only four survivors of the expedition, our principal source of information about the tragic events that unfolded.[5] Narváez sailed to Santo Domingo, where he remained for forty-five days, long enough for 140 men to desert. Enough men were recruited from the local population, however, to make up for most of those who had deserted, and a sixth ship was purchased for the armada. The squadron of six ships eventually left Santo Domingo for Santiago, Cuba, probably during the first week of September 1527. In Cuba, Narváez was able to add yet more men to his crew to compensate for those who deserted in Santo Domingo.

While in Santiago, Narváez was offered certain provisions by Vasco Porcallo de Figueroa, who would later visit Florida with Hernando de Soto, but to get them Narváez would have to sail about 300 miles from Santiago to the port of Trinidad on Cuba's south coast. The fleet started toward Trinidad, Cuba, but stopped at Cape Santa Cruz, a make-shift rest stop approximately a third of the way from Santiago to Trinidad. For whatever reason, Narváez sent two ships from Santa Cruz to Trinidad

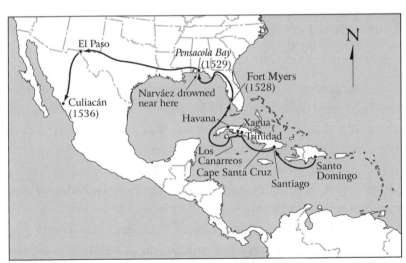

Figure 53. The route of Pánfilo de Narváez and Álvar Núñez Cabeza de Vaca, 1528–1536. Narváez drowned in November, 1528, and Cabeza de Vaca and his small group wandered westward sporadically until they reached Culiacán in 1536.

to get the provisions; one of these ships was commanded by Captain Pantoja and the other by Cabeza de Vaca. The other four ships remained at Santa Cruz. It was at this time that ill fortune began to befall the Narváez expedition.

A major hurricane struck southern Cuba that September and destroyed both ships that Narváez had sent to Trinidad. Cabeza de Vaca barely escaped with his life. Captain Pantoja and thirty men who were on shore with him when the hurricane struck also survived. But the sixty or so men who had remained on the ships perished, along with twenty horses and the supplies that had already been loaded.

Narváez did not reach Trinidad with the four remaining ships until November 5. Yielding to the pleas of the townspeople, Narváez decided to spend the winter at Trinidad and Cabeza de Vaca took the ships to Xagua, the fine harbor that is today Cienfuegos. Here he stayed until Narváez arrived on February 18, 1528, with a small ship, a brigantine, that he had bought in Trinidad. Also with Narváez was Diego Miruelo, the nephew and namesake of Vázquez de Ayllón's incompetent pilot. This Miruelo was also a pilot, and in many ways he was just like his uncle.

Narváez and his entourage departed Xagua on February 20, 1528, and sailed toward Havana with the five ships, 400 men, and eighty horses. In Havana they had planned to pick up another ship that Narváez had purchased during the winter, along with its contingent of forty foot soldiers and twelve cavalrymen. Then, they would sail on to Florida. But, Narváez never reached Havana.

The first thing Miruelo did after sailing from Xagua was to run the squadron aground in the Gulf of Batabanó near the Canarreos Archipelago, east of the Isle of Pines off of Cuba's south coast. All five ships were stuck there for fifteen days.[6] This mishap was followed by three successive storms and, though the ships finally were pulled free from the shoals, they never reached Havana. A strong southerly wind prevented the fleet from entering the harbor at Havana, and the fleet was blown toward Florida — which came into sight on April 12, 1528. On April 14, the fleet anchored at the head of a bay, and on April 15, Good Friday, Governor Narváez and a large number of people went ashore. Formal possession of the land was proclaimed on April 16.[7] There has been no positive identification of this bay, but most likely it was either at Charlotte Harbor or Tampa Bay, Florida. This author leans toward the former site because of the sailing time involved.

On April 19, Narváez ordered the crew of the brigantine to search the coast of west Florida and look for a bay supposedly known to Miruelo. Up to this time, Miruelo had failed to find the harbor, and indeed he had no idea where the Narváez expedition had landed. In the event that the bay was not discovered, Miruelo was to take the brigantine to Havana, get fresh provisions, find the ship that belonged to Narváez, and return to Florida. The bay was not found. Miruelo did make it to Havana, found Narváez's ship, and returned to Florida in May — one of the few things he ever did that turned out to be right — but after joining the ships still in Florida, he was never able to find Narváez or any of his men. He did, however, manage to lose a shore party of four men to the Indians, one of whom survived and was rescued by Hernando de Soto in 1539.

Narváez had made a terrible decision during the last week of April. He had elected to leave the fleet and move overland with all of the men who were not needed to mind the ships. On May 1, he had marched inland with a company of about 300 men. The plan had called for a rendezvous with the ships farther up the coast, somewhere north of today's Tampa. By the time Miruelo with the brigantine and the other ship from Havana had reached Florida, only three of Narváez's ships were at anchor. One of the ships had already been lost to the breakers.

About a hundred men were aboard the five remaining ships, but at least ten women — married to men on the exploring party — were also present. This fleet searched the Florida coast for the governor and his men for most of 1528 without success. Finally, the search was called off and the ships sailed to Veracruz and Cortés.

The trials and tribulations of this doomed exploring party are well-documented by Cabeza de Vaca. On June 18, while attempting to cross the Suwannee River, the first Spaniard in this party was lost. From that time on, things went from bad to worse. Eventually, Narváez and his lieutenants reached the conclusion that the only way out of Florida's swamps and forests, and the only escape from its hostile Indians, was by sea. And to do this the explorers would have to construct five boats. There was only one carpenter among the group, and they had no tools or such basic necessities as nails. Not one single man knew anything about boat building and there was virtually no food. What little there was came from the horses — one was killed for food every third day — and from raiding a nearby Indian village for corn. One third of the force was too ill to work at the beginning of the project, and the number of ill grew as the days passed.

Construction of the boats began on August 4 and lasted until September 20, 1528. A crude forge was built and a bellows was fashioned from deerskin. Nails, hammers, saws, and axes were made from the stirrups, armor, crossbows — anything containing iron that was carried by the explorers. The rigging and caulking came from plants; sails from clothing; resin from pine trees; rope from the manes and tails of horses.

By September 22, after seven weeks of boat construction, only one horse remained alive, more than forty men had died, and thirteen men had been killed or had drowned. All told, 242 men crowded into the five small boats that had been built; one boat held forty-seven people, another held forty-eight, and the other three held forty-nine each. There was no room on the boats to move about, and the gunwales were barely above the water level when the boats were launched and loaded. This launching took place on the shore of Apalachee Bay, somewhere south of today's Saint Marks, Florida. During the rest of September and all of October, the party followed the coast westward until it reached Pensacola Bay on November 2. A few men died during this period, including some who were near death upon departure and some who ingested salt water during the voyage.

Narváez died in November when his boat was blown out to sea from the vicinity of Pensacola Bay. Three other boats capsized and one sank after it was repaired. By April of 1529, only fifteen men were still alive; some of these survived by eating dogs and others turned to cannibalism. Ultimately, there were four survivors: Álvar Núñez Cabeza de Vaca, Alonso del Castillo Maldonado, Andrés Dorantes, and Estéban (Estevanico, a black man). These four men, on foot, wandered from Pensacola to the Rio Grande, across northern Mexico to what is today El Paso, then across the Sonora Desert to the west coast of Mexico; by 1536, they had reached what is today Culiacán on the west coast of Mexico.

The small group of survivors spent the seven years between 1529 and 1536 with various Indian bands. Sometimes the men were together and sometimes they were separated, but the tales they told upon their return to civilization spurred Cortés, and later Francisco Vázquez de Coronado, to search northwestern Mexico and the American southwest for the legendary cities of gold. In effect, the saga of the Narváez survivors triggered a whole new phase of North American exploration. Cabeza de Vaca later served as governor of Rio de la Plata, South America; he built the first road from Santos, Brazil, to

Asunción, Paraguay; and he discovered Iguaçu Falls in 1541. He died in Sevilla in 1560.

It is obvious that Narváez did not live up to the terms of his contract with the king. No towns or forts were established, those Spaniards on the ships sailed away, and there were only four survivors of the original landing party — and they turned up in Mexico seven years later.

~

The next attempt to settle Florida occurred in 1539, more than a decade after the Narváez fiasco. Hernando de Soto had served his New World apprenticeship in Panama (as a student of Pedrarias, his father-in-law and the man who murdered Balboa in 1519), Nicaragua, and Peru, and had returned to Spain in 1536. Wealthy from his exploitation of the Incas and a disciple of that master-of-greed, Francisco Pizarro, de Soto was now ready to sail back to America as a governor and, hopefully, become a very rich governor. To this end, he petitioned Charles V for a royal patent, and one was issued on April 20, 1537.[8] This was the standard capitulación; essentially, it extended the previous contracts made with Vázquez de Ayllón and Narváez to conquer and populate the land between the Rio de las Palmas up to and including the Florida peninsula. The grant to de Soto gave him exclusive rights to explore and settle "two hundred leagues of coast." He was to take at least 500 men on the expedition with supplies for at least eighteen months, and to construct at his own expense three stone forts. Although the contract mentions "settlement of the land" several times, there was no specific requirement to build towns. Lastly, there was the appointment of de Soto as governor of Cuba as well as governor of Florida. This apparently was the first time that the two territories had shared the same governor.

There are four basic sources for the story of Hernando de

Soto's entrada into what is now the southeastern United States. While these sources are in general agreement, they differ greatly in some specifics. Probably the best interpretation of these differing accounts is that of Rolfe F. Schell.[9] No one seems to know exactly how many people sailed from Sanlúcar de Barrameda on April 6, 1538.[10] The numbers range from 600 to more than 1000. Even the number of ships is debatable and we are not certain of the sizes of the vessels.[11] There were probably ten ships of various sizes in de Soto's fleet, and they sailed with twenty other ships bound for Mexico. This group of thirty vessels was one of the largest ever assembled in Spain.

The first problem confronted by the fleet occurred a little after midnight on the first day out.[12] One of the ships bound for Mexico ran ahead of the fleet, against standing orders, and was thought to be an enemy vessel. It was fired upon and damaged to the point that it almost collided with de Soto's flagship. What appeared to be a certain disaster was averted at the last minute. Also, two soldiers got into a fight and both fell overboard and drowned. If this was not enough, one man's dog fell into the sea but the fleet was unable to stop. After swimming for five hours, however, the dog was rescued by another vessel, and the owner was overcome with joy to find him ashore when the ships reached Gomera, in the Canary Islands. A sad footnote to this episode is that, on their departure from Gomera, the dog's master was struck in the head by a boom and knocked into the ocean. He was never seen again.

The necessary supplies were replenished in the Canaries, and the seventeen-year-old daughter of the Count and Countess of Gomera joined the passengers at this time. The count's wife was a cousin of de Soto's wife, who was also on this voyage, and the count and countess allowed the beautiful girl to sail away with them on April 24. None of the chroniclers speculates on de Soto's motives. And what did the governor's wife think about this?

Around the middle of May, the ships bound for Mexico sailed away on a new course, and de Soto's fleet made directly for Santiago, Cuba. During the latter part of May, the Cuban town of Santiago came into sight and a new adventure unfolded. It seems as though a French pirate ship had attacked a Spanish ship in the port a few days before the de Soto fleet arrived. This fight had gone on for four days, with the opposing ships' captains calling off the battle from sundown to sunrise, and even visiting one another in the evenings. Eventually the French ship slipped away in the dead of night after concluding that the struggle would forever be a draw. With this as a backdrop, we have de Soto entering the harbor in the lead ship. Thinking that the French ship had returned, a sentinel on shore attempted to lure de Soto's vessel onto some rocks by shouting incorrect sailing instructions. As soon as the error was detected, and the correct instructions given, the sailors tried to alter their course. But it was too late. There was a sudden jolt as the ship hit the rocks, and the crew furiously began to pump a mixture of wine, vinegar, oil, and honey from the hold — but little or no water! The grounding only smashed a number of storage jars, and no serious damage was done. However, from the outset of this mishap, many abandoned the ship, including de Soto's wife, the teen-ager from Gomera, and several ladies-in-waiting.

The town of Santiago was able to provide de Soto with everything he needed.[13] He even received unexpected help from Vasco Porcallo de Figueroa of Trinidad, Cuba. Porcallo visited de Soto in Santiago and provided men, food, horses, and money. And, in return, de Soto named him lieutenant general of the expedition. This position had become vacant when de Soto discovered that his current lieutenant general, Nuño de Tovar, had secretly wed Doña Leonor, the daughter of the Count and Countess of Gomera. Nuño de Tovar had been removed from office as soon as de Soto became aware of what had happened.

The people and the ships were moved to Havana, and final preparations for the journey to Florida were made there. Juan de Añasco was sent with two brigantines to carefully survey the coast of Florida for a landing spot. While Añasco was absent for about two months, de Soto purchased another ship, the large and beautiful *Santa Ana*. When Añasco returned, he was sent back to make an even closer study of the coast. This survey took three months, and every nook and cranny of coastal west Florida was plotted. It is truly unfortunate that nothing from this survey has survived. There is no doubt that de Soto was better prepared than anyone had ever been for entering and exploring a new land. Not only was de Soto prepared to take up his new duties as governor of Florida, but he also had made arrangements for the governance of Cuba — he left his wife in charge.

The principal sources for information about the voyage of de Soto do not agree on the day of departure from Havana.[14] The most likely date was May 18, 1539. There is also disagreement as to the total number of people on the expedition and even the types and numbers of the ships.[15] There were at least five ships, two caravels, and two brigantines; Vega states that there was yet another ship.[16] No less than 620 men took part in the expedition as infantry or calvary, and there were an additional 130 sailors manning the ships. Besides the necessary equipment, arms, and provisions, 223 horses would survive the journey.

After a pleasant sail of a week, landfall occurred on May 25. Formal possession of the land was probably made on June 1, 1539, but some men had gone ashore before this time to get water and grass for the horses. De Soto went ashore on May 25 for a quick reconnaissance, became separated from the fleet, and almost caused a panic while everyone anxiously awaited

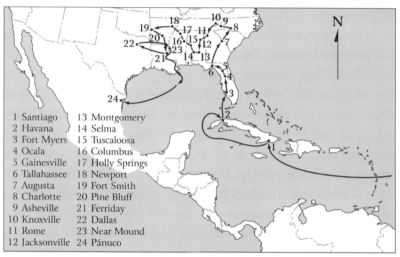

1 Santiago   13 Montgomery
2 Havana   14 Selma
3 Fort Myers   15 Tuscaloosa
4 Ocala   16 Columbus
5 Gainesville   17 Holly Springs
6 Tallahassee   18 Newport
7 Augusta   19 Fort Smith
8 Charlotte   20 Pine Bluff
9 Asheville   21 Ferriday
10 Knoxville   22 Dallas
11 Rome   23 Near Mound
12 Jacksonville   24 Pánuco

Figure 54. The route of Hernando de Soto and his successor, Luis de Moscoso de Alvarado, 1539–1543. De Soto died near what is today Ferriday, Louisiana, in May, 1542.

his safe return.[17]

And just where did this landing take place? Even though many people over many years have poured through the documents, we are not sure and there is disagreement among scholars as to the actual location of the site. Geographically, the best candidate for the landing is Punta Rassa, at the mouth of the Caloosahatchee River. The Caloosahatchee is also known as the Bahía del Espíritu Santo (Bay of the Holy Ghost). Most scholars, however, have chosen Tampa Bay — or the Manatee River, a little south of Tampa Bay near what is today Bradenton, Florida — as the Bahía del Espíritu Santo.[18]

Not long after landing and unloading, the Spaniards discovered one of their own.[19] Juan Ortíz, a native of Sevilla, had been on the brigantine that Narváez had sent to Havana under Miruelo's command in 1528. Upon returning to Florida, the crew had searched for Narváez and while doing so, the Indians, by trickery, had captured four men from the brigantine. Three of

190

the Spaniards had been executed by the Indian cacique Hirrihigua in the Indian village of Ucita (Ocita, or Ecita), but Ortíz had survived. He had been literally snatched from the jaws of death by the wife and daughter of the cacique. Later, he managed to escape from Hirrihigua and received the protection of another cacique, Mucozo. Ortíz, who was eighteen years old at the time of his capture, had lived with these Indians, as an Indian, for eleven years. He almost had forgotten how to speak Spanish but, because he was fluent in the local dialect, he was to become de Soto's interpreter. From that time on, every time the Spaniards came to a linguistic boundary — and there were many — they would seek out an Indian who knew the native language on each side of the boundary. By the time de Soto and his entourage reached the Mississippi River four years later, in 1542, the governor's words would have to pass through more than a dozen people before they reached the intended recipient. Even in the same language the accuracy and meaning of a message always changes before it passes through a dozen people, so it is easy to imagine the difficulty faced by de Soto when he had to communicate via twelve or more interpreters, all speaking different languages.

In order to prevent desertion or mutiny by his colonists, de Soto, like Cortés before him, removed his ships from the scene once the party moved onto land. At least five of the largest vessels were sent back to Havana. De Soto's lieutenant general, Figueroa, had had a horse shot out from under him with an arrow and decided that he preferred the plush life on his vast estate near Trinidad, Cuba, to that of a conquistador. He returned to Cuba with the ships.

De Soto explored the lands northward from his landing site from 1539 to 1542.[20] His entrada departed modern Florida for Georgia, somewhere north of Tallahassee, in March 1540. Eventually, his party was to explore portions of Florida, Georgia, South Carolina, North Carolina, Tennessee, Alabama, Mississippi, Arkansas, Louisiana, and Texas. In May 1542, de Soto became ill with a fever and — certain of his impending death because an astrologer had predicted he would die when he reached the age at which Balboa died — he called in all of his men and formally passed his authority to Luis de Moscoso de Alvarado. De Soto died on May 21 near Guachoya (today's Ferriday, Louisiana). At first, he was buried in a field and, though the site was well-hidden from the Indians, there was a general feeling among the Spaniards that the Indians knew of the location and would eventually desecrate the body. To prevent that, de Soto was disinterred, placed in the hollowed-out trunk of a live oak tree, weighted down with his armor, and reburied in the main channel of the Mississippi River.

Moscoso then led the men into Texas, somewhere near what is today Dallas, at which point they turned around and returned to the Mississippi River. Here, beginning about January 1543, they constructed a small fleet of seven brigantines. Around July 1, 1543, they left the Indian village of Aminoya, about fifty miles upstream from Guachoya; they traveled down the Mississippi River to the Gulf of Mexico and then sailed to Pánuco, Mexico. It took nineteen days to reach the Gulf of Mexico from Aminoya and another fifty-three days to reach Pánuco. Thirty of these travel days were spent sailing, rowing, or navigating; and twenty-three days were spent repairing the boats, resting, or fishing. According to two of the principal sources for information about this journey — the reports of Elvas and Biedma — 311 men reached Pánuco, Mexico, on September 10, 1543.[21]

After the failure of de Soto's expedition became well known in Spain, many made petitions to the king seeking the governorship of Florida. All of these applicants were rejected by Charles V and, at his own expense, he sent a group of Dominican friars to Tampa Bay in 1549. Apparently, the Crown had reached the conclusion that military might was not the way to conquer Florida. To this end, five friars, led by Luis Cáncer de Balbastro, were dispatched.

Garcilaso de la Vega tells the story this way:[22]

> *These friars had offered to convert the Indians to the Evangelical faith with their preaching, but when they arrived in Florida and disembarked for the purpose, the natives, who had learned a lesson in their previous contact with the Spaniards, refused to listen. Instead they fell upon them and slew Friar Luis as well as two of his companions. The remainder of the brothers then took refuge in their ship and, returning to Spain, proclaimed that people so barbarous and inhuman as Indians had no desire to hear sermons.*

～

Spain seemed to operate on a ten-year cycle with regard to the conquest and settlement of Florida, and so another decade passed before — in 1559 — there was yet another major attempt to establish a permanent Spanish presence on the Gulf Coast of Florida. But this time there was a slight difference in the plan. Spain had a new king. Felipe II had come to the throne in 1556. Whether because of Felipe or in spite of Felipe, the Crown had decided to finance a new expedition to Florida, and it would be organized and administered directly from New Spain (Mexico). In 1551, Antonio de Mendoza, the viceroy of New Spain since the inception of that office, had been promoted to the viceroyalty of Peru. Luis de Velasco had assumed the viceregal office in New Spain and became the administrator of the 1559 expedition to Florida. Velasco then appointed Tristán de Luna y Arellano to be the next governor of Florida.

Tristán de Luna is one of modern Florida's "forgotten governors." Very little has been written about him and some Florida histories skip him altogether. What little information is known about Luna comes mostly from the documents that were collected, translated, and edited by Herbert Ingram Priestley in

193

the 1920s.[23] From Luna's own papers we learn that he came to Mexico about 1530.[24] At that time he had a son, Carlos, who was eight years old, and a younger daughter, Juana.[25] If Luna had an eight-year-old son in 1530, the child would have been born in 1522. Luna, therefore, was probably born around 1500. He was married to Isabel de Rojas, who died before 1559. Luna came from a distinguished family in Spain, where his only brother, seventy-year-old Pedro de Luna y Arellano, was, in 1559, the lord of the towns of Cicia and Borobia. Don Tristán was the only legitimate heir of the estate.

From 1539 to 1541, Luna was with Francisco Vázquez de Coronado in what is now northern Mexico and the southwestern United States, searching for the Seven Golden Cities of Cíbola. Luna went as a calvary captain and returned as Coronado's lieutenant general. He truly distinguished himself on the Coronado expedition, so much so that in 1548 he was sent to Oaxaca in south-central Mexico by then-Viceroy Mendoza to quell an Indian rebellion. Not only did he do this at his own expense, but he pacified the region and in the process very few lives were lost on either side.

Tristán de Luna's appointment as captain-general and governor of Florida was made in 1558. While preparations for the expedition were being made in Veracruz, Viceroy Luis de Velasco took the prudent step of sending three small vessels to survey the coast of the Gulf of Mexico and to "examine, sound, and mark the rivers and ports [harbors]."[26] They were also to find the best place — the most secure and the most convenient place — to land. The location chosen was supposed to be about 250 miles from Santa Elena, for the plan anticipated an overland connection between Luna's colony and the rather vaguely-known Santa Elena.

The survey ships departed Veracruz on September 3, 1558, under the command of Guido de la Bazares (sometimes las

Bazares or Lavazares).[27] The tiny fleet reached the Pánuco River on September 5 and, for some unknown reason, was there until September 14. The fleet covered most of the coast from Mexico to Florida, but movement of the mission appears to have slowed at Mobile Bay, which de la Bazares named Bahía Filipina, in honor of Felipe II. The description of Mobile Bay prepared by Luna at this time is excellent and includes consideration of the flora, fauna, topography, hydrology, soils, climatology, native population, and domestic plants. Other places were named at this time, including Ancón de Velasco (Velasco Bay) in honor of the viceroy. It is possible that Velasco Bay is the modern Perdido Bay, which lies on the Alabama-Florida boundary. On the other hand, the fleet might have sailed farther east, past the bays of Pensacola, Choctawhatchee, West, Andrews, and East, and Velasco Bay could have been one of these or even another bay. The fleet departed the coast of Alabama and western Florida on December 3 and was back in Veracruz by December 14, 1558. The viceroy received the report in Mexico City on February 1, 1559.

While the survey was underway, six large barks, each capable of carrying 100 men and four pieces of artillery, were under construction for use in the expedition.[28] The original plan called for the ships to sail to Florida in May 1559 and transport 500 Spaniards — 200 calvary soldiers, 200 with crossbows and arquebuses, and 100 artisans of all sorts — plus horses and servants. This scheduled departure date was almost met. Luna sailed from Veracruz on June 11, 1559, only eleven days late.

When Luna departed, he carried far more people than the 500 mentioned in the original plan.[29] There were 500 Spaniards, but there were also 1000 servants and 240 horses — 110 of which died enroute to Florida. It is obvious that the six barks built in Veracruz were in addition to other ships, for it was not possible to carry all of those people and animals on six barks. There is

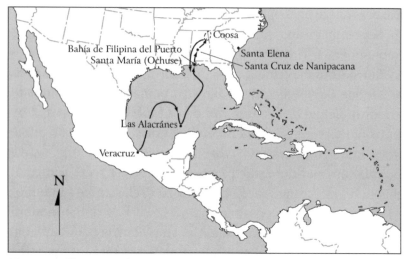

Figure 55. The route of Tristán de Luna y Arellano, 1559–1561. When Luna left Florida in 1561, he traveled to Havana, then to Spain.

some corroboration given for these numbers by Alonso de Montalván, who was a calvaryman with the Luna expedition and who testified at a hearing in Ocoa, Española, August 11, 1561.[30] Montalván placed the total number of Spanish soldiers at 540 — 200 of them were calvary and 340 were infantry, arquebus men, shield bearers, and crossbowmen. There were 800 other people, including married Spanish women, African and European servants and slaves, and friendly Indians.

The attempt by Luna to conquer, settle, and govern Florida began on August 15, 1559, at Pensacola Bay. But it did not begin as smoothly as it should have. Luna's fleet seemed to have had trouble finding the landing place that had been selected by Guido de la Bazares. The voyage from Veracruz to Pensacola Bay had lasted sixty-six days — far in excess of what a normal sail using that route should have taken. According to Luna's report to the viceroy, which was received by Luis de Velasco on September 9, 1559, the first seventeen days consisted of fair weather and mild winds.[31] At that point, Luna's pilot estimated

196

that the fleet was about sixty-five miles south of the Mississippi Delta. From there they sailed six days to the southeast, south-southeast, and south until they came to Las Alacránes, a cluster of small, low-lying islands on the Tropic of Cancer, about 375 miles due south of the mouth of the Mississippi River. From there they sailed northeast for eight days, and sighted the Florida coast about twenty-five miles west of Apalachee Bay, probably at Cape San Blas or Cape Saint George. The vessels anchored — about July 11 — to take on water, wood, and grass for the horses. They apparently rode at anchor for a week, then departed the site on July 17. Luna dispatched a frigate to sail ahead and find the harbor everyone was looking for. The frigate, however, did not see Pensacola Bay and sailed right past it to Mobile Bay, and Luna's ships followed. Another search by the frigate — this time toward the east and over the same route already covered by Luna's vessels — found Pensacola Bay, to which the fleet moved on August 15, 1559. The horses, however, were unloaded at Mobile Bay and were taken overland to Pensacola Bay. Luna named his new base of operations Bahía Filipina del Puerto de Santa María (The Port of Saint Mary on Philippine Bay), but the Indian name, Ochuse, became the vernacular and preferred name. The name Pensacola — used today for the city and the bay — dates from the late seventeenth century and may be a corruption of a Choctaw name. None of Luna's party ever used this name and probably never heard of it. Occasionally, one will run across the name Polonza as a synonym for Ochuse. Its origin is unclear.

Viceroy Velasco had already drawn up a master plan for Luna's first settlement before the expedition got under way.[32] The population was to consist of 100 heads of families who, with their families, would live in 100 houses, each located on a lot fitted to a master plan for the settlement. There were to be forty lots in the center of the town for a plaza, church, monastery, and royal house. The latter would serve as a residence for the governor and as a storehouse for small and large arms, munitions, and food supplies. There was to be a wall around the town, and entry would be controlled by four gates, all visible from the plaza.

On September 19, 1559, a major hurricane struck the area of Pensacola and, for all practical purposes, the fledgling colony was devastated.[33] There was great loss of life and property. All of the ships were either destroyed or grounded except one caravel, two barks, and possibly one frigate. Fortunately the best ship, the *San Juan*, was in Mexico at the time. Many of the ships had not been unloaded and those provisions that were still on board were lost. In addition, the few provisions that had been unloaded were either destroyed or damaged by the wind and rain.

According to the testimony given in Española on August 11, 1561, the colony had become completely dependent on relief supplies sent by Viceroy Velasco following the 1559 hurricane.[34] At first, the only thing that saved the colony was the return of the *San Juan*, accompanied by a bark loaded with provisions. Despite worsening conditions, Luna was adamant in his refusal to move the colony, and he and the colonists survived for several months on the supplies brought from Mexico.

After the hurricane, a detachment of about 150 men was sent north into what is today Alabama in search of the Indian town of Nanipacana, where they hoped to find food. This part of southern Alabama had been a well-populated and prosperous agricultural area when de Soto passed by two decades earlier. By Luna's time, however, the region was becoming depopulated and most of the maize fields had vanished. Even so, there was more food there than on the storm-ravaged coast, and the Spaniards who had been sent to Nanicapana begged Luna to move the entire population of Ochuse north.

At about the time the relief supplies ran out — in January or February, 1560 — Tristán de Luna became very ill. It was reported that he lost his senses and began to say nonsensical and foolish things. In a few days, when he reacquired his faculties, he agreed to move to Nanicapana and, around the middle of February 1560, most of Luna's colony departed Ochuse. About half of the people traveled to Nanicapana via Mobile Bay and the Alabama River and the other half or so traveled overland. A token force of some fifty men and a few black slaves were left at Pensacola Bay. On the way to Nanicapana, Luna again became irrational.

Once the two groups assembled in Nanicapana, which the Spaniards renamed Santa Cruz de Nanicapana, it was learned that the Indians had rebelled and run away with all the corn. Again the governor regained his wits and agreed with his lieutenants that a party should go out and seek more food. A hundred men went up the Alabama River for many miles but found only abandoned houses and fields. The men returned within three weeks. A force of 150 men was then dispatched to the province ruled by Tascalusa (Taxcalusa), the Atahachi cacique who in 1540 had attacked de Soto at the town of Mabila.[35] The Spaniards found corn at Tascalusa and approximately 125 bushels of it were rafted downstream to the governor.

Luna's Florida colony suffered greatly during the spring of 1560, and on June 24, 1560, Santa Cruz de Nanicapana was abandoned and all of the colonists then in the settlement moved to Mobile Bay, then to Ochuse. A note was left in a tree for the force of 150 men who had gone to Tascalusa, directing them to dig for a sealed jar that contained information concerning the move. Despite the constant arrival of supplies from Mexico (at least seven shiploads), by September 1560 there was no more than a one-month supply for the 330 people. They had eaten all of their horses and were even eating cowhide. During this same time, the Spaniards up north had pushed on from Tascalusa to Coosa, arriving there about October 1560 after an arduous journey of four months. This site, visited earlier by de Soto, was probably in what is today northern Georgia. Twelve horsemen were sent back to Ochuse to plead with the governor to join the force in Coosa but, in January or February 1561, Luna sent an order to the men at Coosa to return to Ochuse. This order was obeyed, and the force returned, probably in May or June 1561.

Sometime between January and April 1561, Ángel de Villafañe arrived at Ochuse with fifty men, more supplies, and two ships. Luna requested a ship from Villafañe who complied by giving Luna a frigate. On April 10, 1561, Luna — taking only two servants and a black woman — sailed for Spain by way of Havana. By August 20, 1561, he was in Madrid.

The day after his arrival at Ochuse, Villafañe explained his real mission and his reason for visiting Ochuse. He had been ordered by the king and the viceroy to go to the Punta de Santa Elena (Saint Elena Point) and establish a colony — and he was seeking recruits. About 160 of the colonists at Ochuse took the oath of service and sailed with him to Havana. The others remained at Ochuse, free to leave if they received no orders to the contrary from the viceroy in four or five months.

Villafañe sailed from Havana in late summer with the nao *San Juan*, a caravel, and two frigates. Even though 160 people had taken the oath of service at Ochuse, Villafañe had designated only ninety to accompany him. Fifteen of the ninety had hidden from him in Havana, so his crew numbered only about seventy-five when his fleet left Havana. The sail along the Bahama Channel (Gulf Stream) was smooth, and Santa Elena was located with no problem. Because of the shoals, Villafañe anchored offshore and took a frigate close-in to find a good river harbor. When he landed, he took possession of the land for His Majesty. This ceremony occurred on what is now part

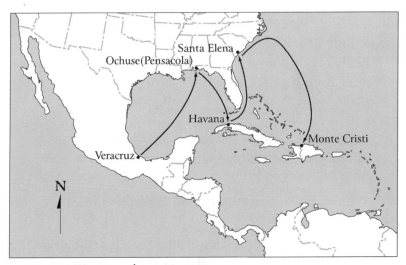

Figure 56. The route of Ángel de Villafañe, 1561.

of the golf course at the United States Marine Corps Base, Parris Island, South Carolina.

Later, Villafañe's fleet sailed northward to North Carolina, and then a hurricane hit. It is difficult to imagine why the Spaniards were still sailing these waters at this time of the year. Surely, hurricanes were frequent meteorological events in this part of the Atlantic at this time of the year, and by the 1560s they should have been anticipated. The two frigates and their crews were lost. The *San Juan* broke loose from its anchor and was blown out to sea. Villafañe took the remaining caravel and headed for Española, the closest place with a Spanish population. To everyone's surprise, the *San Juan* was spotted at sea, and both vessels sailed together to Monte Cristi on the north coast of Española. About twenty-five days were necessary to repair both vessels. Eleven soldiers and four sailors fled the *San Juan* while it was under repair and were never found.

There was no formal dissolution of Luna's Florida colony. It just seems to have evaporated after the summer of 1561. And the settlement at Santa Elena, which was not only a part of Span-

201

ish Florida but was also to be governed by Luna, was not established until 1566, a year after Saint Augustine was settled.

Some concluding words about Luna's 1559–1561 expedition come from James R. Robertson. In 1936 he wrote:[36]

> And yet, the expedition failed — failed in spite of all the care taken to make it a success. Storms, loneliness, the terror of the unknown, illness, starvation, and other sufferings broke the morale of the commander and men, and the immediate project ended in the bushes where it began.

With this as a legacy Luna died in Spain in 1573.

~

After Luna's failures, King Felipe abandoned Florida for all practical purposes. To say the least, this Spanish inaction got the attention of the French. The earlier voyages of Jean Verrazano (1524) and Jacques Cartier (1534) had given France a legitimate claim to the northern portion of La Florida. To strengthen that claim, Cartier actually attempted to establish a colony at Montreal in 1541.[37] These claims, coupled with internal disputes in France brought on by the Reformation and an international crisis that saw Austrian and Spanish forces encircling France, set the stage for heightened French involvement in North America.

To a large degree, French efforts to colonize parts of America stemmed from the efforts of one man, Gaspard de Coligny, Admiral of France and Seigneur de Châtillon.[38] Coligny was a sincere patriot and a devout Protestant, a Huguenot, who viewed colonization as a means to avoid fratricide at home, lift French morale, and improve the nation's economy. To these ends, he was supported by Catherine de Médicis, regent in the name of her twelve-year-old son, Charles IX.

Coligny had attempted to establish a colony in Brazil in 1555, but it ended in failure. By 1561, the year of Luna's demise in Florida, Coligny was anxious to try to establish another

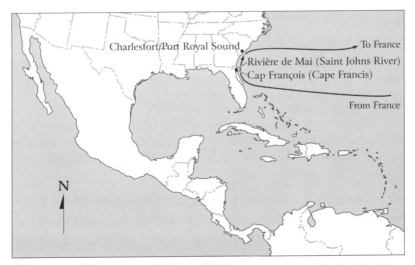

Figure 57. The route of Jean Ribault and René de Goulaine de Laudonnière, 1562.

colony. He chose Jean Ribault to be his commander. Second in command was René de Goulaine de Laudonnière, a geographer, mariner, and the man destiny had selected to establish a French settlement, in 1564, in what is today Florida.[39] Approximately 150 volunteers signed on; most of them were Protestants, but some were Catholics. Two were Spaniards and one was an Englishman.

The fleet of five ships sailed from Le Havre-de-Grâce, a port located on the Atlantic coast of France, on February 18, 1562, and followed a long, circuitous route across the Atlantic, carefully planned to avoid Spanish shipping lanes and territories under Spanish control. Land was first sighted on April 30, 1562, along the coast of what is today Florida at approximately 30° N latitude. It was at this point, where today Saint Augustine Inlet provides access from the Atlantic Ocean to the city of Saint Augustine, that Ribault assigned the first French placename to modern Florida, that being Cap François in honor of François II who had died in 1560. This name, which disappeared from maps after 1565, was restored in March 1985 by the United States Board on Geographic Names.[40]

Decision List 8501 of the US Board on Geographic Names reads:

> Cape Francis: *point of land, on N end of Conch Island, at S entrance to Saint Augustine Inlet 3.2 km [2 mi] ENE of Saint Augustine; named Cap François by the French explorer Jean Ribault on April 30, 1562; St. Johns Co., Fla.; 29⁰54' 30" N, 81⁰17' 00" W. Not: Cap François.*

Ribault did not elect to settle at the present site of Saint Augustine because the water behind the barrier island was too shallow. Instead, he sailed northward and, on May 1, 1562, his flotilla entered a large river which he named the Rivière de Mai (River of May; now the Saint Johns River). On May 2, 1562, on a bluff overlooking the River of May, Jean Ribault erected a stone monument to mark the French claim. Mayport, the United States Naval Station at the mouth of the Saint Johns River, is a lasting

Figure 58. The restored Ribault Monument at Fort Caroline, Florida. (Photograph by R. H. Fuson)

memorial to the French name.

Although pleased with the friendly nature of the Indians and the natural setting of the River of May, the French continued their sail northward. There may have been a desire to stay clear of the Spanish territory, even if it was unoccupied or if the Spanish claims were of questionable validity. Beginning with the Saint Mary's River, which Ribault called the Seine, every large river that they passed was named. By sheer coincidence, they found what the Spanish had called, since 1524, the Punta de Santa Elena, and on May 17 they entered and named Port Royal Sound, an estuary which still bears that name. On Port Royal Island, just north of what is now the United States Marine Corps Base, Ribault planted his colony and named it Charlesfort in honor of the young king, Charles IX. Located three or four miles west of today's Beaufort, South Carolina, this colony was the first French settlement in what is now the United States and the first Protestant colony in North America. On May 22, 1562, the French erected another stone monument, across the Libourne (now Broad) River from Charlesfort. This column marked the northern extent of Ribault's claim and was probably placed on Libourne Island (now Lemon Island). As an aside, the monument was later removed by the Spanish, as was the one on the banks of the River of May, but a replica of the column was erected by local citizens in 1925 to mark the site. Unfortunately, it was placed on the wrong side of the river in the middle of Fort San Marcos, a Spanish installation that existed from 1577 to 1587, a mile or so south of Charlesfort. And, to add insult to injury, Ribault's name was misspelled on the monument!

Charlesfort failed. There was internal dissention in the colony after Ribault and de Laudonnière sailed back to France on June 11, 1562, to seek additional colonists. Ribault had left thirty volunteers at Charlesfort. One of these was hanged by

Figure 59. The recreated Ribault Monument at Parris Island, South Carolina. The monument was erroneously placed atop the ruins of the Spanish site of Santa Elena and the inscription contains a misspelling of Ribault's name. (Official USMC photograph)

the commandant. The latter, in turn, was killed by a soldier. Two men drowned. One fifteen-year-old boy stayed behind with the Indians while twenty-five sailed for France in a home-made boat. The English rescued the pitiful survivors before they reached France, but only a few lived to tell of this voyage — including the fact that some of them had turned to cannibalism.

Perhaps the biggest problem facing the Charlesfort colony, however, was one that the Spaniards had faced time after time — the settlers had not established an agricultural base for their survival. Of all the explorers since Columbus, only Juan Ponce de León seems to have really understood the necessity of producing food before a colony could become self sufficient.

Ribault and de Laudonnière landed in Dieppe on July 20, in the midst of a civil war between Catholics and Protestants;

206

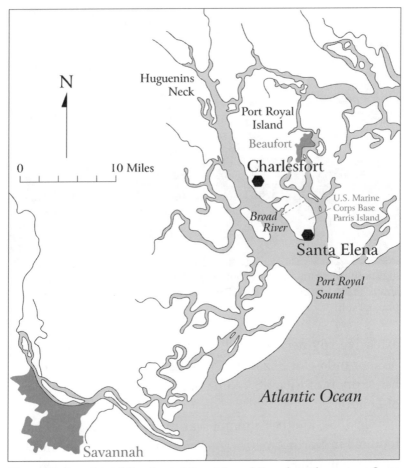

Figure 60. Location of the aborted Spanish and French settlements at Santa Elena and Charlesfort, respectively, along what are now the Broad River and Port Royal Sound, South Carolina.

under such circumstances the country was not able to resupply or reinforce the colony. The Protestants surrendered on October 20, 1562, and though de Laudonnière remained in France, Ribault fled to England. While there, he wrote a book about his adventures that was published in English in May 1563.[41] For a while it looked as if Ribault was going to lead a joint French-English expedition to America, but Felipe II of Spain had an

207

Figure 61. The Santa Elena Monument is on the officer's golf course at the United States Marine Corps Base, Parris Island, South Carolina. (Official USMC photograph)

extensive spy network in England and he was, after all, the brother-in-law of Elizabeth I.[42] Elizabeth eventually withdrew her support of Ribault, and he became her guest in the Tower of London.

In 1564, another attempt was made to establish a French foothold in North America. As before, Coligny was the mastermind behind the expedition; he chose de Laudonnière to lead the second attempt.[43] Once again, the fleet sailed from Le Havre-de-Grâce. Three ships departed on April 22, 1564, carrying 120 soldiers, 110 sailors, and approximately seventy colonists. There were a few women and fifty Moors, but not one single farmer.

It took two months for the ships to reach Florida, after a long journey that stopped briefly in the Canary Islands and Dominica, where one man was lost to the Caribs. The ships had also passed dangerously close to a number of Spanish-controlled islands in the Caribbean. On June 22, de Laudonnière and his entourage reached Cap François and named the lagoon there the Rivière des Dauphins (River of Dolphins; now the Matanzas River). This was the second time that a French name was applied to the area where the Spanish colony of Saint Augustine soon would be established. They visited the River of May on June 24 and sailed part of the route to Charlesfort before turning around and returning to the River of May on June 29. A site about five miles up-river was selected for the new colony.

The French established their settlement and fort of La Caroline, named in honor of Charles IX, on the south side of the River of May. La Caroline almost suffered the same fate as Charlesfort — voluntary abandonment — and for many of the same reasons. As with Charlesfort and the Spanish antecedents in Florida, these colonists, too, had failed to establish an agricultural base and too many demands had been made on the Indians for food. Besides hunger — greed, laziness, and internal dissention were also factors. Even though the colony was established and de Laudonnière had sent two ships back to France for fresh supplies and another 500 colonists, there was turmoil. In November and December 1564, there was a major

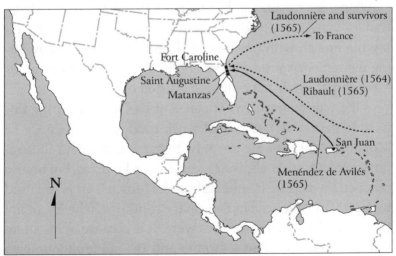

Figure 62. The routes of de Laudonnière in 1564 and Ribault and Pedro Menéndez de Avilés in 1565.

Figure 63. The fort at La Caroline, Florida, was erected by French colonists in 1564. Although the exact location of the original fort is not known, a one-third scale model of the structure was built at Fort Caroline National Memorial in 1964. This replica flies the blue and gold *fleur-de-lis*, a symbol of the kings of France during the sixteenth century. (Courtesy Fort Caroline National Memorial, National Park Service)

desertion and a serious mutiny. While those who were still at La Caroline waited for relief, the colony was visited by John Hawkins, one of England's leading navigators — and slave-traders. Hawkins stayed for three days in August 1565, providing the French with much-needed provisions and clearly lifting the settlers' spirits. He even offered to give them one of his three ships, but de Laudonnière insisted on trading for it.

If anything positive happened at La Caroline during this terrible period, it was the art work produced by Jacques Le Moyne de Morgues. He not only prepared meticulous illustrations of plants, animals, water features, and Indians, but he also mapped towns, coasts, and harbors. Le Moyne's art is still used to depict the American Indians of the southeast, whether or not they were Timucuans — as his were. It is because of his attention to detail that Fort Caroline and the stone monuments Ribault placed at the southern and northern limits of his claim

Figure 64. Saint Johns Bluff, Florida, was settled as La Caroline in 1564 — one year before Saint Augustine. (Photograph by R. H. Fuson)

have been reconstructed with such a high level of accuracy.

While Le Moyne was painting and de Laudonnière was trying to manage the unmanageable, Ribault had been released from jail, had returned to France, and was putting together a new expedition to relieve the colony. On May 22, 1565, he sailed from Dieppe with seven ships and over 600 people, including some families with children.[44] Ribault reached La Caroline on August 28 — the same day that Pedro Menéndez de Avilés sighted Florida.

The Spaniards were determined to prevent French encroachment upon territory that they had discovered and claimed, and in which they had invested so much time, money, and human life. Further, the Spaniards did not want a base for French pirates so close to their possessions to the south and to the Gulf Stream, their primary shipping lane to Europe. Last,

Figure 65. Jacques Le Moyne's sketch of the little French fort at La Caroline on the south side of the River of May. The detailed graphic renderings of Le Moyne prepared while he lived at La Caroline in 1564 and 1565 are important sources of information about the land and people of northern Florida in the middle part of the sixteenth century. (Courtesy Fort Caroline National Memorial, National Park Service)

the Spaniards had absolutely no tolerance for a "heretic camp" of Protestants in their midst; in their eyes, there was only one true religion, the Catholic religion, and defending it was God's will. The French, on the other hand, viewed the east coast of what is now the United States and Canada as a wilderness uninhabited by Europeans and up for grabs. In fact, there was even a legal basis for this in the Treaty of Cateau Cambresis (1559), where America was considered to be a region where the strongest power would be recognized as the master.[45] Such an agreement produced the ironic situation where two powers could be at war in the New World and at peace in Europe. Yet another part of the mix was the growing power of the Reformation in France, where strange ideas such as "freedom of the seas" and the denial of any validity to earlier papal divisions of the earth were gaining in popularity.

Spain lost no time in responding to the French presence at La Caroline. Pedro Menéndez de Avilés departed Cádiz about a month after Ribault sailed from Dieppe, and Menéndez was being sent to Florida by Felipe II for one purpose — to eliminate La Caroline.[46] Although Menéndez claimed he sailed with 1504 people, the official count based on muster rolls indicated there was only a little over 1000.[47] After the fleet set sail on June 27, 1565, Menéndez said that the winds were contrary so he returned to port. It is widely believed that an additional 300 men were added to the passenger list during this one-night layover. On June 28, 1565, the ships departed once again.

Most of Menéndez's sailors came from the northern Spanish cities of Avilés (Menéndez's home), Gijón, and Santander. Almost all of his closest advisors and officers were fellow Asturians and many of them were relatives. The skills represented by the members of this expedition included almost every trade known in Spain at that time. Clearly this group was well-qualified to transfer European culture across the Atlantic. Even so, the logistics of the voyage were almost beyond credulity.

Menéndez had drawn up a plan that required certain elements of the expedition to rendezvous at specific locations and at specific times. This plan made no allowances for vagaries of weather or mechanical failure. Yet, when one considers the state of communications and technology in the sixteenth century, it was almost a certainty that something would go wrong.

Only eight ships departed from the Canary Islands on July 8, 1565 — but there should have been more. Of the eight ships that sailed, one started leaking severely and had to turn back. Another sank at Guadeloupe in a storm. A third was unable to reach San Juan, Puerto Rico, the last rendezvous point, because of the same storm. In fact, of the five ships that did reach San

Juan, the bad weather made it impossible to adhere to the original course: two ships eventually reached San Juan on August 8, and the other three arrived on August 13. About the only sun that shone on Menéndez while he was in Puerto Rico was his meeting the grandson of Juan Ponce de León — also named Juan Ponce de León — who was alcaide of the fortress and a wealthy and influential person. Juan Ponce assisted Menéndez then and later.

The Spanish fleet that sailed for Florida from San Juan on August 15, 1565, consisted of five vessels and about 600 men. The Ribault expedition, unaware that Menéndez was almost on top of them, had sighted Florida on the preceding day. If Ribault had not been delayed at the outset of his voyage by a storm and had not sailed so leisurely through the West Indies, he might have had time to prepare for a Spanish attack — one that he knew was inevitable.

Menéndez arrived at the River of May on September 4, but would not enter the river for fear of entrapment. The French,

Figure 66. The Saint Johns River, Florida, looking eastward over one of the cannons of Fort Caroline. (Photograph by R. H. Fuson)

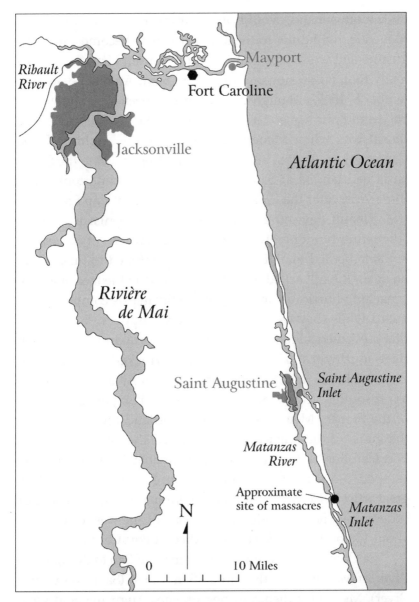

Figure 67. Fort Caroline, Saint Augustine, and Matanzas — places where France and Spain collided on the Atlantic coast of northern Florida in 1565. Menéndez's slaughter of French forces at Matanzas and rout of the colonists at Fort Caroline secured this part of the Atlantic coast of North America for Spain for more than two centuries.

on the other hand, would not venture from their sanctuary. Menéndez withdrew to the site that was to become Saint Augustine and waited for addtional forces from Havana. He formally took possession of Florida and Saint Augustine on September 8, 1565, although the harbor had been seen a few days before and was named San Augustín in honor of the saint whose day it was when Menéndez first came into sight of Cape Canaveral on August 28. This marked the first time the Spaniards had landed at Saint Augustine; the landing took place three years after the French had named nearby Cap François.

Ribault devised a plan to attack the Spaniards at Saint Augustine, but it involved stripping La Caroline of almost every able-bodied man. De Laudonnière objected to this, but to no avail. Ribault sailed to Saint Augustine in the face of an approaching hurricane and caught the Spaniards completely off guard while they were unloading their supplies. But the low tide prevented a French attack, and the storm drove the French fleet southward. Three ships were wrecked near modern Daytona Beach, and the one carrying Jean Ribault was blown as far south as Cape Canaveral. Upon realizing the misfortune of the French, Menéndez marched overland for four days in the midst of the hurricane and attacked the lightly defended Fort Caroline on the morning of September 20. Though a few escaped — including de Laudonnière, Ribault's son, and the great artist Le Moyne — and some were spared when Menéndez ordered that no one under fifteen years of age was to be killed, about 150 of the French colonists died at Fort Caroline.

La Caroline was immediately renamed San Mateo and the River of May became the Rio de San Mateo (Saint Matthew's River). Menéndez then returned to Saint Augustine and went south along the beach for about fifteen miles. At this location, on September 29, Menéndez encountered the survivors of three of the wrecked French ships. After they surrendered and were

Figure 68. Matanzas, Florida. The name Matanzas, meaning "slaughters" in Spanish, has been given to the beach and the lagoon behind it. The French called this lagoon the River of Dolphins. (Photograph by R. H. Fuson)

bound, each one was run through systematically with a lance. Two weeks later, on October 12, Ribault's crew was ambushed in the same place and all were killed, one by one, after they had surrendered and agreed to Menéndez's terms. The location of this savagery became known as Matanzas, the Spanish word for "slaughters." Later, the peaceful lagoon that the French once had called the River of Dolphins became the Matanzas River, a fitting name truly born in violence.

Although the French did avenge the massacre at Fort Caroline when Dominique de Gourgues destroyed San Mateo and its garrison in 1568, the Spaniards immediately reoccupied San Mateo and remained there throughout the colonial period. La Caroline, therefore, marked the beginning of the first permanent European occupation of the territory that now includes Canada and the United States. It was one year older than Saint Augustine, forty-four years older than Québec, and forty-five years older than Jamestown.

Jean Ribault died on a lonely Florida beach at the age of forty-five. René de Goulaine de Laudonnière, who escaped the massacre and returned to France, died at the same age in 1574. Ironically, Pedro Menéndez de Avilés died in Spain the same year as de Laudonnière, at the age of fifty-five.

~

The political control of Florida by Spain was, by 1565, a *fait accompli*, although it is not likely that Juan Ponce de León would have approved of the manner in which his country finally established itself on the peninsula he discovered and sought to settle and govern. He certainly never imagined the blood that would flow near the place where he first stepped ashore so many years before. In retrospect, it had taken more than half a century for Spain to gain its first permanent foothold in what was to become the continental United States, and Spain accomplished that by forceably taking a colony that had been founded by a European rival. But the native population had not been conquered or Christianized, and neither the French nor the English were going to go away. In a way, the conquest of Florida began with the arrival and success of Pedro Menéndez de Avilés. Perhaps that is why so many books about Florida's history begin with Menéndez, Saint Augustine, and the year 1565.

Epilogue

The young Juan Ponce de León, fresh from the Moorish wars, sailed to the New World from Cádiz, Castilla, in 1493, and died in that New World in 1521. In the eighteen-year period from 1503 to 1521, he had a major impact on the course of events in three places: today's Dominican Republic, Puerto Rico, and Florida. Juan Ponce accomplished many things in the New World, and he failed attempting others. Unfortunately, history and historians have tended to slight his accomplishments and emphasize his failures — and all too strongly to associate him with a myth that was not even of his own making. Juan Ponce lives on as a participant in the history of the Dominican Republic and Puerto Rico, but he has all but disappeared from Florida history. For most, Florida's written history begins with the founding of Saint Augustine in 1565, an event that took place more than fifty years after Juan Ponce de León became the first European to officially set foot on Florida soil.

In retrospect, the historical record reveals that Juan Ponce de León was an unusual man for his time. He was a man whose ambitions followed paths different from many of his contemporaries, yet they led him to personal, social, political, and financial success – achievements made all the more noteworthy when one considers the distractions and pitfalls that existed during this turbulent period of history. A review of the accomplishments of Ponce de León suggests the following:

Juan Ponce first came to what is now the Dominican Re-

Table 5. The Voyages and Discoveries of Juan Ponce de León, 1493–1521.

Date	From	To	Purpose
1493	Cádiz	La Navidad	To accompany Columbus on the Second Voyage of Discovery
1494	Isabela	Cádiz	Disenchantment with Española (?)
1502	Sanlúcar de Barrameda	Santo Domingo	To accompany Fray Don Nicolás de Ovando
1506	Salvaleón	Aguada	First reconnaissance of Puerto Rico
1507	Aguada	Salvaleón	Return from Puerto Rico
1508	Salvaleón	Caparra	Official colonization of Puerto Rico
1513	San Germán	Florida	First official voyage to Florida
1513	Florida	San Juan	Return from Florida
1514	San Juan	Castilla (Bayona)	To protest treatment of Indians and other activities of Diego Columbus
1515	Sanlúcar de Barrameda	San Juan	Return from Castilla with privileges, titles, and armada
1516	San Juan	Sanlúcar de Barrameda	To protect rights and privileges after death of Ferdinand, and to return armada
1518	Sanlúcar de Barrameda	San Juan	Return from Spain
1521	San Juan	Florida	Second voyage to Florida
1521	Florida	Havana	Withdrawal from Florida following attack by Indians; died July 1521

public with Christopher Columbus's Second Voyage of Discovery late in December 1493. Strong circumstantial evidence indicates that he returned to Castilla, probably in 1494 or 1495, but came back to Española in 1502 with the colony's newly appointed Governor Ovando. Ovando found Juan Ponce to be a loyal and trustworthy subject. By 1504 Juan Ponce was commander of the Santo Domingo troops that were sent into Higüey Province in eastern Española to pacify the Taino Indians. As a reward for his service he was given a land grant of at least 225 acres and named provincial governor of Higüey. The next year (1505), Juan Ponce was given permission to establish a town (the sixteenth on Española), which he named Salvaleón after his grandmother's estate in Castilla. Here he built a solid stone house, married a Castilian girl, raised a family, and became a successful farmer.

At Salvaleón, Juan Ponce became a very successful farmer and rancher, he proved to be a just and compassionate governor, and he held the respect of both the Indians and the Castilians. When he asked for the governor's approval to explore the Island of San Juan Bautista, Governor Ovando gave such permission quickly. Juan Ponce probably made his first exploratory visit to San Juan Bautista in 1506.

Juan Ponce de León was with Christopher Columbus and others when San Juan Bautista was discovered by Europeans on November 18, 1493. There is strong evidence that Juan Ponce began the conquest and colonization of San Juan Bautista on June 24, 1506, at the same place on the northwestern part of the island he visited with Columbus in 1493. Although this was an unofficial exploration — one off-the-record but approved by Ferdinand and Ovando — it marks the beginning of the Europeanization of San Juan Bautista. The official colonization of San Juan Bautista commenced on August 12, 1508. The first permanent European settlement was established at a site visited by Juan Ponce in 1506 and later named Caparra.

When Diego Columbus arrived in Santo Domingo as interim viceroy in 1509, Juan Ponce found him to be less supportive than were Ferdinand and Ovando. There was a period, however, when Juan Ponce was Diego Columbus's deputy, and this made him the virtual governor of San Juan Bautista. He was also appointed interim governor of San Juan Bautista by Ferdinand. Although he was an excellent governor and a successful farmer on San Juan Bautista, neither Governor Ovando nor King Ferdinand could protect him any longer from his differences with Diego Columbus — at least while he was in San Juan Bautista. The king indirectly suggested that Juan Ponce consider searching for new lands, a recommendation he followed in 1513 with his first voyage to Bimini — Florida.

When Juan Ponce returned to San Juan Bautista from Florida in 1513 he was confronted by a number of problems. First, while he was away, Carib Indians — probably from the Virgin Islands — had attacked Caparra and burned most of the settlement, including the stone house Juan Ponce had erected for himself, his wife, and their four children. Second, Diego Columbus had come to San Juan Bautista and suggested moving all of the Castilians in Caparra to San Germán. Third, Diego Columbus had allowed his underlings to attack any Indians, including Tainos, people who had nothing to do with the attack on Caparra. Juan Ponce saw this as a means of taking more Taino land and more slaves to work it. Perhaps if Juan Ponce had seized land from the Tainos, established more settlements in San Juan Bautista, and spent more time seeking gold, his stature in the eyes of Diego Columbus might have been enhanced. But he viewed protection of the Tainos and farming to be accomplishments, not failures. His only solution was to take his complaints directly to Ferdinand, a dangerous initiative which no conquistador had ever done before.

Epilogue

Juan Ponce went to Castilla in the spring of 1514. He was knighted by the king, becoming Don Juan Ponce de León, and he was given a personal coat-of-arms. No other conquistador had ever received these honors before. Juan Ponce also won other concessions from Ferdinand — he was: awarded a contract for a second voyage of exploration to Florida and Bimini, named governor and chief justice of Florida, named captain of the armada to subdue the Caribs, named captain-general of San Juan Bautista for life, named a perpetual member of the city council of what became the city of San Juan, named captain of the Regiment of San Juan Bautista, reimbursed for past expenses, and given an annual salary of 50,000 maravedis. The most ambitious of these awards were the contract to explore and settle Florida and the commission to subdue the Caribs. Juan Ponce spent nearly twelve months in 1515 and 1516 calming the hostilities between Castilians and Caribs, and most of the year 1520 preparing for the second voyage to Florida.

Juan Ponce departed La Aguada, San Juan Bautista, on his first voyage to "the Islands of Benimy" on March 4, 1513. On April 2, 1513, the flotilla reached what everyone thought was a large island, and the next day the party went ashore; among them were the first black man and the first European woman ever to set foot on what is now the United States. This landing probably occurred along an uninhabited stretch of coast just north of today's Daytona Beach.

Juan Ponce and his people sailed south along the Atlantic coast of Florida, naming capes, rivers, and islands. During this southerly cruise, Juan Ponce and his pilot, Antón de Alaminos, discovered the Gulf Stream, a discovery that seems to have gone unnoticed by most historians. This was, however, probably the single most important accomplishment of the voyage because the Gulf Stream became the oceanic highway from America to Europe and remained such until the middle of the nineteenth century. Before the discovery of the Gulf Stream in 1513, Castilian vessels sailing for Europe typically sought the westerly winds that blew steadily across the Atlantic Ocean somewhere between 25° N latitude and 40° N latitude, depending upon the season. East of the Bahamas a ship might have to struggle to find the westerlies, and there was an ever-present danger of being becalmed — stranded when the winds were not blowing. Fortunately for the Castilians, there was no serious European competition for the sea lanes in the late fifteenth and very early sixteenth centuries. In fact, until the discovery of the great wealth of Mexico (gold and silver) after 1519 there was not even much concern about European pirates. Not long after the discovery that, unlike the wandering and unreliable westerly winds, the Gulf Stream provided a permanently flowing current to Europe, Antón de Alaminos found that the great ocean current not only passed between Florida and the Bahamas, but also between Cuba and Florida. This made Havana, Cuba, the most important commercial city in the West Indies. Once ships from Havana started to travel the Gulf Stream to Europe, the Atlantic coast of Florida became more strategically important to Spain and this became one of the reasons why Saint Augustine, Florida, was later established.

After Juan Ponce's fleet discovered the Gulf Stream, the little fleet continued south past Miami Beach (named Chequescá) and Biscayne Bay (described but not named), then west along the Florida Keys (called Los Mártires). At some point, perhaps near Key West, Juan Ponce turned north and sailed to the barrier islands near present-day Fort Myers on Florida's Gulf coast. At an island Juan Ponce called Matanza (Slaughter), which may have been modern Pine Island, the Europeans and Indians had a major battle — a fight that might have prevented the establishment of a colony in Florida at that time.

From the barrier islands the fleet went south to the Dry

Tortugas (named Las Tortugas). In terms of age, Tortuga is second only to Florida among place-names of European origin in the United States. From there, via Cuba, the Florida Keys, and the Bahamas, Juan Ponce went home. He did, however, leave his best ship and his best pilot, with the necessary crew, to look for Bimini and the magic fountain. This occurred on day 208 of a 230-day sail. Bimini (Benimy) was not mentioned until day 144, with no mention of the magic Fountain of Bimini. There is no evidence that Juan Ponce made any serious effort to locate the Fountain of Youth — he certainly did not make any overland marches to Florida's numerous artesian springs.

Juan Ponce's second voyage to Florida, this in 1521, fell short of its goals in all respects. Despite a number of accomplishments, essentially all from the first voyage in 1513, there were two glaring failures on both Florida voyages. First, no colony was founded, and second, the question of whether Florida was an island or a peninsula was not resolved. A third failure, as far as Ferdinand was concerned, was Juan Ponce's inability to locate the magic fountain. Unfortunately, Juan Ponce's greatest personal loss came during the first week in July 1521: he died at the age of forty-seven, probably from an infection in his thigh, brought on by a Caloosa arrow.

So, what of the legacy of Juan Ponce de León? What record of his presence endures, and what lasting effects, if any, have come from his ambitious undertakings? What can every citizen of the Dominican Republic, Puerto Rico, or Florida share with Ponce de León?

Santo Domingo, capital of the Dominican Republic on the island of Hispaniola (Española), is the oldest European city in the New World. It was founded on August 4, 1494, by Bartholomew Columbus shortly after the first European town, Isabela (1493), failed. Almost everyone who was anyone in the Spanish colonial world of the late fifteenth and early sixteenth centuries lived in or passed through Santo Domingo at one time or another. Today, there are statues, plaques, monuments, buildings, parks, and streets throughout this city named for the heroes of the last half-millennium, including even George Washington. But there is nothing of significance dedicated to Don Juan Ponce de León in the city where he once lived and whose soldiers he once commanded.

Juan Ponce is, however, mentioned in Dominican history books, and about eighty-five miles east of Santo Domingo one may find the house he built in 1505 in the province he governed (then Higüey; now La Altagracia). The house, standing on the estate Juan Ponce called Salvaleón, was once the administrative headquarters for the entire eastern part of Española and was part of the sixteenth town founded by Castilians in the New World. The modern town is called San Rafael del Yuma. It was from here that the exploration and settlement of San Juan Bautista began. Also, the first voyage to Florida was largely a product of Salvaleón and San Rafael del Yuma. Most of the food and provisions, two of the three ships, and many of the participants came from there. Salvaleón also prospered while providing basic foodstuffs for east-bound Castilian ships heading back to home ports on the coast of Iberia.

The shadow of Juan Ponce is ever-present in modern Puerto Rico. The site where Columbus's party first made landfall in 1493 is indicated on most maps. Juan Ponce's tomb, within the Cathedral of San Juan, is a historic national icon. Juan Ponce's remains were moved to the present location in 1909. From 1521 until 1559, Juan Ponce lay at rest in Havana, Cuba, but in 1559 his remains were moved to the church of Saint Thomas Aquinas (now San José) in San Juan. A large statue of Juan Ponce stands in the plaza facing the church of San José.

The first capital of San Juan Bautista, Caparra, now lies within the metropolitan area of San Juan, about ten miles south

Figure 69. A statue of Juan Ponce in the Plaza de San José, San Juan, Puerto Rico. (Courtesy San Juan National Historic Site, National Park Service)

of Old San Juan. Here one may see the ruins of Juan Ponce's house and the location of the first church in the Western Hemisphere. There is a small museum that contains artifacts from the site.

A principal street in San Juan is the Avenida Ponce de León, which runs from Columbus Park in Old San Juan to the University of Puerto Rico in the new city. Many imposing governmental buildings line this broad avenue, including the Capitol.

Puerto Rico's second largest metropolitan area — Ponce — was named for the first governor. Despite the fact that it is a

Figure 70. Casa Blanca, San Juan, Puerto Rico. Casa Blanca was the fortified residence of the Ponce de León family for 250 years. Juan Ponce died two years before the house was completed. (Photograph by George Barford)

relatively new city by Spanish colonial standards, founded in 1670, Ponce is the largest city on Puerto Rico's Caribbean (south) coast.

Juan Ponce de León's legacy in Florida has always had to compete with that of Pedro Menéndez de Avilés and the settlement he founded — Saint Augustine. It is ironic that the one place in Florida that most strongly touts the legacy of Juan Ponce de León — Saint Augustine — occupies a site he never visited and perpetuates a myth at the expense of historical fact. Indeed, when viewed from a different perspective, the popular history of Saint Augustine has absorbed bits and pieces of a past that really belonged to Juan Ponce and to other places. The material expression of Saint Augustine's affinity with Juan Ponce does perpetuate memory of the man, however, and does so in the forms of a statue, a park, a purported landing place, a stone cross, the Ponce de León Golf and Conference Center, and the Fountain of Youth — all in a place Juan Ponce never saw.

228

Figure 71. The entrance to the Fountain of Youth, Saint Augustine, Florida. This tourist attraction is based upon the myth that Juan Ponce actually landed at Saint Augustine and there discovered the Fountain of Youth. (Photograph by R. H. Fuson)

Figure 72. The Fountain of Youth in Saint Augustine, Florida — a place that Juan Ponce never visited. (Photograph by R. H. Fuson)

Figure 73. A statue of Juan Ponce in Saint Augustine, Florida. (Photograph by R. H. Fuson)

In stark and unfortunate contrast, there are virtually no historical markers within the state of Florida that identify or suggest places actually visited by Juan Ponce in either 1513 or 1521, or that commemorate his discovering and attempting to bring about the European colonization of the state. This is part of the legacy of Juan Ponce de León for which recognition is long overdue, and it needs to be addressed by appropriate public or private entities.

The state capital, Tallahassee, is situated in the only one of Florida's sixty-seven counties that is named for Juan Ponce, but that county — Leon — is incorrectly named. Either Ponce or Ponce de León would be an accurate name, but not simply Leon.

Only the state can solve this problem.

There is a small town in Holmes County named Ponce de Leon, and in Volusia County there is De Leon Springs and Ponce Inlet. There are two important bodies of water named for Juan Ponce: Ponce de Leon Inlet in Volusia County and Ponce de Leon Bay in Monroe County. Additionally, there is a variety of streets, subdivisions, motels, and businesses that display all or part of the name Juan Ponce de León.

Perhaps the most unfortunate legacy is the one concerning the Fountain of Youth and the true motivations for both of Juan Ponce's voyages from Puerto Rico to Florida. Juan Ponce is best remembered for something he did not find — a magic fountain, the pursuit of which was not even his idea — while all but forgotten are his important discoveries. The historical documents are clear that Ponce de León undertook the voyages to Florida at the suggestion of King Ferdinand and that the voyages were first and foremost to expolore for new lands, to determine what resources they might yield, and to colonize those lands for the benefit of Castilla. Juan Ponce's voyages were not motivated by the magical fountain. The idea that a magical fountain might exist in Bimini, or Florida, originated among the Taino (Lucayo) Indians encountered by Columbus in the Bahamas in 1492, and this information was communicated to Juan Ponce by King Ferdinand so that the explorer might be alert to the possibility of finding such a fountain, among other resources, in the lands he was about to visit. Truly important, however, were Juan Ponce's discovery of the Gulf Stream, his being the first European documented to have seen and set foot upon the land that became the state of Florida, and his assigning the name to that part of the continent that is still in use today.

Appendix I

Principal Chroniclers of Fifteenth- and Sixteenth-Century Spanish America

FERDINAND COLUMBUS

Period Covered: 1451 – 1506

Document: *The Life of the Admiral Christopher Columbus*

Significance: Compiled documents and first person accounts of his father, Christopher Columbus, who explored much of early Spanish America.

BARTOLOMÉ DE LAS CASAS

Period Covered: 1492 – 1528

Documents: *Diario de Colón; Historia de las indias*

Significance: Came to the Americas in 1502; knew the Columbus family well and had access to all of the Columbus papers from 1492 – 1528 and participated in many New World events between 1502 and 1514.

GONZALO FERNÁNDEZ DE OVIEDO Y VALDÉS

Period Covered: 1492 – 1548

Document: *Historia general y natural de las indias*

Significance: Came to the Americas in 1514; knew Juan Ponce well.

MARTÍN FERNÁNDEZ DE NAVARRETE

Period Covered: 1492 – 1565

Documents: *Colección de los viages y descubrimientos; Viajes de Cristóbal Colón*

Significance: Compiler of many important documents of colonial activity during the fifteenth and sixteenth centuries.

ANTONIO DE HERRERA Y TORDESILLAS
Period Covered: 1492 – 1565
Document: *Historia general*
Significance: Chief historian to Felipe II and Felipe III of Spain; had access to all official documents of Spain and compiled accounts of Spanish colonial activities, including voyages of Juan Ponce.

PETER MARTYR D'ANGHIERA
Period Covered: 1511 – 1530
Document: *De Orbe Novo*
Significance: Member of the Council of the Indies; published first map of Florida in 1511.

GARCILASO DE LA VEGA
Period Covered: 1513 – 1568
Document: *The Florida of the Inca*
Significance: Compiler of accounts of de Soto's expedition to Florida in 1539.

BERNAL DÍAZ DEL CASTILLO
Period Covered: 1514 – 1521
Document: *The Discovery and Conquest of Mexico*
Significance: Included account of visit to first landing site of Juan Ponce in western Florida.

HERNÁN CORTÉS
Period Covered: 1519 – 1526
Documents: Five letters
Significance: Conqueror of Mexico; one letter includes reference to one of Juan Ponce's ships that sailed to Veracruz in 1521.

ÁLVAR NÚÑEZ CABEZA DE VACA
Period Covered: 1528 – 1536
Document: *Relation of Álvar Núñez Cabeza de Vaca*
Significance: Accompanied the Narváez expedition to Florida in 1528.

TRISTÁN DE LUNA Y ARELLANO
Period Covered: 1530 – 1561
Document: *The Luna Papers* (compiled by Herbert Ingram Priestley)
Significance: Participated in Coronado expedition 1539 – 1541; attempted to establish colony at what is now Pensacola, Florida, in 1559.

RENÉ DE GOULAINE DE LAUDONNIÈRE

Period Covered: 1562 – 1565

Document: *Three Voyages*

Significance: Established first French colony in Florida at Fort Caroline in 1564.

Appendix II

Political and Administrative Organization of the Colonies in Spanish America, 1474–1565

THE CROWN (King and Queen; King; Queen; Regent)

The king, queen, or regent was the head of state for Castilla and Spain during the period of concern here. The reigning monarchs of Castilla and Spain from 1474 to 1565 were as follows:

CASTILLA

Ferdinand V and Isabela I (1474 – 1504)

Juana the Mad (Ferdinand and Isabela's daughter) (1504 – 1506)

Ferdinand V (Regent) (1504 – 1506)

Felipe I (Juana's husband; died three weeks after becoming king) (1506)

Ferdinand V (married Germaine de Foix in 1507, but she did not become queen) (1507 – 1516)

SPAIN

Carlos I (in 1519 became Charles V, Emperor of the Holy Roman Empire) (1516 – 1556)

Felipe II (1556 – 1598)

VICEROY

The viceroy in Spanish colonial days was an "assistant king" and enjoyed a life style not unlike that found in the royal household of Spain. This included all of the pomp and circumstance — and even a palace — that went with the office.

Technically speaking, Christopher Columbus was the first Spanish viceroy in the New World. In the contracts with Isabela and Ferdinand (April 17 and 30, 1492), Columbus was named viceroy and governor-general of all the islands and mainland in the Ocean Sea. This was an appointment in perpetuity, so all of his heirs and successors were to enjoy these rights and privileges. Christopher Columbus reigned supreme in the West Indies for about three years; after 1495 his power became less and less. Following protracted litigation through which he claimed rights and privileges that had been granted to his father, Diego Columbus became the second viceroy in 1511 and held that office until his death in 1526.

In 1524, Spain created the *Consejo de las Indias* (Council of the Indies) which became the supreme executive, legislative, and judicial body of the colonial government. Generally speaking, the viceroy dealt directly with the Council, not with the Crown. In the sixteenth century the viceroyalty became a political division, governed by a viceroy. Excluding the title inherited by Diego Columbus, only four viceroyalties were established after Christopher Columbus; two were in the sixteenth century and two were in the eighteenth century. Of the sixteenth-century viceroyalties, the only one other than Diego Columbus's that concerns us is that of New Spain. The other sixteenth-century viceroyalty, Peru, is not pertinent to the subject at hand.

New Spain, established in 1535 with its capital in Mexico City, was very large. It originally included all of the territory from Panama, through Central America and Mexico, to San Francisco Bay; the American Southwest and eastward to where Saint Louis is today; all of the Gulf of Mexico littoral, including Florida; and the West Indies. The first viceroy of New Spain was Antonio de Mendoza.

AUDIENCIA

The viceroyalty was typically divided into *audiencias* (judicial districts). Each political unit called an *audiencia* contained an institution called an *audiencia*. This was, in effect, an appeals court, presided over by an *oidor* (judge). In Mexico City, however, the viceroy usually presided at court. Some of the *audiencias* predate the viceroyalties.

Some Important Sixteenth-century *Audiencias*	
1511 Santo Domingo	West Indies and Venezuela
1527 Mexico	Southeastern Mexico, Gulf of Mexico Coast, and Florida
1535 Panama	Panama
1543 Guatemala	Southern Mexico to Panama
1548 New Galicia	Northwestern Mexico and north-central Mexico

CAPTAIN-GENERAL

A captain-general was beneath a viceroy but, for all practical purposes, ruled a vast territory within the viceroyalty and was essentially independent of the viceroy. In a few cases — if he had been appointed by the Crown and reported directly to the king — the captain-general was equal to the viceroy; Ferdinand II used this method with Juan Ponce to bypass the viceregal authority of Diego Columbus. The political subdivision ruled by a captain-general was called a captaincy-general.

PRESIDENT

A president was on a par with a captain-general, but lacked the military authority of the latter. The president governed a subdivision of an audiencia called a *presidencia*. If military authority was required, it had to be requested from the viceroy.

GOVERNOR and ADELANTADO

Any chief executive of a territorial unit larger than a town or municipality could also be called *gobernador*, or governor. Typically the territory governed was a *presidencia* or a captaincy-general or a portion of one of these; sometimes it was called a province. A viceroy might also have been a governor-general. The term governor was usually used for the executive of a settled, or "pacified," region. If a frontier region, and especially if it were not under total control, the term *adelantado* was used. An *adelantado* was a governor, but he might also have been a captain-general.

Another person who could properly be called governor was a *corregidor*, the governor of a unit called a *corregimiento*. The territory governed could have been as large as a province, but it was usually a district within a province and might contain only one town of any consequence. In practice, the *corregidor* was the Crown's link to the local municipality.

LOCAL INSTITUTIONS

The municipal council was called the *cabildo* or *ayuntamiento* and was composed of *regidores* (councilmen or aldermen) elected by Iberian landowners. Collectively the members of a *cabildo* were known as the *regimiento*. The councilmen chose the *alcaldes* (judges) from the council's own ranks, and the judges selected one of their own to be *alcalde mayor* (chief judge). The judicial district of the *alcalde* was known as the *alcaldía*.

Every town had an *alguacil*. His function was typically law-related; he was a constable or bailiff, the closest thing the Spanish colonial world had to a sheriff. But he could be a jailer or a governor! At times the *alguacil* became a very important person in Spanish America. Typically the jailer or warden was called the *alcaide*, and he usually assisted the *alguacil*.

Endnotes

Chapter 1: 1474–1493
The Early Years and the Discovery of Puerto Rico

1. Turespaña, *Costa de la luz*, 15, 17.
2. *Ibid.*, 14–15.
3. *Encyclopaedia Britannica*, X:223.
4. Fuson, *Geography of Geography*, 34.
5. Tió, *Nuevas fuentes*, 537.
6. Gómez de Silva, *Etymological Dictionary*, 35, 539.
7. Fuson, *Legendary Islands*, 135.
8. Turespaña, *Costa de la luz*, 15.
9. Las Casas, *Historia*, 1:346.
10. Anderson, *Old Panama*, 67.
11. Thacher, *Columbus*, 3:96–113.
12. Las Casas, *Historia*, 1:331–345.
13. Fuson, *The Log*, 195.
14. Allen, ed. *North American Exploration*, 1:167.
15. Winsor, *Christopher Columbus*, 258.
16. Las Casas, *Historia*, 1:346.
17. Navarrete, *Viajes*, 255–275.
18. Morison, *Journals*, 211, 225.
19. *Ibid.*, 234.
20. Anderson, *Old Panama*, 67–68.
21. Morison, *Journals*, 229–245.
22. *Ibid.*, 209–228.
23. Friede and Keen, *Las Casas*, 67–69; Tió, *Nuevas fuentes*, 541; Las Casas, *Historia*, 1: 347. The rather informal way of choosing either the paternal surname or the maternal surname in fifteenth-century Castilla (and later Spain) makes it very difficult to trace a person's lineage. This was certainly

the case with Juan Ponce.

24. *Encyclopaedia Britannica*, VIII: 855.
25. *Ibid.*, II: 605; Winsor, *Christopher Columbus*, 481.
26. Columbus, *The Life of the Admiral*, 109.
27. Thacher, *Columbus*, 2: 244–245.
28. Columbus, *The Life of the Admiral*, 109.
29. Morison, *Journals*, 210.
30. Tió, *Nuevas fuentes*, 5, 182, 516, 521, 532–547.
31. *Ibid.*, 537; Devereux, *Juan Ponce*, 1–3.
32. Tió, *Nuevas fuentes*, 532–547.
33. Oviedo, *Historia*, 3:193–194.
34. *Colección de documentos inéditos*, 1:620.
35. Tió, *Nuevas fuentes*, 183.
36. Devereux, *Juan Ponce*, 4–5.
37. *Ibid.*, 5.
38. Fuson, *Legendary Islands*, 115.
39. Phillips, *Life at Sea*, 4.
40. *Ibid.*, 6–25.
41. Columbus, *The Life of the Admiral*, 110.
42. *Ibid.*, 111–116.
43. *Ibid.*, 116.
44. Morison, *Journals*, 212–213.
45. Columbus, *The Life of the Admiral*, 117.
46. *Ibid.*
47. *Ibid.*

Chapter 2: 1493–1511
Peón, Conquistador, Explorer, Governor

1. Columbus, *The Life of the Admiral*, 119.
2. Fuson, *The Log*, 150–151.
3. *Ibid.*, 161.
4. Columbus, *The Life of the Admiral*, 121.
5. Morison, *Journals*, 242; Thacher, *Columbus*, 2:257, 282.
6. Columbus, *The Life of the Admiral*, 122.
7. Morison, *Journals*, 244, 229–251; Winsor, *Christopher Columbus*, 280.
8. Ballesteros, *La idea colonial*, 32.
9. Oviedo, *Historia*, 3:191.
10. Las Casas, *Historia*, 1:366, 409.
11. Navarrete, *Viajes*, 255.

12. Thacher, *Columbus*, 2:297–308. The English version of the *De Torres Memorandum* may be found in Thacher; the Spanish version, in Navarrete (*Viajes*, 255–275).

13. *Ibid.*

14. Las Casas, *Historia*, 1:405.

15. Columbus, *The Life of the Admiral*, 222.

16. *Ibid.*, 224–226.

17. Las Casas, *Historia*, 2:214.

18. Friede and Keen, *Las Casas*, 69.

19. Las Casas, *Historia*, 2:215.

20. *Ibid.*, 2:223–224; Columbus, *The Life of the Admiral*, 228–229.

21. Columbus, *The Life of the Admiral*, 228.

22. Las Casas, *Historia*, 2:230.

23. *Ibid.*, 231.

24. Varner and Varner, *Dogs of the Conquest*, 23, 36, 46. Dogs played a major role in the Conquest and the Castilians were using them at least as early as 1493. Ponce de León had a large dog named Becerrillo ("little bull") that was a vicious attack dog. A puppy sired by Becerrillo was given to Vasco Núñez de Balboa. This animal, named Leoncico ("little lion"), is mentioned in many accounts for his ferocity and was with Balboa when he crossed the Isthmus of Panama and discovered the South Sea (Pacific Ocean).

25. Las Casas, *Historia*, 2:258.

26. *Ibid.*, 269.

27. *Ibid.*, 355.

28. Van Middeldyk, *The History of Puerto Rico*, 92.

29. Oviedo, *Historia*, 2:166–176.

30. Fuson, "Land Tenure in Central Panama," 164.

31. *Colección de documentos inéditos*, 1:260.

32. Las Casas, *Historia*, 2:270.

33. *Colección de documentos inéditos*, 1:260; Tió, *Nuevas fuentes*, 542.

34. Tió, *Nuevas fuentes*, 542.

35. Biesanz and Biesanz, *The People of Panama*, 33.

36. Tió, *Nuevas fuentes*, 113.

37. Las Casas, *Historia*, 2:338.

38. Sarramía, *Los gobernadores de Puerto Rico*, 2.

39. Tió, *Nuevas fuentes*, 17–18, 27, 110, 167, 183, 198–199.

40. *Ibid.*, 17–18.

41. *Ibid.*, 17, 126, 136–143, 146–147, 229–230. Many of the place-names in east-central Dominican Republic are common to west-cental Puerto Rico. Some of these represent Spanish attempts to transcribe Taino names for "water" or "wells." These shared place-names also establish the fact that there was

frequent contact between Indians on either side of the Mona Passage.

42. Gaztambide, *Tras las huellas de Cristóbal Colón*, 90–91.

43. Oviedo, *Historia*, 3:191.

44. *Ibid.*

45. Tió, *Nuevas fuentes*, 112.

46. *Ibid.*, 31–108.

47. *Ibid.*, 164.

48. Van Middeldyk, *The History of Puerto Rico*, 24.

49. Oviedo, *Historia*, 3:195.

50. *Ibid.*

51. Murga Sanz, *Juan Ponce*, 50–51. The ruins of the Roman Capera (Caparra) may still be seen in Ovando's native province of Cáceras, in Extremadura. Still standing is a triumphal arch and a bridge. These are located just north of Plasencia and a few miles west of highway N-630, the main route from Salamanca, through Plesencia, to Cáceras.

52. Ballesteros, *La idea colonial*, 34.

53. *Ibid.*

54. *Ibid.*, 35.

55. Devereux, *Juan Ponce*, 35–36.

56. Ballesteros, *La idea colonial*, 35.

57. *Ibid.*, 35–36.

58. *Ibid.*, 37.

59. Las Casas, *Historia*, 2:371–372. Among the reasons given by Las Casas are: Sotomayor had no idea what it was to settle a land, other than find water and wood; he had no idea where gold came from; he came to the New World with practically nothing, not even money to spend; the king sent Diego Columbus to govern and there was no need for another governor; a lawsuit was pending in Castilla that would make a final determination concerning the governorship; and finally, Juan Ponce was more qualified.

60. Tió, *Nuevas fuentes*, 467.

61. Sarramía, *Los gobernadores de Puerto Rico*, 4–5.

62. Ballesteros, *La idea colonial*, 44–45.

63. Sarramía, *Los gobernadores de Puerto Rico*, 6.

64. Devereux, *Juan Ponce*, 30–60.

65. Ballesteros, *La idea colonial*, 40.

66. *Ibid.*, 39–47.

67. *Ibid.*, 48.

CHAPTER 3: *1511–1514*
THE DISCOVERY OF FLORIDA

1. Fuson, *The Log*, 8. A classic case in point is the insularity of Cuba. The

official circumnavigation of Cuba occurred in 1508, when the island was coasted by Sebastián de Ocampo, acting under orders from the governor, Nicolás de Ovando. Cuba, however, appeared as an island on the very first map of the New World, drawn by Juan de la Cosa in 1500. After 1500 (but before 1508) Cuba was depicted as an island on numerous charts. In other words, Cuba was known to be an island at least eight years before it was officially surveyed.

2. *Ibid.*, 71.

3. *Ibid.*, 76–78.

4. *Ibid.*, 96–100.

5. *Ibid.*, 92.

6. Fuson, *Legendary Islands*, 158.

7. *Ibid.*, 159–160.

8. Harrisse, *The Discovery of North America*, 77–95, 289–374; Fuson, *Legendary Islands*, 160.

9. Fuson, *Legendary Islands*, 160–165; Harrisse, *The Discovery of North America*, 134–141; Las Casas, *Historia*, 2:501–504.

10. Sale, *The Conquest of Paradise*, 159–162.

11. Las Casas, *Historia*, 2:501–504; Fuson, *Legendary Islands*, 162–163.

12. Fuson, *Legendary Islands*, 163.

13. *Ibid.*, 161–162.

14. Nebenzahl, *Atlas of Columbus*, 60.

15. Fuson, *Legendary Islands*, 162.

16. Harrisse, *The Discovery of North America*, 139–141.

17. Balseiro, ed., *The Hispanic Presence*, 44–50; Lawson, *The Discovery of Florida*, 77–79.

18. Ballesteros, *La idea colonial*, 268.

19. *Ibid.*, 270; Devereux, *Juan Ponce*, 77.

20. *Colección de documentos inéditos*, 22:26–32.

21. Ballesteros, *La idea colonial*, 67.

22. *Ibid.*, 68.

23. *Colección de documentos inéditos*, 22:26–32. The translation of the contract between Juan Ponce de León and Ferdinand, for the first voyage to Florida (Benimy or Bimini), is a modern English version, made by the author. A more formal English version may be found in either Davis (*History of Juan Ponce*, 9–14) or Lawson (*The Discovery of Florida*, 84–88). There is also an excellent synopsis in Spanish by Ballesteros (*La idea colonial*, 70–71) and in English by Devereux (*Juan Ponce*, 81–83).

24. Morison, *Journals*, 310–311.

25. Balseiro, ed., *The Hispanic Presence*, 37.

26. Sarramía, *Los gobernadores de Puerto Rico*, 11.

27. Balseiro, ed., *The Hispanic Presence*, 42–43.

28. Ballesteros, *La idea colonial*, 71–72; Devereux, *Juan Ponce*, 108–113; Murga Sanz, *Juan Ponce*, 104–106.

29. Ballesteros, *La idea colonial*, 71–72.

30. Antón de Alaminos came to the New World as a teen-age apprentice pilot on the Fourth Voyage of Christopher Columbus (1502–1504) and had seen all of the Central American coast from Honduras to Panama. He had also been on all of the islands of the Greater Antilles. He was pilot of the *Santiago* on Juan Ponce's first voyage to Florida (1513) at the time that the Gulf Stream was discovered. Alaminos returned to Florida in 1517 when he was piloting a vessel for Francisco Hernández de Córdoba. This voyage had sailed from Cuba, discovered Yucatan, and carried among its passengers Bernal Díaz del Castillo. In 1518 Alaminos was a pilot for Juan de Grijalva who sailed from Cuba to Yucatan to the site where Veracruz was founded. It was probably Alaminos who selected the Veracruz site for the Cortés landing and Mexico's first Spanish colony (1519). He became the chief pilot for Cortés, led the Cortés armada to the preselected site at Veracruz, and his was the only ship not destroyed by Cortés in order to prevent desertions.

31. Ballesteros, *La idea colonial*, 71–72.

32. Herrera, *Historia general*, 2:207–212.

33. *Ibid.*, 1: 5–9 ("Prologue" by J. Natalicio González); Fuson, *Legendary Islands*, 165.

34. Fuson, *Legendary Islands*, 165.

35. *Ibid.*, 166.

36. *Ibid.*

37. Harrisse, *The Discovery of North America*, 147–153.

38. Judge, ed., *A Columbus Casebook*, 64–69.

39. Herrera, *Historia general*, 2:207–212.

40. Judge, ed., *A Columbus Casebook*, 65–69.

41. Fuson, *Legendary Islands*, 166.

42. Harrisse, *The Discovery of North America*, 17, 710, 736.

43. *Ibid.*, 14.

44. *Ibid.*, 13–22. The men associated with the *Casa de Contratación*, especially those who held the office of Pilot-Major or Royal Cosmographer, form a veritable Who's Who of early sixteenth-century Castilian/Spanish navigation: Amerigo Vespucci, Juan Díaz de Solis, Vicente Yáñez Pinzón, Sebastián Cabot, Diego de Ribero, Alonso de Cháves, and Alonso de Santa Cruz. An excellent summary of the development of the *Casa* and the *Padrón Real* (official map) may be found in Harrisse.

45. Fuson, *Legendary Islands*, 167–176; Herrera, *Historia general*, 2:207–212. The account of Juan Ponce's first voyage to Florida, as published by Antonio de Herrera y Tordesillas, has been translated by the author. All dates are those of the Julian Calendar then in use. To correct for modern (Gregorian) dates, add nine days to each date. Modern place-names are given in brackets.

46. Fuson, *Legendary Islands*, 157–184.

47. By the 1540s Cabo de Corrientes (Cape of the Currents) was being called Cabo Cañaveral (Cape Canaveral) and, under that name, was mapped correctly by Alonso de Santa Cruz who placed it at Jupiter Inlet. By the 1600s, the name Cabo Cañaveral moved northward and replaced the name Cabo de la Cruz (Cape of the Cross), also called Punta de Arrecifes (Reef Point), and has remained there ever since. After Cape Canaveral's name migrated to the north, the original name (Cape of the Currents) never returned. Although an historic lighthouse stands today at Jupiter Inlet, not one single marker identifies the original Cape Canaveral or its predecessor, Cape of the Currents.

48. The name did vanish in the eighteenth century, and was replaced by the name Florida Keys. "Key" is from the Lucayan (Bahamian Taino) word *cay* or *cayo*, meaning "small island." It is interesting to note the way Herrera wrote, when referring to *Los Mártires* (Florida Keys), "And also the name has survived [i.e., *Los Mártires*], for the many men who have been lost there since." If the Herrera account was from Juan Ponce's log, this is not the way this sentence would be crafted. The first person to see the Keys would not have mentioned a surviving name or the many people who had been lost there. This implies a long span of time between the voyage and the account of it.

49. Gore, *The Gulf of Mexico*, 163–164.

50. *Pola* is an interesting name. If it is not misspelled, or mistranscribed, then it can only mean village or small settlement. It is an archaic form of *puebla*. This may be correct, for when it was named (on May 13) it was not *Santa Pola* but just plain *Pola*. Perhaps Herrera added the *Santa* to the name the second time around, on July 3 or 4. There is no female saint named *Pola* or anything close to that name. There is an Andalucian song by that name but it has nothing to do with saints.

51. Fuson, *Legendary Islands*, 177–179.

52. Devereux, *Juan Ponce*, 87–104.

53. Fuson, *Legendary Islands*, 84.

54. Davis, *History of Juan Ponce*, 11–13, 108–112; Devereux, *Juan Ponce*, 87–104.

55. Fuson, *Legendary Islands*, 177.

56. *Ibid.*, 179.

57. Ballesteros, *La idea colonial*, 73–75.

58. Balseiro, ed., *The Hispanic Presence*, 43.

Chapter 4: 1514–1521
The Years Between the Florida Voyages

1. Ballesteros, *La idea colonial*, 75.

2. Devereux, *Juan Ponce*, 144.

3. Balseiro, *The Hispanic Presence*, 51.

4. Devereux, *Juan Ponce*, 144.

5. *Ibid.*, 145.

6. Balseiro, *The Hispanic Presence*, 51.

7. Ballesteros, *La idea colonial*, 77.

8. *Colección de documentos inéditos*, 22:33–37. The contract (*capitulación*) between Ponce de León and Ferdinand for a second voyage to Florida has been translated by the author. The date on the contract — 1512 — is an error, probably made by an anonymous copyist in the *Archivo General de Indias* in Sevilla. The correct date is September 27, 1514. A very formal, but excellent English translation of the contract can be found in Lawson (*The Discovery of Florida*, 92–94); a poorer English version can be found in Davis (*History of Juan Ponce*, 53–56).

9. Helps, *The Spanish Conquest*, 1:358–361; Las Casas, *Historia*, 3:26–27.

10. Harrisse, *The Discovery of North America*, 801.

11. Oviedo, *Historia*, 7:128.

12. Friede and Keen, *Las Casas*, 444.

13. Madariaga, *Rise of the Spanish American Empire*, 1:12.

14. Friede and Keen, *Las Casas*, 150.

15. Anderson, *Old Panama*, 148.

16. *Ibid.*

17. Helps, *The Spanish Conquest*, 1:271.

18. Oviedo, *Historia*, 7:125–126.

19. *Ibid.*

20. *Ibid.*, 126–128.

21. *Ibid.*, 131.

22. Helps, *The Spanish Conquest*, 1:264–267.

23. Ballesteros, *La idea colonial*, 279–280; Sarramía, *Los gobernadores de Puerto Rico*, 8; Balseiro, *The Hispanic Presence*, 55.

24. Ballesteros, *La idea colonial*, 82.

25. Eden, trans., *Three English books*, 181.

26. Fuson, *The Log*, 237.

27. Lawson, *The Discovery of Florida*, 11–12, 108–110.

28. Devereux, *Juan Ponce*, 153.

29. Ballesteros, *La idea colonial*, 83.

30. Balseiro, *The Hispanic Presence*, 54.

31. Tió, *Nuevas fuentes*, 330–331.

32. Sarramía, *Los gobernadores de Puerto Rico*, 12.

33. Spain, as we know it today, came into being when Carlos I became king upon the death of his grandfather, Ferdinand. At that time, however, Carlos (Charles) was king of the Netherlands and heir to the Hapsburg thrones in

Germany and Austria. He was also only sixteen years old and did not speak Castilian or Catalán; French was his native tongue. Until Carlos reached Spain, in September 1517, Castilla and Aragón were ruled by regents who had been proscribed by Ferdinand before his death.

34. Devereux, *Juan Ponce*, 164.

35. Ballesteros, *La idea colonial*, 94.

36. *Ibid.*, 95.

37. *Ibid.*, 97, 287.

38. *Ibid.*, 97.

39. Ballesteros, *La idea colonial*, 288; Devereux, *Juan Ponce*, 164; Raisz, *Atlas of Florida*, 17–18.

40. Díaz, *Discovery and Conquest of Mexico*, xv, 14–16. Very few accounts of sixteenth-century events in America have received the attention of those of Bernal Díaz. There are sixteen Spanish-language editions of his version of the Mexican conquest and at least seven in English. In addition, there are many translations in other languages. The visit to Florida in 1517 is in all of these. Perhaps the edition best-known to Americans is the translation by A. P. Maudslay of Genaro García's Spanish version, first published by the Hakluyt Society in 1908.

41. *Ibid.*, xxiv–xxv.

42. *Ibid.*, 14.

43. *Ibid.*, 16.

44. The Mayan culture encountered by Córdoba's expedition is called "Renaissance Maya" by some anthropologists, but actually this is a misnomer. The Spaniards discovered a Toltec (central Mexican) revival of a Mayan civilization that had lost much of its grandeur. Classical Mayan culture had vanished six centuries earlier.

45. Oviedo, *Historia*, 1:7.

46. Friede and Keen, *Las Casas*, 77.

47. Balseiro, *The Hispanic Presence*, 57–58; Devereux, *Juan Ponce*, 164.

48. Tió, *Nuevas fuentes*, 423.

49. *Ibid.*

50. *Ibid.*, 532–547.

51. Ballesteros, *La idea colonial*, 97–100.

52. Devereux, *Juan Ponce*, 168–169.

53. Ballesteros, *La idea colonial*, 101.

54. Díaz, *The Discovery and Conquest of Mexico*, 40.

55. Fuson, *Legendary Islands*, 180.

56. Navarrete, *Colección de los viages*, 3:160.

57. Winsor, *Christopher Columbus*, 560. For reasons unknown to the author, credit for the discovery of the Mississippi River has also been assigned to Álvar Núñez Cabeza de Vaca (1528) and to Hernando de Soto (1541). Not

only did Alonso Álvarez Pineda discover the Mississippi River in 1519, but he correctly located it on his map!

58. Fuson, *Legendary Islands*, 180.

59. *Ibid.*, 180–181.

60. *Colección de los documentos inéditos*, 35:5–18.

61. Prescott, *Conquest of Mexico*, 1:264.

62. Díaz, *The Discovery and Conquest of Mexico*, 69.

63. Prescott, *Conquest of Mexico*, 1:365.

64. *Ibid.*, 1:367.

65. *Ibid.*, 1:372–376.

66. *Ibid.*, 2:217–226.

67. *Ibid.*, 2:226.

68. *Ibid.*, 2:222–223.

69. *Ibid.*, 2:223.

70. *Ibid.*, 2:224.

71. *Ibid.*, 2:226.

72. *Ibid.*, 2:228.

73. *Ibid.*

74. *Ibid.*, 2:229–233.

75. *Ibid.*, 3:247.

76. *Ibid.*, 2:437.

77. *Ibid.*, 2:438; Díaz, *The Discovery and Conquest of Mexico*, 330–331.

78. Willey, *An Introduction to American Archaeology*, 1:247–252.

79. *Ibid.*, 329–332.

80. Nebenzahl, *Atlas of Columbus*, 76.

81. Willey, *An Introduction to American Archaeology*, 1:169.

82. Díaz, *The Discovery and Conquest of Mexico*, 330; Prescott, *Conquest of Mexico*, 2:438.

83. *Ibid.*

84. Prescott, *Conquest of Mexico*, 2:438–439.

85. Díaz, *The Discovery and Conquest of Mexico*, 330–331.

86. *Colección de documentos inéditos*, 28:500–501.

87. Navarrete, *Colección de los viages*, 3:160.

88. Prescott, *Conquest of Mexico*, 2:440–441.

89. Harrisse, *The Discovery of North America*, 502–503. What is thought to be the original Pineda/Garay map of 1519 is preserved in Sevilla at the Archive of the Indies. It is a small map (about nine by seventeen inches) and it is untitled and unsigned.

90. *Ibid.*, 509–510.

91. *Ibid.*; Nebenzahl, *Atlas of Columbus*, 74–75. A beautiful color reproduction of the *Cortés Map of the Gulf of Mexico* and the plan of Mexico City appear in

the atlas by Nebenzahl.

92. Allen, ed., *North American Exploration*, 1:228.

93. Harrisse, *The Discovery of North America*, 503. It is interesting to note that Pineda's 1519 map clearly and accurately depicts Yucatan as a peninsula. Harrisse (*Ibid.*) calls this "an extremely remarkable configuration in a Spanish map of 1519." Despite Pineda's correct representation of the peninsula, however, Yucatan was represented as an island on almost all, if not all, maps until the middle of the sixteenth century, including the well-known maps of Weimer (1527, 1529), Mercator (1538), Vopel (1543), and the 1548 edition of Ptolemy that was published in Venice (see: Nordenskiöld, *Facsimile-Atlas*, 25–26, plate xl, plate xliii). The 1524 German edition of the *Cortés Map of the Gulf of Mexico* continued, or perhaps started, the tradition of mapping Yucatan as an island, almost as a "correction" to Pineda's rough sketch made five years earlier.

Chapter 5: 1521
The Second Voyage to Florida

1. Ballesteros, *La idea colonial*, 103; Murga Sanz, *Juan Ponce*, 240.

2. Harrisse, *The Discovery of North America*, 156–162.

3. *Colección de documentos inéditos*, 40:47–54.

4. *Ibid.*, 47–49.

5. *Ibid.*, 50–52.

6. *Ibid.*, 54.

7. Murga Sanz, *Juan Ponce*, 240.

8. Harrisse, *The Discovery of North America*, 158.

9. Herrera, *Historia general*, 4:48.

10. Oviedo, *Historia*, 10:256–259.

11. Harrisse, *The Discovery of North America*, 158. Harrisse offers an incorrect translation of this passage, for he refers to "leagues" as "degrees" and confuses length and width with geographical longitude and latitude. Oviedo, on the other hand, had a distinct advantage over Juan Ponce: he wrote his history *after* Florida's peninsular nature was understood and its size was generally fixed.

12. Oviedo, *Historia*, 3:223–224.

13. Las Casas, *Historia*, 2:504–505.

14. Herrera, *Historia general*, 4:48.

15. Díaz, *The Discovery and Conquest of Mexico*, 454.

16. Cameron, *Magellan*, 81, 140–143, 192, 209.

17. Ballesteros, *La idea colonial*, 288.

18. Devereux, *Juan Ponce*, 191; Murga Sanz, *Juan Ponce*, 240.

19. Devereux, *Juan Ponce*, 168–169.

20. Oviedo, *Historia*, 10:256–259.

21. Archeology might one day help identify the site or sites visited by Ponce de León's colony. If the colony remained in one place for four months, there should be some evidence of it that is yet to be discovered. It would also be prudent to reexamine all of the material dealing with Cortés's Veracruz colony during July 1521. There is always the possibility that some survivor of Ponce de León's colony told the story while in Veracruz and, for whatever reason, this information has never been gleaned from the documents.

22. Díaz, *The Discovery and Conquest of Mexico*, 444; Prescott, *Conquest of Mexico*, 3:163–164.

23. Ballesteros, *La idea colonial*, 241.

Chapter 6: 1521–1565
From the Dream of Juan Ponce
to the Reality of Saint Augustine

1. de la Vega, *The Florida of the Inca*, 9.

2. *Ibid.*, 11.

3. Cabeza de Vaca, *Relation*, 13.

4. *Colección de documentos inéditos*, 22:224–245.

5. Cabeza de Vaca, *Relation*, 14–15.

6. *Ibid.*, 19.

7. *Ibid.*, 20–21.

8. *Colección de documentos inéditos*, 22:534–546.

9. Schell, *De Soto Didn't Land at Tampa*.

10. de la Vega, *The Florida of the Inca*, 22–23; Schell, *De Soto*, 29.

11. Schell, *De Soto*, 19–21.

12. de la Vega, *The Florida of the Inca*, 24–31.

13. *Ibid.*, 41–55.

14. Clayton, Knight, and Moore, eds., *De Soto Chronicles*, 1:19–219 (Elvas), 1:225–246 (Biedma), 1:251–305 (Rangel), 2:25–559 (de la Vega).

15. Schell, *De Soto*, 20, 29.

16. *Ibid.*, 20.

17. *Ibid.*, 23–25.

18. *Ibid.* Do not confuse this location with others of the same name. The Spaniards used the name Espíritu Santo many times — it was one of their favorite place-names.

19. de la Vega, *The Florida of the Inca*, 63–85.

20. Clayton, Knight, and Moore, eds., *De Soto Chronicles*, 1:19–219 (Elvas), 1:225–246 (Biedma), 1:251–305 (Rangel), 2:25–559 (de la Vega).

21. Clayton, Knight, and Moore, eds., *De Soto Chronicles*, 1:354.

22. de la Vega, *The Florida of the Inca*, 12–13.

23. Priestley, ed. and trans., *The Luna Papers*, 2 vols.

24. *Ibid.*, 2:199–207.

25. *Ibid.*, 1:xxv, 2:205.

26. *Ibid.*, 2:257.

27. *Ibid.*, 2:333–337.

28. *Ibid.*, 2:257.

29. *Ibid.*, 2:211.

30. *Ibid.*, 2:283, 285.

31. *Ibid.*, 2:271–277.

32. *Ibid.*, 2:225.

33. *Ibid.*, 2:245.

34. *Ibid.*, 2:281–301.

35. Duncan, *Hernando de Soto*, 370–384. Some historians believe that the Battle of Mabila, one of the bloodiest fought between Indians and Europeans in the last 500 years, altered the course of history in what is now the United States. This site was probably located west of today's Montgomery, Alabama, on the Alabama River.

36. Priestley, *Tristán de Luna*, 12.

37. Fuson and Klingen, "La Floride," 421.

38. *Ibid.*

39. *Ibid.*

40. Personal correspondence from Donald J. Orth, Executive Secretary, Domestic Geographic Names, United States Board on Geographic Names, March 28, 1985. This letter informed the author that the Board on Geographic Names had, in its March 1985 meeting, restored the name *Cape Francis* to the map.

41. Ribault, *The Whole and True Discouerye of Terra Florida*, 1563. A facsimile of this London edition was published by the University of Florida Press, Gainesville, in 1964.

42. Klingen, *Early French Attempts*, 37–41.

43. Laudonnière, *Three Voyages*, 53.

44. Klingen, *Early French Attempts*, 107.

45. *Ibid.*, 4.

46. The saga of Ribault and Menéndez is both fascinating and complicated. The serious reader is referred to Laudonnière and Lyon, cited in the Bibliography. One of the reasons that the episode is complicated is that two historical dramas were being played out at the same time and on the same stage.

47. Lyon, *The Enterprise of Florida*, 97–98.

Bibliography

Allen, John L., ed. *North American Exploration*. 3 vols. Lincoln, NE: University of Nebraska Press, 1997.

Anderson, C. L. G. *Old Panama and Castilla del Oro*. New York, NY: North River Press, 1944.

Ballesteros Gaibrois, Manuel. *La idea colonial de Ponce de León* (The Colonial Idea of Ponce de León). San Juan, PR: Insituto de Cultura Puertorriqueña, 1960.

Balseiro, José Augustín, ed. *The Hispanic Presence in Florida*. Miami, FL: E. A. Seemann Publishing, 1977.

Biesanz, John, and Mavis Biesanz. *The People of Panama*. New York, NY: Columbia University Press, 1955.

Cabeza de Vaca, Álvar Núñez. *Relation of Álvar Núñez Cabeza de Vaca*. Translated by Buckingham Smith. New York, NY: Estate of Buckingham Smith, 1871. Facsimile reprint, Ann Arbor, MI: University Microfilms, 1966.

Cameron, Ian. *Magellan and the First Circumnavigation of the World*. New York, NY: Saturday Review Press, 1973.

Clayton, L. A., V. K. Knight, Jr., and E. C. Moore, eds. *The De Soto Chronicles*. 2 vols. Tuscaloosa, AL: The University of Alabama Press, 1993.

Colección de documentos inéditos relativos al descubrimiento, conquista y organización de las antiguas posesiones españolas de América y Oceanía, sacados de los Archivos del Reino y muy especialmente del de indias (Collection of unedited documents relative to the discovery, conquest and organization of the old Spanish possessions in America and Oceania, taken from the royal archives and very especially from the [Archive] of [the] Indies). 42 vols. Madrid, Spain: Imprenta de Manuel G. Hernández, 1864–1884.

Columbus, Ferdinand. *The Life of the Admiral Christopher Columbus By His Son Ferdinand.* Translated and with a new introduction by Benjamin Keen. New Brunswick, NJ: Rutgers University Press, 1992.

Cortesão, Armando, ed. Portvgaliae Monvmenta Cartographica. 6 vols. Lisbon, PORT, 1960.

Davis, T. Frederick. *History of Juan Ponce de Leon's Voyages to Florida.* Jacksonville, FL: T. Frederick Davis, 1935.

de la Vega, Garcilaso. *The Florida of the Inca.* Translated and edited by John Grier Varner and Jeannette Johnson Varner. Austin, TX: University of Texas Press, 1980.

Devereux, Anthony Q. *Juan Ponce de León, King Ferdinand, and the Fountain of Youth.* Spartanburg, SC: The Reprint Company, 1993.

Díaz del Castillo, Bernal. *The Discovery and Conquest of Mexico.* Edited by Genaro García and translated by A. P. Maudslay. New York, NY: Farrar, Straus and Cudahy, 1956.

Duncan, David Ewing. *Hernando de Soto: A Savage Quest in the Americas.* New York, NY: Crown Publishers, 1995.

Eden, Richard, trans. *The first Three English books on America.* [?1511] — 1535 A.D. Edited by Edward Arber. Birmingham, England: [Printed by Turnbull & Spears, Edinburgh, Scotland], 1885. Facsimile reprint, New York, NY: Kraus Reprint, 1971.

Encyclopaedia Britannica. Fifteenth edition. 30 vols. Chicago, IL: Encyclopaedia Britannica, Inc., 1974.

Friede, Juan, and Benjamin Keen, eds. *Bartolomé de Las Casas: Toward an Understanding of the Man and His Work.* DeKalb, IL: Northern Illinois University Press, 1971.

Fuson, Robert H. "Land Tenure in Central Panama." *Journal of Geography* 43, no.4 (April 1964): 161–168.

_____. *A Geography of Geography.* Dubuque, IA: Wm. C. Brown, 1969.

_____, trans. *The Log of Christopher Columbus.* Camden, ME: International Marine Publishing Company, 1987.

_____. *Legendary Islands of the Ocean Sea.* Sarasota, FL: Pineapple Press, 1995.

Fuson, Robert H., and Françoise Klingen. "Noms de lieux français de la Floride" (French place-names in Florida). *450 ans de noms de*

Bibliography

lieux français en Amérique du nord. Gouvernement du Québec, Commission de toponymie, Premier congrès international, July 11–15, 1984, 421–432.

Gaztambide, Miriam Añeses de. *Tras las huellas de Cristóbal Colón* (In the wake of Christopher Columbus), San Juan, PR: Cultural Panamericana, 1991.

Gómez de Silva, Guido. *Elsevier's Concise Etymological Dictionary.* Amsterdam, Netherlands: Elsevier Science Publishers, 1985.

Gore, Robert H. *The Gulf of Mexico.* Sarasota, FL: Pineapple Press, 1992.

Harrisse, Henry. *The Discovery of North America.* London, England: H. Stevens and Son, and Paris, France: H. Welter Rochdale, 1892. Facsimile reprint, Amsterdam, Netherlands: N. Israel, 1961.

Helps, Arthur. *The Spanish Conquest in America.* 4 vols. New York, NY: Harper and Brothers, 1856–1868.

Herrera y Tordesillas, Antonio de. *Historia general de los hechos de los castellanos en las islas, y tierra-firme de el Mar Occeano* (General history of the Castilians in the islands and mainland of the ocean). 10 vols. Asunción, Paraguay: Editorial Guarania, 1945.

Judge, Joseph, ed. *A Columbus Casebook.* Washington, DC: National Geographic Society, 1986.

Klingen, Françoise. "Early French Attempts at Colonization in North America: The Huguenot Settlements in The Florida of the 1560's." Master's thesis, Université de la Sorbonne Nouvelle-Paris III, 1982.

Las Casas, Bartolomé de. *Historia de las indias.* 3 vols. Mexico City, DF: Fondo de Cultura Económica, 1951.

Laudonnière, René de Goulaine de. *Three Voyages: René Laudonnière.* Translated by Charles E. Bennett. Gainesville, FL: University Presses of Florida, 1975.

Lawson, Edward W. *The Discovery of Florida and Its Discoverer Juan Ponce de León.* Nashville, TN: Cullom and Ghertner, 1946.

Lyon, Eugene. *The Enterprise of Florida: Pedro Menéndez de Avilés and the Spanish Conquest of 1565–1568.* Gainesville, FL: The University Presses of Florida, 1983.

Madariaga, Salvador de. *The Rise of the Spanish American Empire.* London, England: Hollis and Carter, 1947.

_____. *The Fall of the Spanish American Empire.* London, England: Hollis and Carter, 1947.

Martyr d'Anghiera, Peter (also Peter Martyr and Pietro Martire). *De Orbe Novo: The Eight Decades of Peter Martyr d'Anghiera*. 2 vols. Translated by Francis A. MacNutt. New York, NY: Burt Franklin, 1970.

Morison, Samuel Eliot. *Journals and Other Documents on the Life and Voyages of Christopher Columbus*. New York, NY: The Heritage Press, 1963.

Murga Sanz, Vicente. *Juan Ponce de León*. San Juan, PR: Ediciones de la Universidad de Puerto Rico, 1959.

Navarrete, Martín Fernández de. *Viajes de Cristóbal Colón*. Second edition. Madrid, Spain: Espasa-Calpe, 1934.

_____. *Colección de los viages y descubrimientos que hicieron por mar los españoles desde fines del siglo XV* (Collection of the voyages and discoveries that the Spanish made by sea from the end of the fifteenth century). 5 vols. Buenos Aires, Argentina: Editorial Guarania, 1945.

Nebenzahl, Kenneth. *Atlas of Columbus and the Great Discoveries*. Chicago, IL: Rand McNally, 1990.

Nordenskiöld, A. E. *Facsimile-Atlas to the Early History of Cartography*. Translated by J. A. Ekelof and C. R. Markham. Stockholm, Sweden: P. A. Norstedt & Soner, 1889. Facsimile reprint, with a new Introduction by J. B. Post, New York, NY: Dover, 1973.

Oviedo y Valdés, Gonzalo Fernández de. *Historia general y natural de las indias, islas y tierra-firme del mar océano* (General and natural history of the Indies, islands and mainland of the ocean). 14 vols. Asunción, Paraguay: Editorial Guarania, 1944.

Phillips, Carla Rahn. *Life at Sea in the Sixteenth Century: The Landlubber's Lament of Eugenio de Salazar*. Minneapolis, MN: James Ford Bell Library, 1987.

Prescott, William H. *History of the Conquest of Mexico*. Twenty-second edition. 3 vols. New York, NY: Harper & Brothers, 1852.

Priestley, Herbert Ingram, trans. and ed. *The Luna Papers*. 2 vols. Deland, FL: The Florida State Historical Society, 1928.

_____. *Tristán de Luna: Conquistador of the Old South*. Glendale, CA: Arthur H. Clark, 1936.

Bibliography

Raisz, Erwin, comp. *Atlas of Florida.* Text by John R. Dunkle. Gainesville, FL: University of Florida Press, 1964.

Ribault, Jean. *The Whole and True Discouerye of Terra Florida.* London, England: 1563. Facsimile reprint, Gainesville, FL: University of Florida Press, 1964.

Sale, Kirkpatrick. *The Conquest of Paradise: Christopher Columbus and the Columbian Legacy.* New York, NY: Plume, 1991.

Sarramía Roncero, Tomás. *Los gobernadores de Puerto Rico* (The governors of Puerto Rico). San Juan, PR: Publicaciones Puertorriqueñas, 1993.

Schell, Rolfe F. *De Soto Didn't Land At Tampa.* Fort Myers Beach, FL: Island Press, 1966.

Thacher, John Boyd. *Columbus: His Life, His Work, His Remains.* 3 vols. New York, NY: G. P. Putnam's Sons, 1903–1904.

Tió, Aurelio. *Nuevas fuentes para la historia de Puerto Rico* (New sources for the history of Puerto Rico). San Germán, PR: Ediciones de la Universidad Interamericana de Puerto Rico, 1961.

Turespaña. *Costa de la luz* (Coast of Light). Madrid, Spain: Secretaria General de Turismo, 1991.

_____. *In the Footsteps of Columbus.* Madrid, Spain: Secretaria General de Turismo, 1991.

Van Middeldyk, R. A. *The History of Puerto Rico.* Facsimile reprint, New York, NY: Arno Press, 1975.

Varner, John G., and Jeannette J. Varner. *Dogs of the Conquest.* Norman, OK: University of Oklahoma Press, 1983.

Willey, Gordon R. *An Introduction to American Archaeology.* 2 vols. Englewood Cliffs, NJ: Prentice-Hall, 1966.

Winsor, Justin. *Christopher Columbus.* Boston, MA: Houghton, Mifflin & Co. Facsimile reprint, Stanford, CT: Longmeadow Press, 1991.

Index

Lucayos. *See* Bahama Islands
Luna y Arellano, Tristán de, 193–95, 196f, 197–200, 202

Mabila (Alabama Indian village), 199, 253n.35
Madeira Islands, ix, 10–11, 14
Madrid, 30f
Magellan, Ferdinand (Fernão de Magalhaes; Fernando de Magallanes), xii, 33, 167
Málaga, 5
Manatee River, 190
Mangi Peninsula, 86, 87f, 88
Manso, Alonso, 96, 121
Marchena, Antonio de, 29
Margarite, Pedro, 59
María Galante (island), 49, 52f
Martín, Benito, 149
Martín de Jérez, Alonso, 169
Martinique, 22f, 24t, 49, 52f
Mártires, Los. *See* Florida Keys
Martyr, Peter (Peter Martyr d'Anghiera), 89, 90f, 137–38
Martyrs, The. *See* Florida Keys
Matacumbe Indians, 141
Matanza (Pine Island, Florida), 111f, 116, 117t
Matanzas River, 209, 209f, 217, 217f, 218f
Matinino. *See* Martinique
Maya; Mayan civilization, 144, 152, 249n.44
Mayagüez, 71, 79
Medini-Celi, Duke of, 29, 31
Mendoza, Antonio de, 103–04
Menéndez de Avilés, Pedro, xiv, 209f, 211, 213–14, 215f, 216–18
Mexican conquest, xiv, 141, 146–49, 155, 167
Mexico, 28, 55t, 142f, 146–50, 152–53, 156, 159, 166, 180f, 185–87, 193–94, 198
Mexico City, 72, 150, 152f, 155, 157, 195
Miami, 104f, 116
Miami Beach, 83, 116, 117t
Miruelo, Diego (uncle), 120, 155, 168, 178–79
Miruelo, Diego (nephew), 182–83, 190
Mississippi River, 147, 148f, 151, 156, 178, 191–92, 197, 249–50n.57
Mobile Bay, 195, 197, 199
Moguer, 22, 30f, 31, 33
Mona Island, 62f, 71, 76
Mona Passage, 62f, 64, 71

Montalván, Alonso de, 196
Monte Cristi, 52f, 54, 62f, 201, 201f
Montejo, Francisco de, 149
Montón system, 66
Montserrat, 49, 52f
Moors. *See* Arabs and Berbers
Morales, Andrés de, 89, 90f
Morales, Diego de, 79
Moreno, Pedro, 163
Moscoso, Rodrigo de, 96
Moscoso de Alvarado, Luis de, 190f, 192
Mucozo (cacique), 191
Muskogean Indians, 151–52
Muslims, 7–10, 15–16, 19, 24, 37–38. *See also* Arabs and Berbers

Names, xv–xvi, 29, 49, 49t, 115–16, 117t, 119, 145, 243n.41, 247n.50. *See also* Genealogy
Nanipacana (Alabama Indian village), 196f, 198–99
Narváez, Pánfilo de, xi, xiii, 149–51, 179, 181f, 182–86, 190
Navarra (Navarre), 8, 30f
Navidad, La, 22f, 50, 52–55, 52f, 53f, 62f
Neanderthal Man, 3
New Spain. *See* Mexico
Nicaragua, 24t, 186
Nueva Isabela. *See* Santo Domingo
Núñez de Balboa, Vasco. *See* Balboa

Oaxaca, 194
Ocampo, Sebastián de, 244–45n.1
Ochuse. *See* Pensacola Bay
Ocoa (Azul), 63, 196
Ojeda, Alonso de, 29, 55, 55t
Ortíz, Juan, 100
Ortubia, Juan Pérez de, 98, 120, 126
Ovando, Nicolás de, xvi, 31f, 33, 51, 56–57, 60–65, 67, 72, 74–76, 149
Oviedo y Valdés, Gonzalo Fernández de, 39, 56–57, 72, 74, 133–34, 144, 159, 164–66, 171

Padrón Real, 101–03, 127
Palacios Rubios, Juan López de, 132
Palm Coast, 105f, 114
Palos, 14, 22, 24t, 29, 30f, 31, 33
Panama, 24t, 55t, 133, 146, 186
Panama City, Panama, 55t
Pánuco River, 146, 151–55, 190f, 192, 195
Papal Demarcation Line, 23
Parris Island. *See* Santa Elena